MongoDB, Express, Angular, and Node.js Fundamentals

Become a MEAN master and rule the world of web applications

Paul Oluyege

MongoDB, Express, Angular, and Node.js Fundamentals

Author: Paul Oluyege

Technical Reviewer: Sam Anderson

Managing Editor: Mahesh Dhyani

Acquisitions Editor: Koushik Sen

Production Editor: Samita Warang

Editorial Board: David Barnes, Ewan Buckingham, Shivangi Chatterji, Simon Cox, Manasa Kumar, Alex Mazonowicz, Douglas Paterson, Dominic Pereira, Shiny Poojary, Saman Siddiqui, Erol Staveley, Ankita Thakur, and Mohita Vyas.

First Published: January 2019

Production Reference: 2270219

ISBN: 978-1-78980-873-5

Published by Packt Publishing Ltd.

Livery Place, 35 Livery Street

Birmingham B3 2PB, UK

Table of Contents

Developing RESTful APIs to Perform CRUD Operations   39

The MEAN Stack Security   117

Angular Declarables, Bootstrapping, and Modularity   167

Testing and Optimizing Angular Applications 201

Preface

This section briefly introduces the author, the coverage of this book, the technical skills you'll need to get started, and the hardware and software requirements required to complete all of the included activities and exercises.

About the Book

MongoDB, Express, Angular, and Node.js Fundamentals begins by demystifying the MEAN architecture. You will take a look at the features of the JavaScript technologies, frameworks, and libraries that make up the MEAN stack. You will learn how to develop a RESTful API using Node.js, Express.js, and MongoDB Atlas. You will also learn how to build a blogging application using the MEAN stack. Next, you will learn about authentication using the MEAN stack, and explore the features of Angular, such as pipes, reactive forms, modules, optimizing apps, animations, and unit testing, and much more. By the end of the book, you will have all the knowledge you need to become a pro at developing efficient web applications using JavaScript technologies.

About the Author

Paul Oluyege is a full-stack software engineer who currently works as the software engineering lead in a top consumer credit company in Nigeria. With over 5 years of experience in all fields of the software development life cycle and after playing integral roles in building well-tested, rock-solid software projects, Paul is dedicated to constantly improving tools and infrastructure to maximize productivity, minimize system downtime, and quickly respond to the changing needs of a business. He is a proactive problem solver and a determined achiever looking for opportunities to prove himself.

Objectives

* Understand the MEAN architecture
* Create RESTful APIs to complete CRUD tasks
* Build a blogging application with basic features
* Create simple animations using Angular
* Perform unit testing on Angular applications

Audience

MongoDB, Express, Angular, and Node.js Fundamentals is ideal for beginner and intermediate frontend developers who want to become full-stack developers. You will need some prior working knowledge of JavaScript and MongoDB as we skim over its basics and get straight to work.

Approach

MongoDB, Express, Angular, and Node.js Fundamentals takes a hands-on approach to teach you how to build professional full-stack web applications. It contains multiple activities that use real-life business scenarios for you to practice and apply your new skills in a highly relevant context.

Hardware Requirements

For an optimal student experience, we recommend the following hardware configuration:

- Processor: Intel Core i5 or equivalent
- Memory: 4 GB RAM
- Storage: 35 GB available space

Software Requirements

You'll also need the following software installed in advance:

- OS: Windows 7 SP1 64-bit, Windows 8.1 64-bit, or Windows 10 64-bit
- Browser: Google Chrome, latest version
- Postman | API Development Environment, latest version
- Visual Studio Code, latest version
- Node.js LTS 8.9.1 installed
- Angular 7 CLI 7.21 installed
- Express.js
- MongoDB Atlas

Installation and Setup

Before you start this book, we'll install Node.js, set up a MongoDB Atlas account, and install Angular 7 CLI, Express, Postman, and the other libraries used throughout this book. You will find the steps to install and set them up here.

Installing Node.js

Install Node.js by following the instructions at this link: https://nodejs.org/en/download/.

Setting up MongoDB Atlas

To set up a MongoDB Atlas account, go to the following link: https://www.mongodb.com/cloud/atlas

Installing Angular 7 CLI

Install Angular 7 CLI by following the instructions at this link: https://cli.angular.io/.

Installing libraries

Install Node.js libraries using the following command format:

```
npm install <library-name> --save
```

To install Express.js, for example, use this command:

```
npm install express --save
```

Installing Postman

Install Postman by following the instructions at this link: https://www.getpostman.com/downloads/.

Installing Visual Studio Code

Install Visual Studio Code by following the instructions at this link: https://code.visualstudio.com/download/.

Additional Resources

The code bundle for this course is also hosted on GitHub at https://github.com/TrainingByPackt/MongoDB-Express-Angular-and-Node.js-Fundamentals.

We also have other code bundles from our rich catalog of books and videos available at https://github.com/PacktPublishing/. Check them out!

Conventions

Code words in text, database table names, folder names, filenames, file extensions, pathnames, dummy URLs, user input, and Twitter handles are shown as follows: "We use **var fs = require('fs')** to declare **fs** (a filesystem variable) and assign the filesystem module to it."

A block of code is set as follows:

```
interface LoginResponse {
  accessToken: string;
  accessExpiration: number;
}
```

```
this.http.post<LoginResponse>('api/login', {
  login: 'foo',
  password: 'bar'
}).subscribe(data => {
  console.log(data.accessToken, data.accessExpiration);
});
```

New terms and important words are shown in bold. Words that you see on the screen, for example, in menus or dialog boxes, appear in the text like this: "Create the **Post Create/Edit** form components."

Introduction to the MEAN Stack

Learning Objectives

By the end of this chapter, you will be able to:

- Describe the MEAN architecture
- Run a Node server
- Create, read from, and write to buffers
- Perform various filesystem operations
- Create readable and writable streams

This chapter presents the fundamentals of the MEAN stack, along with practical exercises that implement several features that are described in the chapter.

Introduction

The **MEAN** stack is comprised of four technologies: **MongoDB**, **Express.js**, **Angular.js**, and **Node.js**, and is one of the best tools available for solving contemporary business challenges. This technology results in low maintenance costs, fewer resources being required, and entails less development time. Furthermore, it provides flexibility, high scalability, and several features that help businesses deliver high-performance solutions.

For developers or aspiring developers, learning MEAN is essential as it has become an indispensable tool for web applications. Businesses and developers are increasingly skipping Ruby, Python, and PHP, and choosing **JavaScript** for development. Also, JavaScript boasts the most active developer community.

Other stacks also exist, such as the **Linux**, **Apache**, **MySQL**, and **PHP** (**LAMP**) stacks. However, the flexible simplicity of the MEAN stack is highly desirable. Also, factors such as Node being super-fast and the fact that MongoDB is a compelling database with which apps can be developed, tested, and hosted in the cloud with ease, add to the popularity of the MEAN stack. In comparison, LAMP is MySQL-based and has a confining structure, and thus is not as popular as the MEAN stack.

This chapter introduces the components, libraries, and framework that make up the MEAN stack architecture. We will also describe various contemporary commercial applications that can be built with the MEAN stack. Finally, we will build web servers with Node.js and implement various features that are provided by the backend runtime environment.

MEAN Architecture Demystification

MEAN is a software stack for building active websites and web applications. It is a collection of JavaScript-based technologies for developing web applications. Thus, from the client to the database, everything is based on JavaScript. This free and open source stack is an acronym that's made up of the first letters of MongoDB, Express.js, Angular.js, and Node.js, as shown here:

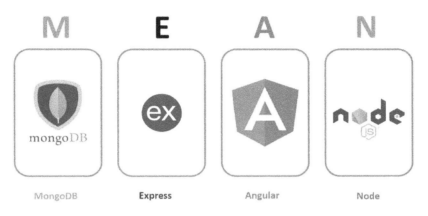

Figure 1.1: The MEAN stack

MEAN Architecture

The MEAN architecture is comprised of four different JavaScript technologies when they are stacked successively. The architecture is designed so that each component performs specific tasks individually as well as in sync with other layers in the stack to achieve an end goal.

In the MEAN architecture that's shown in the following diagram, the client initiates the requests, which flow right from the first layer down to the last. Appropriate responses to those requests then flow right through all the layers back up to the client.

The client first interacts with the user interface, which is built using the **Angular** frontend framework. Requests made on the interface are passed to Node.js, the server-side engine. Then, the middleware framework known as Express.js makes a request to **MongoDB**, which is the database. **Express.js** retrieves the response in the form of data from the database. Finally, this response is then returned by **Node.js** to the client via the user display:

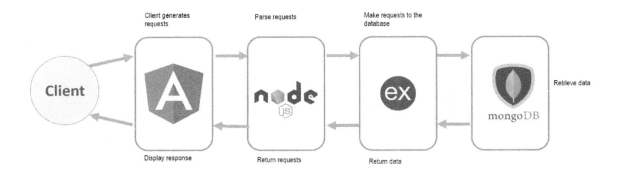

Figure 1.2: Workings of the MEAN architecture

> **Note**
>
> For further information on the MEAN stack, refer to the following page: https://blog.meanjs.org.

There are several advantages to using the various MEAN components, which has made it a technology stack to reckon with for start-ups and big companies alike. There are several reasons why the MEAN stack is preferred in web application development. A few of these reasons are listed here:

- Reduced development time and cost
- Speedy MVP development and scalability
- Increased developer flexibility and efficiency
- Excellent performance
- Speedy data storage and retrieval
- Uniform programming language
- Operating system compatibility

- Agility and quality of apps
- The MEAN stack supports the MVC architecture

Owing to its performance benefits, the MEAN stack has been adopted by many contemporary commercial organizations, such as Uber, PayPal, Netflix, and so on to build their websites and web applications. Ulbora and Trakit.me are a couple of other web applications that are built using the MEAN stack.

> **Note**
>
> A few live applications that have been built with the MEAN stack can be viewed here: https://github.com/linnovate/mean/wiki/Built-with-Mean.

Before going into MEAN application development, we will briefly discuss the individual technologies that make up the MEAN stack. We will start with MongoDB.

MongoDB

MongoDB is a document-oriented database program. The database, which is classified as NoSQL, is developed by MongoDB Inc. It's a free and open source database that uses JSON-like documents with schemas. Described here are some of the major features that make MongoDB stand out in application development:

Strong consistency: Strong consistency is a default feature in MongoDB, and thus it takes no additional upgrades to create consistency. It's also highly guaranteed: as long as a write is successful, you will be able to read it. Automatic failover of the replica set makes it highly available. Also, flexibility and scalability are not readily available in traditional databases that only rely on a defined schema. In comparison, MongoDB, which is NoSQL, relies on the key-to-value pair approach. This enables flexibility and scalability in MongoDB.

Real-time aggregation: This is a built-in MongoDB feature that allows real-time statistical analysis and the generation of pre-aggregated reports on request.

Ad hoc queries: These are impromptu queries that are written to extract information from the database, but only when necessary.

Indexing: Indexing in MongoDB makes it easy to search documents without performing a collection-wide scan by matching specific queries with documents.

Database-as-a-service: Database-as-a-service offerings by MongoDB enable users to access databases without having to install software or set up hardware. MongoDB Atlas, which is a cloud-hosted service offering by MongoDB Inc., will be used in this book. As we progress in the next chapter, we will go through all the processes involved in its setup.

> **Note**
>
> For more features and pricing information on different tiers, refer to this link: https://www.mongodb.com/cloud/atlas.

Despite having several advantages, there are a few limitations of MongoDB that we need to be aware of:

Limited data size: Documents have a maximum data size of 16 MB.

Limited nesting: The maximum number of documents that can be nested is 100.

Joins not supported: This is one of the main differences between RDBMS and NoSQL. MongoDB is not designed to have related columns. Rather, it stores de-normalized data and thus joins are not supported.

However, these limitations cannot overshadow the fact that MongoDB provides high performance, high availability, and automatic scaling, thus mitigating—if not completely eliminating—the preceding limitations.

So far, we have introduced the MEAN stack and its database component, MongoDB. We will now continue with the introduction of the second component, Express.js—a middleware application framework for developing web applications.

Express.js

Express.js or simply Express is a Node.js web application framework that provides a strong set of features for web and mobile applications. It's free, open source, fast, un-opinionated (that is, there is no "right way" to complete a certain task in Express), and is comprised of a simple web framework that's designed for building web applications and APIs. The framework has achieved a dominant position in the industry as the server framework for Node.js. Express possesses rich features and advantages. A few of these are listed as follows:

- Configuration
- Middleware
- Views and templates

- Routing
- Session
- Security

The preceding list includes a few of the most dominant features and advantages of Express, and each of them contribute to the performance benefits afforded by this framework. In Express, third-party plugins (middleware) can be set up to respond to HTTP/RESTful requests, and a routing table can also be defined to perform different HTTP operations. HTML pages are dynamically rendered by Express based on passing arguments to templates. Express supports a wide range of templating languages, such as **Pug**, **React**, **hbs**, and **h4e**. Furthermore, it has detailed documentation to help developers maximize its uses. The community support is huge: as of now, Express has gathered over 30,000 GitHub stars, which means that it is well accepted and supported in the open source community. Also, Express allows for the addition of custom code. In terms of performance, Express leads other frameworks because of its inherent properties that make the routing process efficient and faster.

Express presents a thin layer that enables the addition of robust features and functionalities to your web applications. It organizes web applications into a **model view controller** (**MVC**) architecture and manages everything from routes, to rendering views, and pre-forming HTTP requests.

However, we do need to be aware of certain limitations while developing apps in Express. In a real-life situation, when projects become more complex and code base size increases, refactoring becomes very complex and a lot of manual labor is required. This is because the absence of organization makes the handling of complex applications difficult as Express is not designed to manage complexity by itself. Furthermore, the cost of scaling increases with application complexity.

> **Note**
>
> To explore popular Node.js frameworks that have been built on Express.js, refer to this link: https://expressjs.com/en/resources/frameworks.html.

In this section, we introduced another MEAN stack component – Express.js. We described its features and viewed popular Node.js frameworks that have been built using Express.js. In the next section, we will continue with the introduction of the third component, Angular.

The next component after Express in the MEAN stack is a JavaScript frontend framework known as **Angular**. We will be introducing Angular features across all of its existing versions, and then we will talk briefly about its advantages and limitations.

Angular

Angular is an open source TypeScript and JavaScript-based frontend web application structural framework and is managed and sustained by Google. Being open source, a community of software developers and corporations provide maintenance and address issues that are encountered when developing single-page applications. Listed here are some of the advantages that make Angular stand out:

- **Use of Typescript**: Angular uses Typescript, which is a better tooling language that compiles to readable, clean code and standards-based JavaScript, which is highly scalable.

- **Component-based architecture**: Angular embraces component-based architecture to ensure high quality code.

- **Platform-agnostic philosophy**: A platform, agnostic philosophy simply means that Angular is unbiased toward the use of different technology tools to solve different problems.

- **High performance**: The Angular framework offers dependency injection, end-to-end tooling, declarative templates, and integrated best practices. These features help to solve development challenges. Thus, web, mobile, and desktop application development is made easier using Angular.

- **Long-term support (LTS) by Google**: Long-term support by Google ensures the there is a continuous and timely release of versions to address any performance issues and bugs.

However, note that no framework is perfect and there have been several Angular versions. The following list shows how Angular has evolved over the years, along with its different versions:

- **Angular.js**: This was the first version and was a library written in **JavaScript** released in 2009. It was developed with a **modular structure** that expresses an application's behavior and manages its data, logic, and rules. Its data binding (binding data to a DOM element) and architecture was based on **model view controller** (**MVC**), but was built with no support for mobile.

- **Angular 2**: This version was written in **TypeScript 1.8** and released in 2016. It was developed to be faster than the previous version and was mobile-oriented. It offers **structured components** and has support for offline compilation and fast change detection. **Dynamic loading** and **asynchronous operation** brought about performance improvements. Furthermore, it provides support for component directives, decorator directives, and template directives. Data binding was improved, compared to the previous version, and it offered support for **component-based architecture**.

- **Angular 4**: This was written in **TypeScript 2.1** and **2.2** and was released in 2017. It was developed to be compact and fast. **Animation packages** and **pipes** were introduced, along with directive improvements and simplified HTTP requests.

- **Angular 5**: This version was released in 2017 and was faster than the previous version. Features such as **watch mode**, **type checking**, **improved metadata structure**, and **better error messages** were introduced. **AOT** (**ahead-of-time**) compilation was set to default.

- **Angular 6**: This was released in early 2018 and was faster than the previous versions with features such as `ng update`, `ng add`, **Angular element**, **Angular Material and Components development kit** (**CDK**), **RxJs** version 6, and improved animation, and a CLI workplace.

- **Angular 7**: This version was released in October 2018 with updated features such as **drag and drop**, **virtual scrolling**, and **CLI prompts**, among many others.

> **Note**
>
> The third version release of Angular was skipped to avoid conflict with the router package version. For more detailed documentation, please refer to this link: https://angular.io/. Information on bug fixes in each version can be found here: https://github.com/angular/angular/blob/master/CHANGELOG.md.

However, you should be aware that no web framework is perfect, and in the case of Angular, its verbosity and complexity renders it a difficult framework to master. Furthermore, Angular has a steep learning curve.

In this section, we introduced the third component of the MEAN stack – Angular. We discussed its features, as well as its limitations. In the next section, we will introduce our final MEAN component, a server-side technology known as Node.js.

Node.js

Node is an open source program that is built on a JavaScript runtime engine (Chrome's V8) and consists of JavaScript libraries that are implemented in the form of modules. The cross-platform server environment is lightweight and efficient because it uses an event-driven, non-blocking I/O model. For example, PayPal employs Node to solve the problem that arises owing to the boundary between the browser (client side) and server (server side) by enabling both to be written in JavaScript. This, in turn, helps PayPal unify their engineering specialties into one team, thus enabling them to focus on user needs and create solutions to meet these on the technology stack level. Some other websites and applications built on Node are eBay, GoDaddy, Groupon, Uber, Netflix, Mozilla, Yahoo, LinkedIn, and so on. The outstanding performance offered by Node makes it the heart of the MEAN stack. According to a number of benchmarks, JavaScript technology for the backend outperforms several other backend programming languages, such as PHP, Python, and Ruby. Listed here are some of the major advantages of Node:

- **Fast code execution**: Google Chrome's V8 JavaScript engine makes the Node library extremely fast at code execution as V8 compiles JavaScript into native machine code.

- **Single-threaded operation**: Node is able to handle concurrent tasks because its architecture is built to use the single-threaded event loop model.

- **Highly Scalable**: Its microservice architecture makes Node highly scalable, thereby making it a highly sought after development environment by most start-ups and established companies alike.

- **Asynchronous and event-driven I/O**: Programs in Node do not run until an event occurs.

- **Open source (MIT license) and community support**: Node is a distributed development project that is governed by the Node.js Foundation. Also, Node has a very active and vibrant community with several code files shared by GitHub users.

- **Easy web-application deployment**: Node allows the automated deployment of web applications. Also, the deployment of further updates can be reduced to a single command with Node. Thus, the deployment of Node applications has also led to the proliferation of **Platform-as-a-service** (**PaaS**) providers such as Heroku, Modulus, and so on.

- **Easy scalability**: Developers find it easy to scale applications horizontally as well as vertically.

However, you should be aware of a few points before beginning application development in Node. Using relational databases in conjunction with Node might be a daunting task because Node does not provide support for them. Also, using Node is unsuitable for heavy-computation applications. Having given an overview of Node, we will now progress and build our first Node application in the next section.

> **Note**
>
> A detailed introduction to Node, implementing node features, and various activities will be covered in future chapters.

Getting Started with Node

Here, we will build on the introduction to Node from the previous topic and concretize our knowledge about Node by completing exercises and activities that will help us understand how application development with Node.js is achieved. To get started with Node, the first step is installation. You have two installation options: the LTS or stable version:

LTS (**Long-Term Support**): Support and maintenance are provided by the Node Foundation for at least 18 months from the date of release. So, it's better to use this version for the production of backend Node applications.

Stable: Stable has support for approximately 8 months after release, with features/updates released more often. This version can be used for production if you're using Node for frontend services (dependency management). If apps can be easily updated without interrupting the environment, this version will work for backend services in Node as well. In this book, we will be using the LTS version.

Before we start with Node application development, we need to understand the built-in modules that make up Node. The set of modules that you can use without any further installation are listed as follows, along with a short description:

- **Assert**: This module provides a set of assertion tests
- **Buffer**: This module is used to handle binary data
- **Child process**: This module is used to run a child process
- **Cluster**: This module is used to handle unhandled errors
- **Events**: This module is used to handle events
- **Filesystem (fs)**: This module is used to handle the filesystem
- **HTTPS**: This module is used to render Node as an HTTPS server

- **Path**: This module is used to handle file paths
- **Readline**: This module is used to handle readable streams one line at a time
- **Stream**: This module is used to handle streaming data
- **String**: This module is a decoder that's used to decode buffer objects into strings
- **Timers**: This module is used to execute a function after a given number of milliseconds

Beginning a Node application involves the following steps:

1. Importing and loading the required modules by invoking the **require** directive.
2. Creating the server that will receive the client's requests.
3. Reading the requests and returning the responses from the server that was created in the preceding step.

We will apply all of these steps in our first exercise.

Exercise 1: Creating Our First Node Program

Before beginning this exercise, make sure you have Node installed. Our aim is to create a Node program that will print **Hello World** on the browser window once the appropriate command is passed on to the server. To do so, the following steps have to be performed:

> **Note**
>
> The code files for this exercise can be found here: http://bit.ly/2TaT32E.

1. Create a JavaScript file and name it **hello.js**. This can be done using the options in the **File** tab.
2. Load the built-in **http** module by using the "require" directive and passing a constant variable (**http**) to it:

   ```
   const http = require ('http');
   ```
3. Declare and initialize the **hostname** and port as constant variables using the following code:

   ```
   const hostname = '127.0.0.1';
   const port = 8000;
   ```

4. Create the server using the **createServer** method and pass **req** and **res**, which denote a request to and a response from the server, respectively:

```
const server = http.createServer((req, res) => {
res.statusCode = 200;
res.setHeader('Content-Type', 'text/plain');
res.end('Hello World\n');
});
```

This created server sends the following response to the browser:

statusCode: 200, the **Content-Type** header in plain text, and a string, **Hello World**.

5. Have the server listen to localhost on port 8000 using the following command:

```
server.listen(port, hostname, () => {
console.log ('Server running at
http://${hostname}:${port}/');
});
```

6. Run the server using the following command prompt, as shown in the following screenshot:

```
node hello.js
```

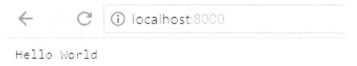

Figure 1.3: Running the server using the command prompt

The output is as follows:

Figure 1.4: Output of the hello.js program

One of the learning objectives of this book is to create the components of a blogging application with basic features. We will commence its development in this chapter. Most of this will be done in the activity section of each topic.

Activity 1: Creating an HTTP Server for a Blogging Application

You have been tasked with developing the HTTP server component for a blogging application. Your aim is to call the server and listen to the **localhost** on a specified port. Before you begin this activity, ensure that you have completed the previous exercise, in addition to creating a project directory named **Blogging Application** and a subfolder named **Server**. You can use an IDE of your choice; however, in this book, we are using Visual Studio.

To complete this activity, the following steps have to be completed:

> **Note**
>
> The code files for this activity can be found here: http://bit.ly/2TZYqz5.

1. Create a **server.js** file.

2. Declare and assign the HTTP server.

3. Declare and assign localhost and port number.

4. Create an HTTP server.

5. Listen to the server.

6. Run the **server.js** file on the command-line terminal.

7. Go to your browser and type in the **localhost:8000** address.

> **Note**
>
> The solution for this activity can be found on page 250.

Understanding Callbacks, Event Loops, and EventEmitters in Node

Callback

Node is built to be asynchronous in everything that it does. In this view, a callback is an asynchronous equivalent of a function that is called after a given task is completed. Alternatively, it can be defined as a function that is passed into another function so that the latter can call it on the completion of a given task. It allows other programs to keep running, thereby preventing blocking.

Let's consider a JavaScript global function, `setTimeout()`, as implemented in the following snippet:

```
setTimeout(function () {
console.log("1…2…3…4…5 secs later.");
}, 5000);
```

`setTimeout()` accepts a callback function and a delay in milliseconds as first and second arguments, respectively. The callback function is fired after 5,000 milliseconds has elapsed, thereby printing "**1…2…3…4…5 secs later.**" to the console.

An interesting thing is that the preceding code can be rewritten and simplified, as shown here:

```
var callback = function () {
console.log("1…2…3…4…5 secs later.");
};
setTimeout(callback, 5000)
```

Another example of callbacks can be seen in filesystem operations. **readFile** (asynchronous) and **readFileSync** (synchronous) are two unique API functions in the Node library that can be used to read a file.

An example of synchronous reading is as follows:

```
var Filedata = fs.readFileSync('fileText.txt');
console.log(FileData);
```

The **readFileSync()** method reads a file synchronously (all of the content is read at the same time). It takes in the file path (this could be in the form of a string, URL, buffer, or integer) and an optional parameter (either an encoder, which could be a string, null, or a flag in the form of a string) as an argument. In the case of the preceding snippet, the synchronous filesystem function takes in a file (**fileText.txt**) from the directory and the next line prints the contents of the file as a buffer. Note that if the encoding option is specified, then this function returns a string. Otherwise, it returns a buffer, just as we've seen here.

An example of asynchronous reading is as follows:

```
var callback = function (err, FileData) {
if (err) return console.error(err);
console.log(FileData);
};
fs.readFile('fileText.txt', callback);
```

In the preceding snippet, the **readFile()** method asynchronously reads the entire contents of a file (read serially until all its content is entirely read). It takes in the file path (this could be in the form of a string, URL, buffer, or integer), an optional parameter (either an encoder, which could be a string or null, or a flag in the form of a string), and a callback as arguments. It can be seen from the first line that the callback function accepts two arguments: **err** and data (**FileData**). The **err** argument is passed first because, as API calls are made, it becomes difficult to track an error, thus, it's best to check whether **err** has a value before you do anything else. If so, stop the execution of the callback and log the error. This is known as **error-first callback**.

In addition, if callbacks are not used (as seen in the previous example on synchronous reading) when dealing with a large file, you will be using massive amounts of memory, and this leads to a delay before the transfer of data begins (network latency). To summarize, from the use of the two filesystem functions, that is, the **readFileSync()**, which works synchronously, and the **readFile()**, which works asynchronously, we can deduce that the latter is safer than the former.

Also, in a situation where a callback is heavily nested (multiple asynchronous operations are serially executed), callback hell (also known as the pyramid of doom) may occur, when the code becomes unreadable and maintenance becomes difficult. Callback hell can be avoided by breaking callbacks into modular units (modularization) by using a generator with promises, implementing async/await, and by employing a control flow library.

> **Note**
>
> For more information on callback hell, refer to this link:
> http://callbackhell.com/.

Event Loops

An event loop is an efficient mechanism in Node that enables single-threaded execution. Everything that happens in Node is a reaction to an event. So, we can say that Node is an event-based platform, and that the event loop ensures that Node keeps running. Node uses event loops similar to a **FIFO** (**first-in first-out**) queue to arrange the tasks it has to do in its free time.

Let's assume that we have three programs running simultaneously. Given that each program is independent of another at any given time, they won't have to wait for the other before the output of each program is printed on the console. The following diagram shows the event loop cycle:

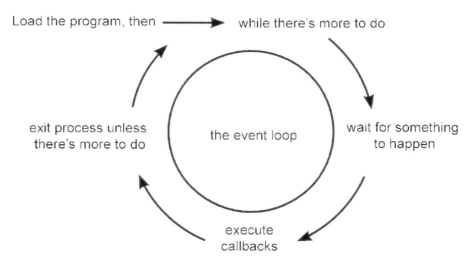

Figure 1.5: Event loop cycle

The following diagram shows the event queue and the call stack operations:

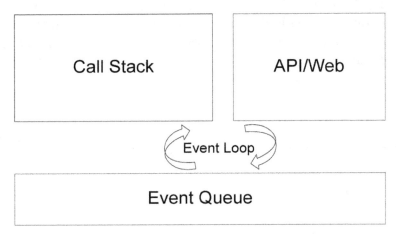

Figure 1.6: Event queue and call stack

To understand the concept of an event loop, we will consider the following implementation of an event loop in a program to calculate a perimeter:

```
const perimeter = function(a,b){
return 2*(a+b);
}
constshowPerimeter = function(){
console.log(perimeter(2,2));
}
const start = function(){
console.log('Initailizing.....');
console.log('Getting Started.....');
setTimeout(showPerimeter,10000);
console.log('Ending program.....');
console.log('Exiting.....');
}
start();
```

The operation sequence of the preceding snippet is listed here:

1. **start()** is pushed to memory, which is known as a call stack.
2. **console.log ('Initializing …..')** is pushed and popped on execution.

3. `console.log ('Getting Started …..')` is pushed and popped on execution.

4. `setTimeout(showPerimiter,10000)` is pushed into the stack, which is where a timer is created by the API, and the program does not wait for the callback.

5. `console.log ('Ending program…')` is pushed and popped on execution.

   If 10 seconds elapse, the `showPerimiter(2,2)` callback function will be sent to the event queue to wait until the stack is empty.

6. `console.log ('Exiting program…')` is pushed and popped on execution.

7. `Executed.start()` is also taken out of the stack.

8. The `showPerimiter(2,2)` function is moved to the stack and is executed.

9. Finally, **8** is printed to the command line, which is the perimeter.

Now, we are able to understand the concept of the event loop in Node. Next, we will explore the **EventEmitter**, which is one of the most important classes in Node.

EventEmitter

Callbacks are emitted and bound to an event by using a consistent interface, which is provided by a class known as **EventEmitter**. In real life, **EventEmitter** can be likened to anything that triggers an event for anyone to listen to.

EventEmitter implementation involves the following steps:

1. Importing and loading the event modules by invoking the "require" directive.

2. Creating the emitter class that extends the loaded event module.

3. Creating an instance of the emitter class.

4. Adding a listener to the instance.

5. Triggering the event.

EventEmitter Implementation

You can implement the **EventEmitter** by creating an **EventEmitter** instance using the following code:

```
var eEmitter = require('events'); // events module from node

class emitter extends eEmitter {} // EventEmitter class extended

var myeEmitter = new emitter(); // EventEmitter instance
```

The AddListener Method

EventEmitter makes it possible for you to add listeners to any random event. For flexibility, multiple callbacks can be added to a single event. Either **addListener(event, listener)** or **on(event, listener)** can be used to add a listener because they perform similar functions. You can use the following code block to add listeners:

```
var emitter = new MyClass();
emitter.on('event', function(arg1) { … });
```

You can also use the following code block to add listeners:

```
emitter.EventEmitter.addListener(event, function(arg1) { … });
```

Trigger Events

To trigger an event, you can use **emit(event, arg1)**, as can be seen here:

```
EventEmitter.emit(event, arg1, arg2……)
```

The **.emit** function takes an unlimited number of arguments and passes them on to the callback(s) associated with the event.

By putting all of this code together, we have the following snippet:

```
var eEmitter = require('events');
class emitter extends eEmitter { }
var myEemitter = new emitter();
myEemitter.on('event', () => {
    console.log('Hey, an event just occurred!');
});
myEemitter.emit('event');
```

Removing Listeners

We can also remove a listener from an event by using the **removeListener(event, listener)** or **removeAllListeners(event)** functions. This can be done using the following code:

```
EventEmitter. removeAllListeners (event, arg1, arg2……)
```

Alternatively, you can use the following code:

```
EventEmitter. removeListener(event, listener)
```

EventEmitter works synchronously; therefore, listeners are called in the order in which they are registered to ensure proper sequencing of events. This also helps avoid race conditions or logic errors. The **setImmediate()** or **process.nextTick()** methods make it possible for a listener to switch to an asynchronous mode.

For example, let's say we wanted an output such as "**Mr. Pick Piper**". We could use the following code:

```
console.log ("Mr.");
console.log("Pick");
console.log("Piper");
```

However, if we want an output such as "**Mr. Piper Pick**" using the preceding snippet, then we would introduce an event sequencing function, **setImmediate()**, to help the listener to switch to an asynchronous mode of operation, such as in the following code:

```
console.log ("Mr.");
console.log("Pick");

setImmediate(function(){
console.log("Piper");
});
```

The output of the preceding function is exactly as expected:

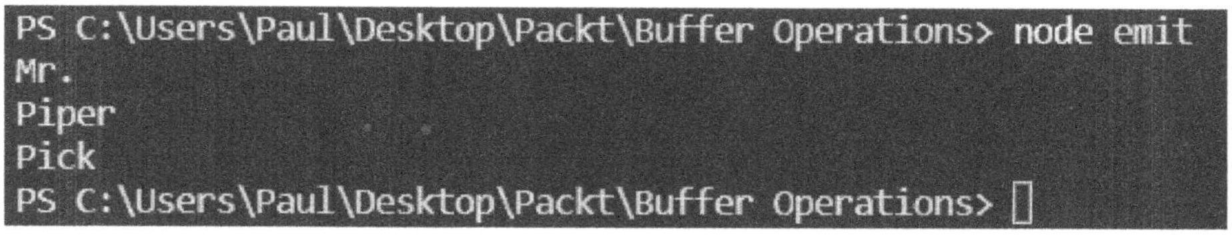

```
PS C:\Users\Paul\Desktop\Packt\Buffer Operations> node emit
Mr.
Piper
Pick
PS C:\Users\Paul\Desktop\Packt\Buffer Operations> []
```

Figure 1.7: Output using the sequencing function

Note

Callbacks, event loops, and event emitters are important concepts in Node.js. However, a more detailed description is beyond the scope of this book. For more information on these topics, please refer to this link: https://nodejs.org/.

Some Other Features of EventEmmitter

`eventEmitter.once()`: This can be used to add a callback that is expected to just trigger once, even when an event occurs repeatedly. It is very important to keep the number of listeners to a minimum (`EventEmitter` expects the `setMaxListeners` method to be called). If more than a maximum of 10 listeners are added to an event, a warning will be flagged.

`myEmitter.emit('error', new Error('whoops!'))`: This emits the typical action for an error event when errors occur within an `EventEmmitter` instance.

Understanding Buffers, Streams, and the Filesystem in Node

We've described several features of Node in the preceding topics. However, our introduction to Node wouldn't be complete without looking at some features, such as buffers, streams, and filesystems, which make Node stand out on the development scene. So, in this topic, we will look at how these features play their respective part in the Node environment.

Buffer

This is a chunk of memory where data is stored temporarily. This non-resizable memory is designed to handle raw binary data, and the integers in it are limited to values from 0 to 255 ($2^8 - 1$), with each integer representing one byte.

Let's look at a real-world scenario so that we have a better understanding of what buffers are and how they work by using the following screenshot from a YouTube video:

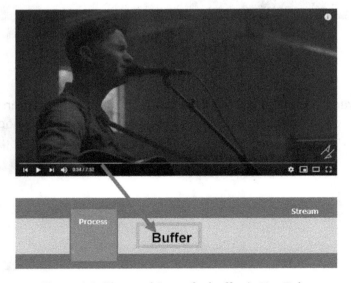

Figure 1.8: The workings of a buffer in YouTube

When a YouTube video starts to play, and if the internet is super fast, a gray area is observed in the playing stream. This area is the buffer zone, where data is being collected and stored temporarily (usually in the RAM) to allow for continuous playing, even when the internet is disconnected. The red zone is the playing zone (data processing zone) whose length is dependent on the video's playing speed and the amount of data that has been buffered. If the browser is refreshed, the temporary storage is re-initialized and the process is restarted.

Now that we have seen a real-time application using a buffer, we will now create, read, and write to buffers in the upcoming exercises.

Exercise 2: Creating, Reading, and Writing to a Buffer

In this exercise, our aim is to create, read from, and write to a buffer. Before attempting this exercise, make sure you have completed all of the previous activities in this chapter. To complete this exercise, perform the following steps:

> **Note**
>
> The code files for this exercise can be found here: http://bit.ly/2SiwAw6.

1. Create a new folder in an appropriate location in your system and rename it **Buffer Operations**.

2. Open the newly created **Buffer Operations** folder from your code editor and create a **buffer.js** file. Buffers can be created in the following ways:

   You can create an uninitialized buffer by passing the buffer size to **Buffer.alloc()**, or you can create an instance of a buffer class; for example, let's create an uninitiated buffer of 5 bytes using the following code:

   ```
   var buf1 = Buffer.alloc(5);
   var buf2 = new Buffer(5);
   console.log(buf1)
   console.log(buf2)
   ```

   The output is as follows:

   ```
   PROBLEMS    OUTPUT    DEBUG CONSOLE    TERMINAL
   PS C:\Users\Paul\Desktop\Packt\Buffer Operations> node buffer
   <Buffer 00 00 00 00 00>
   <Buffer 00 00 00 00 00>
   PS C:\Users\Paul\Desktop\Packt\Buffer Operations>
   ```

   Figure 1.9: A buffer of 5 bytes

You can create a buffer using a given array using **from()** or using an instance of a buffer; for example, let's initialize a buffer with the contents of the array **[10, 20, 30, 40, 50]**:

```
varbuf3 = new Buffer([10, 20, 30, 40, 50]);
varbuf4 = Buffer.from([ 10, 20, 30, 40, 50]);
console.log(buf3)
console.log(buf4)
```

Note that the integers that make up the array's contents represent bytes. The output can be seen as follows:

```
PROBLEMS    OUTPUT    DEBUG CONSOLE    TERMINAL

PS C:\Users\Paul\Desktop\Packt\Buffer Operations> node buffer
<Buffer 0a 14 1e 28 32>
<Buffer 0a 14 1e 28 32>
PS C:\Users\Paul\Desktop\Packt\Buffer Operations>
```

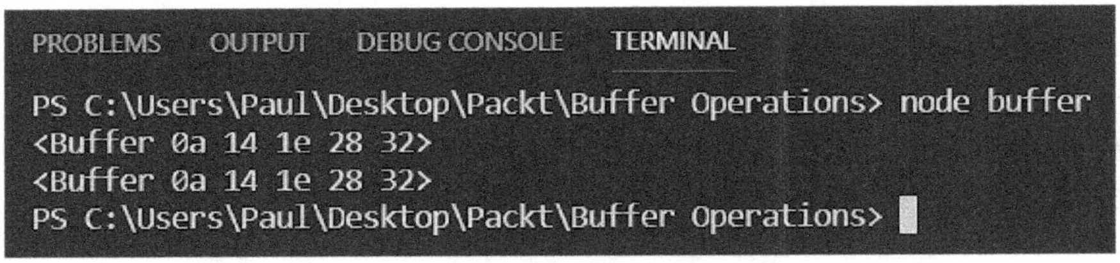

Figure 1.10: A buffer created using array content

Finally, you can create a buffer using a given string and, optionally, the encoding type using **from()** or using an instance of a buffer. The following code initializes the buffer to a binary encoding of the first argument, which is a string that's specified by the second argument, which is an encoding type:

```
var buf5 = new Buffer("Hi Packt students!", "utf-8");
var buf6 = Buffer.from("Hi Packt students!", "utf-8")
console.log(buf5)
console.log(buf6)
```

The output can be seen as follows:

```
PROBLEMS    OUTPUT    DEBUG CONSOLE    TERMINAL

PS C:\Users\Paul\Desktop\Packt\Buffer Operations> node buffer
<Buffer 48 69 20 70 61 63 6b 74 20 73 74 75 64 65 6e 74 73 21>
<Buffer 48 69 20 70 61 63 6b 74 20 73 74 75 64 65 6e 74 73 21>
PS C:\Users\Paul\Desktop\Packt\Buffer Operations>
```

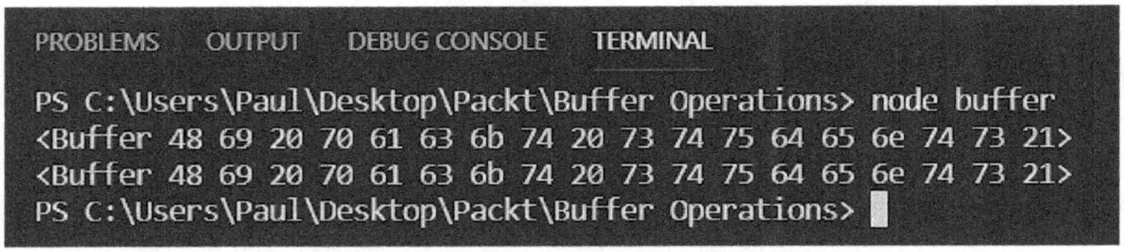

Figure 1.11: Output of the buffer created using a string

The buffer also supports encoding methods such as **ascii**, **ucs2**, **base64**, **binary**, and so on.

3. To write into a buffer, we can use the **buff.write()** method. The output returned after a buffer has been written to (created) is the number of octets written into it:

```
buffer.write(string[, offset][, length][, encoding])
```

Note that the first argument is the string to write to the buffer and the second argument is the encoding. If the encoding is not set, the default encoding, which is **utf-8**, will be used. Write into the buffer that we created in the preceding step using the following code:

```
len = buf5.write("Packt student", "utf-8")
console.log (len) //The length becomes 13 after writing into the buffer
```

The output can be seen as follows:

Figure 1.12: Output of the buffer using utf-8

4. To read from the buffer, the **toString()** method is commonly used, but keep in mind that many buffers contain text. This method is implemented as follows:

```
buffer.toString([encoding][, start][, end])
```

Here, we will read from the buffer that was written into in the preceding step and print the output on the command line using the following code:

```
console.log(buf5.toString("utf-8", 0, 13))
```

```
PROBLEMS    OUTPUT    DEBUG CONSOLE    TERMINAL
PS C:\Users\Paul\Desktop\Packt\Buffer Operations> node buffer
Pactk student
PS C:\Users\Paul\Desktop\Packt\Buffer Operations>
```

Figure 1.13: Reading from the buffer

There are a few more methods for buffers, which will be covered in the following sections.

Uninitialized Buffers

You can also create buffers using the **allocUnsafe(length)** method. The **allocUnsafe(length)** method creates an uninitialized buffer of the assigned length. When compared to the **buffer.alloc()** method, it is much faster, but old data in the returned buffer instance needs to be overwritten using either **fill()** or **write()**.

Let's see how the **allocUnsafe(length)** method is being used in the following snippet:

```
var buf = Buffer.allocUnsafe(15);
var buf1 = Buffer.alloc(15);


console.log(buf);
console.log(buf1);
```

The preceding snippet yields the following output:

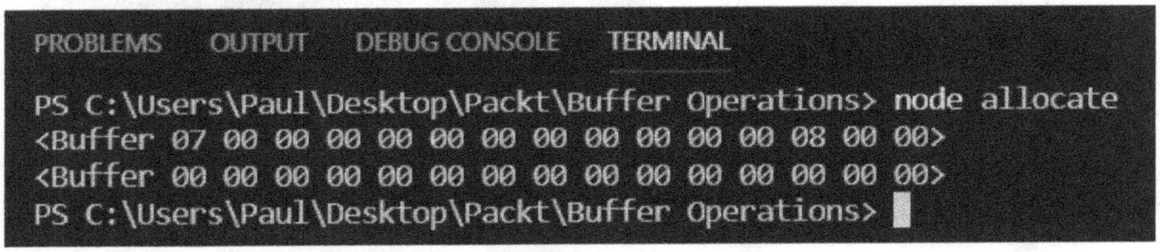

Figure 1.14: Output of the buffer created using allocateUnsafe(length) and alloc(length)

Some Other Buffer Methods

There are a few other methods that you need to be aware of. These are listed here:

- **byteLength(string, encoding)**: This method is used to check the number of bytes required to encode a string with a given encoding.

- **length**: This method is used to check the length of your buffer, that is, how much memory is allocated.

- **copy(target, targetStart=0, sourceStart=0, sourceEnd=buffer.length)**: This method is used to copy the contents of one buffer into another.

- **buffer.slice(start, end=buffer.length)**: This is the same as **Array.prototype. slice**, except modifying the slice will also modify the original buffer.

Streams

Whenever you talk about reading data from a source and writing it to a destination, you're referring to streams (**Unix pipes**). A stream can be likened to an `EventEmitter`. There are four types of streams, and they are as follows:

- **Readable**: Allows you to read data from a source.

- **Writable**: Allows you to write data to a destination.

- **Duplex**: Allows you to read data from a source and write data to a destination.

- **Transform**: Allows you to modify or transform data while data is being read or written.

Reading Data from Streams

A stream is said to be readable if it permits data to be read from a source, irrespective of what the source is, be it another stream, a file in a filesystem, a buffer in memory, and so on. Various data events can be emitted at various points in a stream. Thus, streams can also be referred to as instances of `EventEmitters`. Listening to a data event and attaching a callback are the best ways to read data from a stream. A readable stream emits a data event, and your callback executes when data is available.

Let's observe how a stream is read, a data event is emitted, and a callback is executed using the filesystem module with a readable and writable file. See the following code:

```
const fs = require('fs');
const file = fs.createReadStream('readTextFile.txt');
file.on('data', function(data) {
console.log('Data '+ data);
});
file.on('end', function(){
console.log('Hey!, Am Done reading Data');
});
```

First, we created a file named **readTextFile.txt**. Then, a readable stream is created using the `fs.createReadStream('filename')` function. It is good to know that the stream is in a static state initially, and gets to a flowing state as soon as you listen to a data event and attach a callback. Streams emit an **end** event when there is no more data to read.

Writing to Streams

A stream is said to be writeable if it permits data to be written to a destination, irrespective of what the destination is. It could be another stream, a file in a filesystem, a buffer in memory, and so on. Similar to readable streams, various events that are emitted at various points in writeable streams can also be referred to as instances of **EventEmitter**. The **write()** function is available on the **stream** instance. It makes writing data to a stream possible.

Take a look at the following snippet:

```
const fs = require('fs');
const readableStream = fs.createReadStream('readTextFile.txt');
const writableStream = fs.createWriteStream('writeTextFile.txt');
readableStream.on('data', function (data) {
console.log('Hey!, I am about to write what has been read from the file
readTextFile.txt');
if (writableStream.write(data) === true) {
console.log('Hey!, I am done writing. Open the file writeTextFile.txt to see
what has been written');
    }
else
console.log('Writing is not successful');
});
```

First, we load the filesystem using the **require** directive. Then, we create two files: **readTextFile.txt** and **writeTextFile.txt**. We then write some text string into the **readTextFile.txt** file and leave **writeTextFile.txt** blank. Using the filesystem **createReadStream()** function with the file path or directory as an argument, we create a readable stream. Thereafter, a writeable stream is created using the filesystem **createWriteStream()** function with the file path or directory as an argument. **readableStream.on('data', callback)** listens to a data event and attaches a callback, whereas **writableStream.write(data)** writes data to a writable stream. Once this snippet is run, you will realize that the text string read from **readTextFile.txt** has been written into the **writeTextFile.txt** file.

Duplex

Recall from the short description in the previous section that a duplex is a type of stream that allows you to read data from a source and write data to a destination. Examples of duplex streams are as follows:

- **crypto** streams
- TCP **socket** streams
- **zlib** streams

Transform

This is another stream method that lets you modify or transform data while data is being read or written. In essence, transform streams are duplex streams with the aforementioned functionality. Examples of transform streams are as follows:

- **crypto** streams
- **zlib** streams

Some Other Stream Methods

end(): When this method is called, a finish event is emitted by the stream and a notification is sent to the stream that you have finished writing to.

setEncoding(): Upon being called, the stream becomes encoded. This method is used in a situation where a readable stream needs to be encoded.

pipe(): When this method is called on a readable stream, you can read data from the source and write to the destination without normal flow management.

pause(): When this method is called on a flowing stream, the stream pauses, data will be kept in the buffer, and data events will not be emitted anymore. When this is called on a non-flowing stream, data events will not be emitted, but the stream will start flowing.

resume(): When this method is called on a paused stream, the stream starts to flow again.

unpipe(): When this method is called on a piped readable stream, the destination streams are removed from pipes.

Filesystems

Node has a module name File System (fs) that works with the file systems on a computer. This module, **fs**, performs several methods that can be implemented both synchronously and asynchronously, but there is there is no guaranteed ordering when using them.

Reading, creating, updating, deleting, and renaming are some of the operations that can be performed on any text file that's saved in a directory.

Reading Files

After the required directive has been invoked for the **fs** module, assuming that we have a string of text contained in the text file, the file can be read by calling the **readFile()** function, as shown here:

```
var fs = require('fs');
fs.readFile('readFileName.txt', function(err, data) {
if (err) throw err;
console.log('Read!');
   });
```

Creating Files

The methods that are highlighted here are made available by the **fs** module for creating new files:

fs.appendFile(): This method appends a given content to a file. The file will be created in this case, even if it does not exist. This function can also be used to update a file. Its implementation is as follows:

```
var text = ' Hey John, Welcome to Packt class.'
var fs = require('fs');
fs.appendFile('newTextFile.txt', 'text'
', function (err) {
  if (err) throw err;
  console.log('Saved!');
  });
```

Once the preceding code is run, you will see the designated string written into the file.

fs.open(): When this method is called, a given file is opened for writing, and if the file doesn't exist, an empty file will be created. The implementation is as follows:

```
var fs = require('fs');
fs.open('TextFile.txt', 'w', function (err, file) {
   if (err) throw err;
// let's assume the file doesn't exist
   console.log('An empty file created');
});
```

This method takes a second argument, **w**, which is referred to as a flag for "writing."

fs.writeFile(): When this method is called on a given file and content exists in it, the existing content is replaced by new content. In a situation where the file doesn't exist, a new file containing the given content will be created. This function can also be used to update the file, and the implementation is as follows:

```
Var fs = require('fs');
fs.writeFile('textFile.txt', 'Hello content!', function (err) {
if(err)throwerr;
console.log('Saved!');
});
```

Deleting Files

fs.unlink(): When this method is called on a given file in the filesystem, the file is deleted. The implementation is as follows:

```
var fs = require('fs');
fs.unlink('textFile.txt', function (err) {
   if (err) throw err;
   console.log('File deleted!');
});
```

Renaming Files

`fs.rename()`: This method takes in three arguments: the old name of the file, the new name of the file, and a callback. When this method is called on a given file in the filesystem, the file is renamed. The implementation is as follows:

```
var fs = require('fs');
fs.rename('textFile.txt', 'renamedtextFile.txt', function (err) {
  if (err) throw err;
  console.log('File Renamed!');
});
```

Some Other Methods in the Filesystems Module

`access()`: This method is used to check whether a user has access to the file or directory.

`close()`: This method is used to close a file.

`exists()`: Though this method is deprecated, it's called on a file to check whether a file or folder exists.

`fstat()`: When this method is called on a file, it returns the status of that file.

`link()`: This method is used to create an additional name for a file. The name could either be the old or a new one.

`mkdir()`: This method is used make a new directory.

`readdir()`: This method is used to read the contents of a directory.

`rmdir()`: This method is used to remove a directory.

`stat()`: This method is used to return the status of a file.

`truncate()`: This method is used to truncate a file.

`watch()`: This method is used to watch for changes in a file name or directory name.

> **Note**
>
> For more information on the Node.js APIs, refer to this link:
> https://nodejs.org/api/.

Exercise 3: Reading and Writing Data Using Filesystem Operations

Our aim is to read and write data using the Node filesystem. To complete this exercise, the following steps have to be performed:

> **Note**
>
> The code files for this exercise can be found here: http://bit.ly/2U1FIH5.

1. Create a new folder at an appropriate location and rename it **FileSystemProgram**.

2. Open the newly created **FileSystemProgram** from your code editor and create **write.js**, **read.js**, **write.txt**, and **read.txt**, as shown here:

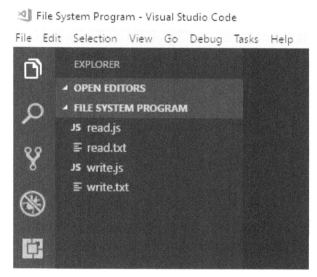

Figure 1.15: Creating filesystem program files

3. Open the **read.txt** file and write some text; for example, "**Welcome to Packt**." To read what has been previously input in the **read.txt** file, open the **read.js** file and type in the following code:

```
var fs = require('fs')
fs.readFile('read.txt', function(err, data) {
if (err) throw err;
console.log('Read!');});
```

First, we will use **var fs = require('fs')** to declare **fs** (a filesystem variable) and assign a filesystem module to it. Then, we will use the **readFile()** function on the **read.txt** file and attach a callback. Next, we will check for errors using **if (err) throw err**. If no errors are present, then we will print "**Read!**" using **console.log('Read!')**.

4. Press *Ctrl + `* to open the integrated command-line terminal in Visual Studio and run the following command:

```
node read.js
```

Figure 1.16: Running the read program

5. Open the **write.js** file to write into the **write.txt** file and run the following command:

```
var fs = require('fs');
fs.writeFile('write.txt','Welcome to packt' function(err, data) {
if (err) throw err;
console.log('Written!');  });
```

We use **var fs = require('fs')** to declare **fs** (a filesystem variable) and assign a filesystem module to it. We then use **fs.writeFile('write.txt', 'Welcome to Packt' function(err, data)** to call the **writeFile()** function on the **write.txt** file, pass the text to be written as the second argument, and attach a callback as the third argument. Thereafter, we check for **if errors** using **if (err) throw err**. If there are no errors, we print **Written!** using **console.log('Written!')**.

6. Press *Ctrl + `* to open the integrated command-line terminal in Visual Studio and run the following command:

```
node write.js
```

You will obtain the following output:

Figure 1.17: Running the write program

7. Open the `write.txt` file to view what has been written from the output, as shown here:

Figure 1.18: Contents written to the file

The previous examples and activities have explored the knowledge and implementation of different built-in modules in Node. The next activity will be a hands-on implementation of streaming data from one file to another.

Activity 2: Streaming Data to a File

You have been tasked with developing an application that streams data (copies some text) from a local file on your system into another local file that's located in a different directory. The aim is to read and write data to a stream.

Before we begin this activity, it is essential that you have completed all the previous exercises and activities. Then, use the IDE to create a project called **StreamingProgram**.

To complete this exercise, the following steps have to be completed:

> **Note**
>
> The code files for this activity can be found here: http://bit.ly/2EkRW8j.

1. Create a folder/directory and name it **StreamingProgram**.
2. Create `stream.js`, `readTextFile.txt`, and `writeTextFile.txt` in the **StreamingProgram** directory.
3. Load and import the filesystem module into `stream.js` file.
4. Create a readable stream on the `readTextFile.txt` file.

5. Create a writeable stream on the `writeTextFile.txt` file.

6. Call the `on()` function on the `readableStream()` method to read data.

7. Call the `write()` method on the `writeableStream() method` to write data.

8. Run the `stream.js` program via the command line and open the `writeTextFile.txt` file to confirm that the text has been written to it.

> **Note**
>
> The solution for this activity can be found on page 251.

Summary

In this chapter, we first described **MEAN** architecture by briefly expanding on the layers that comprise the MEAN stack: **MongoDB**, **Express**, **Angular**, and **Node**. For each of these components, we discussed their features/advantages and limitations. Thereafter, we began by describing the Node framework in detail. We first discussed the various installation options (the LTS and stable versions) that are available. Then, we had a brief look at the built-in modules that make up Node and also learned about the steps that are involved in starting a Node application.

In the subsequent topics, we described some important concepts in Node, such as callbacks, event loops, event emitters, buffers, streams, and the filesystem. For callbacks, we described their implementation in synchronous and asynchronous mode. We also looked into how Node employs event loops in sequencing program operations. Next, we learned how to add event listeners, trigger events, remove listeners, and implement some other features. We then moved on to discuss buffers. Specifically, we learned how to create, read, and write to buffers. The next topic described the various types of streams that are available. We performed an exercise on writing to and reading from a stream. Finally, we discussed the filesystem and implemented different operations that can be performed on a file via an activity.

In the next chapter, we will begin developing RESTful APIs to perform **create**, **read**, **update**, and **delete** (**CRUD**) operations.

Developing RESTful APIs to Perform CRUD Operations

Learning Objectives

By the end of this chapter, you will be able to:

- Describe the design concept of a RESTful API

- Create a MongoDB Atlas cluster with Node

- Connect a Node application to a database with the native MongoDB driver and Mongoose

- Create a database schema and a data model with Mongoose

- Create and export routes

- Implement Express with Node

- Develop a RESTful API

This chapter presents the fundamentals and practical elements that will enable you to develop and test a RESTful API.

Introduction

We began this book by describing the **MEAN** (**MongoDB**, **Express**, **Angular**, and **Node**) architecture. Specifically, we described its technology components in terms of their features/advantages, limitations, and scenarios in which they are best used. We ran a Node server and implemented various Node features, such as callbacks, event loops, event emitters, streams, buffers, and the filesystem.

This chapter will revolve around RESTful APIs, which are a major application of Node that leverage HTTP request types to indicate a desired action. We will also introduce you to the RESTful API and its designs concepts. Later in this chapter, we will talk about some operations of MongoDB Atlas, such as creating clusters, schemas, and connecting the database to applications. This chapter will present the Express framework and its feature implementation on Node and MongoDB Atlas.

Finally, you'll implement Node, MongoDB Atlas, and Express together, with the goal of developing a RESTful API to perform **CRUD** (**Create**, **Read**, **Update**, and **Delete**) operations. The chapter activity will wrap up the backend development for our sample application by creating a RESTful API for our nascent blogging application, which was developed in the first chapter.

Getting Started with RESTful APIs

An **API** (**Application Programming Interface**) is a set of subroutines and protocols that communicate between two components, if possible. To best comprehend the functionality of an API, let's take a look at the following case study.

Consider you have a functioning e-commerce website, and at a point in time you discover the need to track where your customers are actually located so that this data can be used for analytics and marketing purposes. So, you decide to integrate the Google Geolocation API on your e-commerce website instead of creating your own geolocation program from scratch, which would definitely cost you more in terms of both money and time.

Now, how does the Google Geolocation API work?

Whenever a customer visits your website after the Geolocation API is implemented on it, a request is fired to get the location of the GPS-enabled device that was used to access the website. Then, a response is fed back as a result. This response contains a location and address in JSON format, which is then retrieved and stored. A sample of this process is shown in the following code:

```
The API collects the longitude and latitude of the GPS-enabled device
using this URL:
https://maps.googleapis.com/maps/api/geocode/json?latlng=40.714224,
-73.961452&key=YOUR_API_KEY                                          Request


"results" : [
   {
      "address_components" : [
         {
            "long_name" : "277",
            "short_name" : "277",                      Response
            "types" : [ "street_number" ]
         },
         {
            "long_name" : "Bedford Avenue",
            "short_name" : "Bedford Ave",
            "types" : [ "route" ]
         },
         {
```

Figure 2.1: Google Geolocation request and response

In the aforementioned example, the Geolocation API is very robust. Let's assume that you, as a developer, are tasked with developing an API that may some day go public. In such a scenario, you have to think of an API design that will provide room for easy evolution. This is where **REST** (**Representative State Transfer**) APIs come into play.

REST is an architectural style that defines a set of restrictions based on **HTTP** (**Hypertext Transfer Protocol**). Using a REST API design is easy because there's no need to install libraries or additional software. Building APIs that meet your needs and those of your diverse customers has been simplified by the freedom and flexibility that exists in REST API designs. RESTful APIs can be implemented with CRUD HTTP methods such as **GET**, **POST**, **PUT**, and **DELETE**, which are used for mutation, creation, and deletion, respectively. Furthermore, the REST stateless protocol and its interaction with resources through standard operations help systems achieve scalability, fast performance, and reliability.

The reuse of components that can be managed and updated (that is, the ability to handle multiple types of calls, return different data formats, and so on) without affecting the system as a whole, even while it is running, is the major backbone of the REST system.

We have seen the basic definition of a REST API, along with a real-world case study. We have also understood the benefits that are offered by RESTful APIs. Now, we will look into the Node RESTful API design practices that's employed by established companies in the industry to develop scalable, secure, and reliable APIs.

Node RESTful APIs Design Practice

When it comes to designing an API, there's a need to consider and adopt the design practice of successful tech giants whose APIs are being called a million times a day to avoid the aftermath of poor design, such as poor security and the inability to scale, which is often the case when developing APIs. The key success factor in developing a solid API is a strong and robust design. The guiding framework for web standards and designing web services is described by Roy Fielding in his PhD dissertation. This design framework has been adopted by web giants such as **Google**, **Microsoft**, **Facebook**, **PayPal**, and many others. Some of the best practices that developers can emulate from these tech giants are as follows:

1. **Use naming conventions that coincide with standard HTTP URL methods and API routes**:

   Make sure your URLs are simple and intuitive by keeping verbs out of your base URLs. Also, keep singular or plural names short. The following table summarizes HTTP URL methods:

ROUTE	GET	POST	PATCH	PUT	DELETE
/articles	Retrieve all articles	Create a new article	Modify articles	Update articles	Delete all articles
/article:/id:	Retrieve an article	Error	Modify an article-specify key	Update or create an article-specify key	Delete an article-specify key
Incorrect Naming Convention					
/getAllarticles					
/getAnarticle:/id					
/deleteAllatricles					
/deleteOneArticle:/id					

Figure 2.2: HTTP routes and naming conventions

2. **Use HTTP status codes correctly**: It is of utmost importance to ensure that standard responses with correct status codes are returned when something goes wrong while serving a request. The following table shows some recommended status codes:

STATUS CODE	MEANING
200	All ok
400	Bad request; Some required parameter is missing
401	Unauthorized (user not logged-in); Consumer of this API (web/mobile apps) should be redirected to the login page
403	Forbidden/Access denied
500	Internal server error

Figure 2.3: HTTP status codes

3. **Send metadata using HTTP headers**: When sending payloads, their metadata should be attached to the HTTP header. For example, information about authentication and pagination can be passed into the header.

> **Note**
>
> A list of HTTP headers can be found here: https://developer.mozilla.org/en-US/docs/Web/HTTP/Headers.

4. **Use the right framework**: It's best to make a good decision on the right use of technology when embarking on any design and development journey, since technology frameworks and tools perform best when used in their areas of strength. For example, it's highly recommended to use Express when it comes to browser applications, as these applications need to provide templating and rendering to the user-facing side. On the other hand, when the focus is on building "strict" RESTful API services that are maintainable and observable, you can opt for a production framework.

5. **Perform black-box testing**: It is very important to test and validate the functionality of an API before using it. Black-box testing makes it possible to examine an API's functionality without needing to know its internal structures. Functionality testing can be performed on Node RESTful APIs using the **supertest** module. For example, the following snippet shows a test case on a user ID **GET** request; it examines whether a user is returned with some specified properties:

```
const request = require('supertest')
describe('Get /user/:id', function(){
    interface('returns a user', function(){
        return request(app)
        .get('/user')
        .set('Accept', 'application/json')
        .expect(200, {
            id:'1',
            name:'Paul Oluyege',
        }, done)
    })
})
```

6. **Perform JWT-based stateless authentication**: If the state of the user isn't maintained on the server side, then the authentication is said to be stateless. JWT (JSON Web Token) is one of the best methods for implementing stateless authentication, and it's highly recommended for the Node RESTful API.

7. **Create proper API documentation**: The first thing a developer checks before using a third-party API is the documentation. Providing comprehensive API documentation for your Node REST APIs is of great importance. Swagger and API Blueprint are open source projects that can help you with creating API documentation.

> **Note**
>
> To read more about HTTP specification and the Representational State Transfer (REST) architectural style, as described by Roy Fielding, refer to this link: https://tools.ietf.org/html/draft-griffin-bliss-rest-00. For a full list of HTTP status codes, refer to this link: https://www.w3.org/Protocols/rfc2616/rfc2616-sec10.html.

So far, we have explained the design concept of a RESTful API by first describing the relationship between API and REST, and then by listing design practices for Node RESTful APIs. In the next section, we will get started with MongoDB Atlas, which is a database-as-a-service offering by MongoDB. Specifically, we will employ the MongoDB Atlas service to store data and resources that are transferred over the RESTful APIs we aim to develop.

Getting Started with MongoDB Atlas

We covered an introduction to MongoDB in the first chapter. Recall that MongoDB is a document-oriented database program, also classified as a NoSQL database, and it uses JSON-like documents with schemas. In this book, MongoDB Atlas, which was highlighted briefly in the previous chapter as one of the database-as-a -service offerings by MongoDB for addressing the affordability challenges of small-scale start-ups and independent developers, will be used. First, we will set up an account on MongoDB and then set up MongoDB servers, known as clusters, to connect to applications. Finally, we will employ default (native) database drivers and a third-party driver to have the database connect with to Node application. We will also create database schemas and data models.

If you have an existing MongoDB account, you can use your credentials to log in to the MongoDB Atlas dashboard. If you don't, then you can sign up for free at https://www.MongoDB.com/cloud/atlas.

Clusters

Clusters are a set of MongoDB Atlas server components that can connect to applications. Three types of cluster are available: shared, dedicated, and production. The only freely available cluster among these is the shared cluster. In the following exercise, we will create our first free-tier cluster on MongoDB Atlas.

Exercise 4: Creating a Free-Tier Cluster on MongoDB Atlas

In this exercise, we will be creating a free MongoDB cluster. You will need to set up an account on MongoDB Atlas before you attempt this exercise. Perform the following steps to complete this exercise:

1. Log in to MongoDB Atlas to access the dashboard, as shown in the following screenshot:

Figure 2.4: MongoDB Atlas cluster dashboard

2. Click **Build a New Cluster** and input the project name. Then, click **Next**, as shown in the following screenshot:

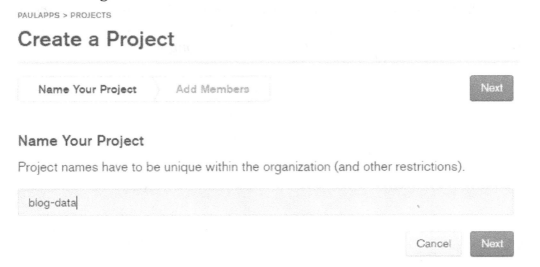

Figure 2.5: Creating a project on MongoDB Atlas

3. Select any free tier that's available, as shown in the following screenshot, and click **NEXT: CLUSTER TIER**:

Figure 2.6: MongoDB free tier

4. Select **M0**, a shared cluster (for the purpose of this book), and click **Create Cluster,** as shown in the following screenshot:

Figure 2.7: Shared cluster tier

5. Select the **Security** tab for the IP whitelist setting, as shown in the following screenshot:

Figure 2.8: Cluster creation on MongoDB Atlas

6. Add a whitelist IP.

   Select either **ADD CURRENT IP ADDRESS** (MongoDB Atlas will automatically detect your IP) or **ADD ACCESS FROM ANYWHERE**, as shown in the following screenshot (MongoDB Atlas will set the IP to **0.0.0.0/0**, which is not recommended). You can also add multiple IP addresses of your choice:

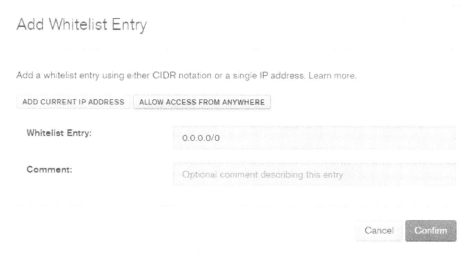

Figure 2.9: IP whitelisting

7. Click **Connect** on the cluster dashboard and observe the **Connect to Cluster0** pop-up page. Then, select the **Connect Your Application** tab under the **Choose a connection method:** label, as shown in the following screenshot:

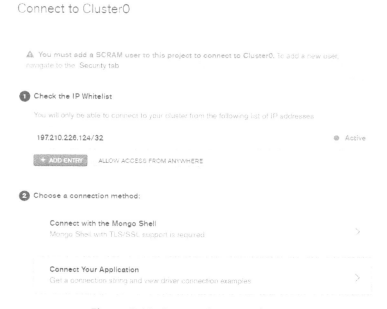

Figure 2.10: Connecting to a cluster

8. To connect the cluster to a Node application, we can use the connection strings that are shown in the following screenshot:

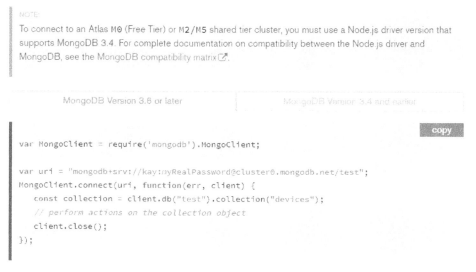

Figure 2.11: Connection strings

Note that MongoDB Atlas has made different connection strings available based on the language or technology that the application has been developed with. In this chapter, we are working with an API that was developed with Node, and the aforementioned procedures are important to successfully connect the cluster to the Node application.

The Native MongoDB Driver and Mongoose (Object Document Mapper)

The native MongoDB driver is the default tool that was developed by MongoDB to control the operations of the document-based database management system. CRUD operations using the native MongoDB driver are much faster than other drivers, such as Mongoose. The conventional method for performing a single **db** operation in each web request using MongoDB is as follows:

1. Open a database connection.

2. Complete your operation.

3. Close the connection.

If you have millions of concurrent requests using the conventional MongoDB method, then your app will crash. The native MongoDB driver makes provisions for developers to handle code that helps optimize the request process. Mongoose is an **Object Document Mapper** (**ODM**) that translates MongoDB documents into program objects, thereby making data access and manipulation in MongoDB easier. Mongoose also employs a principle called **Object Relational Mapping** (**ORM**). This principle is based on having strict models or schemas. You have to define your schema structure, unlike in the case of MongoDB, which doesn't need any fixed schema. You can insert or update documents as per your requirements.

In a situation where you are developing an app for a client that will not have millions of users or very high read/write concurrency, and you want to develop it quickly, then Mongoose is an appropriate choice. Development with Mongoose is really fast. You don't need to create a connection, close it in proper time, optimize the connection, make promises, and so on. The abstraction layer of Mongoose does all of this for you.

We have briefly discussed the fundamentals of the native MongoDB driver and Mongoose. Now, we will learn how to use the driver as well as the Mongoose ODM.

Using the Native MongoDB Driver

Before we establish the Node driver connection, as shown in *Exercise 4, Creating a Free Tier Cluster on MongoDB Atlas*, we first need to install the MongoDB driver using the following command: **npm install mongodb**. Then, we need to use the following command to call the MongoDB driver so that we can reference its properties:

```
var MongoClient = require('MongoDB').MongoClient;
```

Connection to the database is made possible by the **mongoClient.connect** class. The **uri** variable in the following snippet returns a reference to the client instance when establishing a connection. This variable is the connection string to MongoDB Atlas, and it is comprised of the user access parameters to the cluster and the cluster address itself:

```
var uri = "MongoDB+srv://<usernamed>:<password> @cluster0-0wi3e.MongoDB.net/
test?retryWrites=true";
```

Once the connection has been established, the document collection within the database is defined and database access and manipulation is made possible:

```
const options = {
    reconnectTries: Number.MAX_VALUE,
    poolSize: 10
  };
MongoClient.connect(uri, options)
 .then((db) => {
  accountsDb = db;
  collection = accountsDb.db('test');
  console.log('Successfully connected to MongoDB');
})

 .catch((err) => {
  console.log(err);
});
```

Using Mongoose

The first step in using Mongoose is installing the Mongoose package by using the **npm install mongoose** command.

The Mongoose module is required to allow the properties in it to be referenced from within the source file that creates the connection. This can be done with the following command:

```
var Mongoose = require(Mongoose)
```

The **uri** is also declared and assigned the MongoDB Atlas connection string, as seen with the MongoDB driver. Mongoose uses the connection functions that are shown in the following snippet. It provides an abstract layer for the purpose of eliminating the use of collections with the program. Also, function chaining in Mongoose, which is used by queries, makes code more readable, flexible, and maintainable. An example of this is shown as follows:

```
Mongoose.connect(uri, options).then(
    () => {
        console.log("Database connection established!");
    },
    err => {
        console.log("Error connecting Database instance due to: ", err);
    }
);
```

Now that we've gone through the theory and seen, with the aid of snippets, how MongoDB can be connected to an application, let's look at some exercises so that we have a solid understanding of this implementation.

Exercise 5: Connecting a Node Application with the MongoDB Native Driver

In this exercise, we will be connecting the native MongoDB driver to a Node application. Before you begin this exercise, create a folder called **MongoDB Native Driver.** It is assumed that you have already created a MongoDB Atlas cluster in previous exercise. Therefore, use the same cluster credentials (username and password) for this exercise. To complete this exercise, perform the following steps:

> **Note**
>
> The code files for this exercise can be found here: http://bit.ly/2GE5pKM.

1. Create a **db.js** file using the following code:

   ```
   touch db.js
   ```

2. Load the MongoDB module and create a **MongoClient** class instance using the following code:

   ```
   const MongoClient = require('MongoDB').MongoClient;
   ```

3. Declare a variable named **uri** and assign the MongoDB connection string using the following code:

   ```
   var uri = "mongodb+srv://username:password @cluster0-0wi3e.mongodb.net/
   test?retryWrites=true";
   ```

4. Declare a variable named **options** and assign the optional settings using the following code:

   ```
   const options = {
     reconnectTries: Number.MAX_VALUE,
     poolSize: 10,
   };)
     useNewUrlParser:true
   };
   ```

5. Connect MongoDB Atlas using the Mongoose.connect() method by using the following code:

```
MongoClient.connect(uri, options)
  .then((db) => {
    accountsDb = db;
    collection = accountsDb.db('test');
    console.log('Successfully connected to MongoDB');
  })
  .catch((err) => {
    console.log(err);
  });
```

6. Run the **db.js** file to connect the database by running the following code on the command line:

```
node db
```

You will obtain the following output:

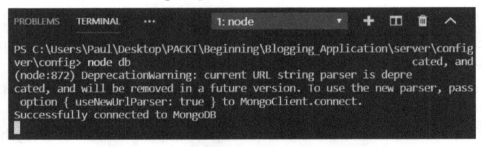

Figure 2.12: Connection with the native MongoDB driver

Now, we will attempt to connect the application using Mongoose.

Exercise 6: Connecting the Node Application with a Third-Party Driver (Mongoose)

In this exercise, we will connect the Node application with a third-party driver, namely, Mongoose.

Before you attempt this exercise, create a folder called **Third Party- Mongoose** and install the mongoose module using npn install mongoose on the CLI. Perform the following steps to complete this exercise:

> **Note**
>
> It is assumed that you have already created a MongoDB Atlas cluster. Therefore, use the same credentials (username and password) for this exercise. The code file for this exercise can be found here: https://bit.ly/2CdnFpO.

1. Create a **db.js** file using the following code:

```
touch db.js
```

2. Load the Mongoose module and set Mongoose default using the following code:

```
const Mongoose = require("Mongoose");
mongoose.set('useCreateIndex', true);// set index
```

3. Declare a variable named uri and assign the MongoDB connection string using the following code:

```
var uri = "mongodb+srv://username:password @cluster0-0wi3e.mongodb.net/
test?retryWrites=true";
```

4. Declare a variable named option and assign the optional settings using the following code:

```
const options = {
  reconnectTries: Number.MAX_VALUE,
  poolSize: 10,
  useNewUrlParser:true
};)
```

5. Connect MongoDB Atlas using the Mongoose connect method by using the following code:

```
Mongoose.connect(uri, options).then(
    () => {
      console.log("Database connection established!");
    },
    err => {
      console.log("Error connecting Database instance due to: ", err);
    }
);
```

6. Run **db.js** to connect to the database:

    ```
    node db
    ```

    You will obtain the following output:

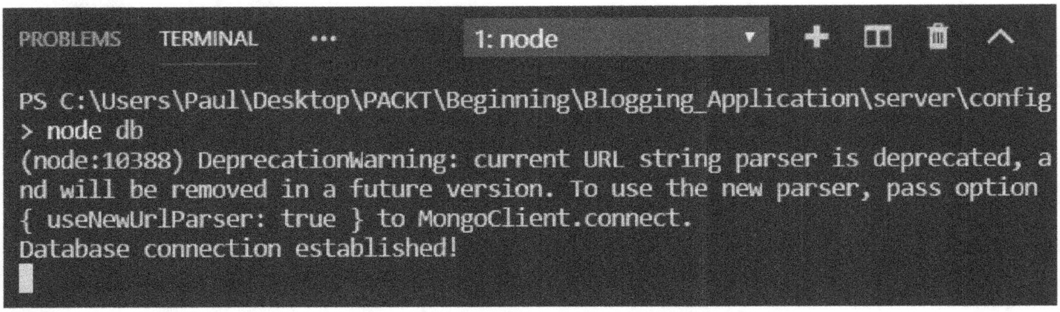

Figure 2.13: Database connection using Mongoose

Creating and Defining a Schema with Mongoose

The creation and management of data has been made convenient by Mongoose via the following features:

- The asynchronous and synchronous validation of models

- Model casting

- Object life cycle management

- Pseudo joins

- Query builder

The schema specifies the attributes of each property, including the data type; for example, during an **insert** or **update** operation, the data type could take either the **required** or **optional** attribute, and the data type values could be set to **unique** or **not**.

For Mongoose, it's best practice for the file to have the same name as that of the model; therefore, we should create a schema models directory. Defining a schema literally means defining the structure or organization of the database and involves the following:

- Mapping a schema to a collection

- Defining the shape and properties of documents within a collection

Mongoose permits a number of **SchemaTypes**, such as **Array**, **Decimal128**, **Map**, **String**, **Buffer**, **Boolean**, **Mixed**, **ObjectId**, **Number**, and **Date**.

Schemas also define document life cycle hooks called middleware, compound indexes, document, static model methods, and instance methods. The following snippet shows a schema being created:

```
// load Mongoose module
const Mongoose = require("Mongoose");


// create mongoose schema
const Schema = Mongoose.Schema;


// create database schema as an instance of Mongoose schema
const BlogSchema = new Schema({
  title: {
    type: String,
    required: true
  },
......
});
```

Creating Models in Mongoose

A model can be likened to a fancy constructor that is compiled after a schema has been defined, and is responsible for creating and reading documents from MongoDB. It is important to know that an instance of a model is referred to as a document.

After a schema is defined, we then convert the schema into a model. It's best practice to create this in the same directory. The following snippet shows an example of a model:

```
Mongoose.model('modelName', definedSchema)
```

The **.model()** function makes a copy of a schema that must be defined before creating the model. The first argument in **.model()** is model name, while the second argument is the name of the defined schema. **Mongoose.model()** tells Mongoose to use the default Mongoose connection for the model being created.

Let's look at some exercises so that we have a better understanding of how a database schema and model is created using Mongoose.

Exercise 7: Creating a Database Schema and a Data Model Using Mongoose

In this exercise, we will create a database schema and a data model using Mongoose. The following steps are a continuation of the previous *Exercise 6*, Connecting the Node Application With a Third-Party Driver (Mongoose) Therefore, it is assumed that a database connection has been successfully established. Before you begin this exercise, make sure that you have created a new **Third Party – Mongoose** folder. Then, create a new folder (model) in the directory and install the Mongoose module using npm install mongoose. Also, save the **db.js** file that was created in the previous exercise in this folder. Perform the following steps to complete this exercise:

> **Note**
>
> The code for the model.js file can be found here: http://bit.ly/2SjFDwM.

1. Create a file named **model.js** inside the model folder using the following code:

   ```
   touch model.js
   ```

2. Load the **Mongoose** module using the following code:

   ```
   const Mongoose = require("Mongoose");
   ```

3. Declare a schema and assign the **Schema** class using the following code:

   ```
   const Schema = Mongoose.Schema;
   ```

4. Create a **Schema** instance and add properties (assuming we're creating for a simple blog) using the following code:

   ```
   const BlogSchema = new Schema({
     title: {
       type: String,
       required: true
     },
     body: String,
     createdOn: {
       type: Date,
       default: Date.now
     }
   });
   ```

5. Call Mongoose on the **model()** function to use the default Mongoose connection:

```
Mongoose.model();
```

6. Pass in the model name, **ArticleModel**, as the first argument using the following code:

```
Mongoose.model("ArticleModel");
```

7. Pass in the schema name **BlogSchema** as the second argument using the following code:

```
Mongoose.model("ArticleModel", BlogSchema);
```

8. Make the model exportable using the following code:

```
module.exports = Mongoose.model("ArticleModel", BlogSchema);
```

9. Create an **output.js** file and import the model using the following code:

```
const Article = require("../models/model");

if(Article){
    console.log('Model Successfully Imported');
}
```

10. Run the **output.js** file on the command line using the following code:

```
node output
```

You will obtain the following output:

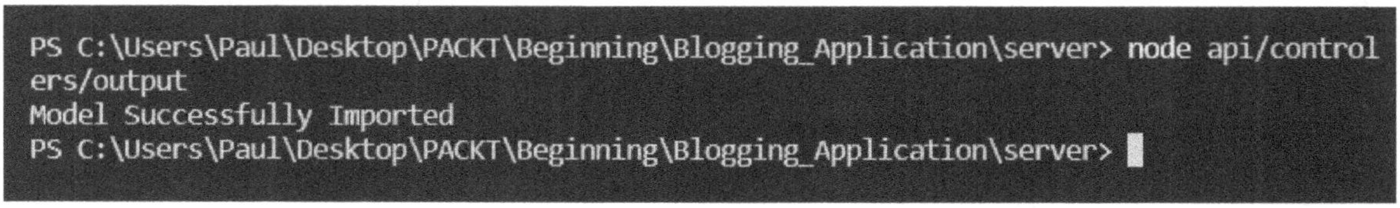

```
PS C:\Users\Paul\Desktop\PACKT\Beginning\Blogging_Application\server> node api/control
ers/output
Model Successfully Imported
PS C:\Users\Paul\Desktop\PACKT\Beginning\Blogging_Application\server>
```

Figure 2.14: Data model successfully imported

Activity 3: Connecting the Node Application to MongoDB Atlas

We created a blogging application, along with a Node server for it, in the previous chapter. In this activity, our aim is to continue server-side development by connecting to MongoDB Atlas, in addition to creating a database schema and data model for the application.

Before you begin this activity, you need to open the **Blogging Application/server** project folder in your IDE (Visual Studio Code).

> **Note**
>
> The code files for this activity can be found here: http://bit.ly/2tuWYsN.

1. Create a subfolder named **config** and create a **db.js** file inside it.

2. Install and import Mongoose in the **db.js** file.

3. Assign a MongoDB connection string to **uri** and declare the options settings.

4. Connect the application to MongoDB Atlas.

5. Create the **api/models** folders and then create an **Article.js** file inside **models**.

6. Declare the schema and assign a schema class in the **Article.js** file.

> **Note**
>
> You will need to install and import Mongoose in the Article.js file once more.

7. Create the default Mongoose model.

8. Create an **output.js** file and import the model.

9. Run the **output.js** file to confirm whether the model has been imported.

10. Run the **node db.js** file inside the config folder to test the connection.

> **Note**
>
> The solution to this activity can be found on page 254.

The previous sections described how to get started with MongoDB Atlas, a database as a service offered by MongoDB. We went through in topics and exercises that taught us about connecting an application to clusters, creating schemas, defining a schema with native and third-party MongoDB drivers, and creating models.

In the next section, we will learn about how to get started with Express, an open source web application framework for Node that's used for building web applications and APIs. We will wrap up the section by understanding the methods for routing HTTP requests, configuring middleware, error handling, rendering HTML views, and registering a template engine.

Getting Started with Express

Express provides a robust set of features for building web applications. In the first chapter, we briefly talked about Express.js, and discussed its advantages and limitations. This topic is about the implementation of Express in an application.

Creating an Express application requires the following steps:

1. Importing the Express module

2. Creating the Express application

3. Defining the route

4. Listening to the server

Take a look at the following example in Express:

```
// load express module
var express = require('express');


//Create express app
var app = express();


// route definition
app.get('/', function (req, res) {
res.send('Hello World');
});


// Start server
app.listen(4000, function () {
```

```
        console.log('App listening at Port 4000..');
    });
```

In the preceding code snippet, the Express module is first loaded and assigned to a variable. Then, an **app** is created using the variable function. The **app.get()** method is used to define the route by passing in a route path and a callback function. The **app.listen()** method starts up the server and prints **Hello World** on the console. The Express **app** object is created by calling the top-level **express()** function, which is exported by the Express module. This function also has methods for routing HTTP requests, configuring middleware, rendering HTML views, registering a template engine, and so on.

Now that we've been introduced to the structure of what an Express application entails, we will be delving into the features that make Express great.

Routing in Express

Routing involves matching a URL in response to an action by a web API. Particular patterns of characters in a URL are matched, and some values that are extracted from the URL are passed as parameters to the route handler, as shown in the following snippet:

```
app.get('/', function(req, res){
    res.send('Hello World!');
});
```

In the preceding code, **app.get()** defines the HTTP GET requests to the site root (/).

Some of the other methods for defining route handlers for all the other HTTP verbs provided by the Express application, which are mostly used in exactly the same way, are as follows: **post()**, **put()**, **delete()**, **subscribe()**, **unsubscribe()**, **patch()**, **search()**, and **connect()**.

Middleware functions can be loaded on a particular path for all request methods using **app.all()**, which is a multipurpose Express route handler. It is also a special routing method that can be called in response to any HTTP method, as shown in the following snippet:

```
app.all('/about', function(req, res, next)
{
console.log('welcome to about page ...');
next(); // next handler takes control
});
```

Route handlers can also be used to group a particular part of a site together so that a common route-prefix is used to access them. This is made possible by the Express **router** object. In the next exercise, we will create a route and export the router object.

Exercise 8: Creating a Route and Exporting the Router Object

In this exercise, we will create a post-route folder (route) and a model named **post. js**, and then export the router object. Perform the following steps to complete this exercise:

> **Note**
>
> The code files for this exercise can be found here: http://bit.ly/2BLDeFU.

1. Load the Express module using the following code:

```
var express = require('express');
```

2. Initialize the router using the following code:

```
var router = express.Router();
```

3. Route to the dashboard using the following code:

```
router.get('/', function(req, res) {
  res.send('Welcome to admin dashboard);
});
```

4. Route to the **About page** using the following code:

```
router.get('/about', function(req, res) {
  res.send('About page');
});
```

5. Export the router using the following code:

```
module.exports = router;
```

6. Verify whether the **router** object has been exported by creating a **test.js** file and pass the following code:

```
//importing route
const routes = require('./routepost');

if(routes){
    console.log('Routes Successfully Imported');
}
```

Note that we are importing the exported route to verify whether the export has been successful.

7. Run the **test.js** file using the following code:

```
node test
```

You will obtain the following output:

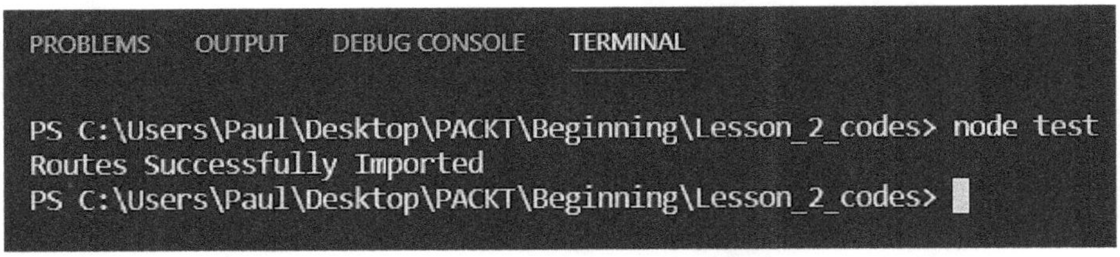

Figure 2.15: Importing the router

If the export hadn't been successful, then we would not have obtained the preceding output.

Before we move on to the next section, you should be aware that Express routing templates can either be one-to-one or one-to-many, as listed here:

- **One-to-one implementation**: `app.get('/users/:id?', function (req, res, next) { //[...]}`

- **One-to-many implementation**: `'/:controller/:action/:id'`

Activity 4: Creating Controller for the API

In *Chapter 1, Introduction to the MEAN Stack*, we created the components of a blogging application, established its database connection, and created the schema and model. In this activity, we aim to create a controller for the application. Before we attempt this activity, all of the previous activities should have been completed. Also, ensure that you open the **Blogging Application/server** project folder in an IDE (Visual Studio Code).

> **Note**
>
> The code files for this activity can be found here: http://bit.ly/2BMvLpZ.

To complete this activity, the following steps have to be executed:

1. Create a folder named **controllers** as a subfolder inside **api**, and then open the **controllers** folder and create an `articleListController.js` file.

2. Open the `articleListController.js` file and import the model.

3. Create a controller to list all articles.

4. Create a controller to create new articles.

5. Create a controller to read articles.

6. Create a controller to update articles.

7. Create a controller to delete articles.

> **Note**
>
> The solution for this activity can be found on page 257.

Middleware in Express

Express is a routing and middleware web framework that has minimal functionality of its own. Alternatively, an Express application can be said to be a series of middleware function calls, as listed here:

```
function myFunMiddleware(request, response, next){
    // Do stuff with the request and response
    // When done, Call next() to defer to the next middleware
    next();
}
```

myFunMiddleware() takes three arguments: a request object (**req**), a response object (**res**), and **next**:

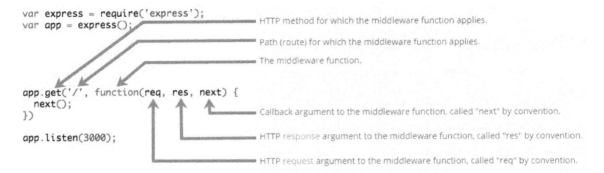

Figure 2.16: Middleware applied on an HTTP method

Third-party middleware can also be added by calling **use()** on the Express application object. For example, **body-parser** is a middleware that extracts the body of an incoming request and exposes it on **res.body** and parses the JSON, buffer, string, and URL encoded data that's submitted using a HTTP **POST** request. This implementation is shown in the following snippet:

```
const express = require("express");
const bodyParser = require("body-parser");


const app = express();


const port = process.env.PORT || 4000;
app.use(bodyParser.urlencoded({ extended: true }));
app.use(bodyParser.json());


app.use((req, res, next) => {
    if (res.body) {
        next();
    }
});
```

Error Handling in Express

Error handling refers to how Express anticipates, detects, catches, processes, and communicates errors that occur both synchronously and asynchronously. Express has been preconfigured with a default error handler to handle both types of errors. The following snippet shows how errors are caught while running route handlers and middleware:

```
app.get('/', function (req, res) {
    throw new Error('Truncated'); // Express will catch this on its own
}
```

This feature is provided by Express, and so there is little or no need to bother about error handling, since all errors are caught and proceed accordingly. You can pass three arguments; the **next()** function can also be added. The **next()** function passes the error to Express. The following snippet shows how the error function is used:

```
app.use(function(err, req, res, next){
    console.error(err.stack);
    res.status(500).send('Something broke!');
});
```

It is strictly recommended that **err** is processed before **res** to avoid the default error handler closing the connection and failing the request in a situation where an error is discovered.

The View Template Engine

The variables in HTML pages are replaced by the actual values with the help of the template engine at runtime. The view template engine makes the design of HTML easier because templates are transformed into HTML files at runtime. Here are some of the advantages of using template engines:

* They improve the productivity of developers, that is, developers can achieve increased productivity over a period of time
* They improve the performance of applications because templates can be accessed from the **CDN** (**Content Delivery Network**)
* They improve code readability and maintainability
* They maximize client-side processing by making it possible to use a single template for multiple pages

The following snippet shows how a template engine is used in an Express application:

```
var express = require('express');
var app = express();
//set view engine
app.set("view engine","pug")
  //route
app.get('/', function (req, res) {
res.render('home');
```

The following are some of the template engines that work with Express:

- **Haml**: This is a markup language that cleanly and simply describes the HTML of any web document without the use of inline code

- **EJS**: This is the embedded JavaScript template engine

- **Pug**: This was formerly known as Jade and it's an Haml-inspired template engine

- **hbs**: This is an extension of the `Mustache.js` template engine that works as an adapter for Handlebars.js

- **React**: Renders React components on a server

- **h4e**: This is an adapter for `Hogan.js` with support for partials and layouts

As highlighted in the preceding list, Express can be used with any template engine. In the following exercise, we will look at how to use Pug (Jade) templates to create HTML pages dynamically and implement error handling in Express.

Exercise 9: Using the Pug (Jade) Template Engine and Implementing Error Handling in the Node Application Using Express

In this exercise, we will use the Pug template to implement error handling in a Node application using Express. Create a Pug-template folder and install the express module using the command npm install express. Perform the following steps to complete this exercise:

> **Note**
>
> The code file for this exercise can be found here: http://bit.ly/2SfZCN9.

1. Install Pug using the following code:

```
npm install pug
```

2. Create an **index.pug** file inside the **views** folder and writing the following Jade Pug template in it:

```
doctype html
html
    head
        title Pug Page
    body
        h1 This page is produced by Pug engine
        p some paragraph here..
```

3. Create an Express application server and render the preceding Pug template using Express by using the following code:

```
var express = require('express');
var app = express();

// initialize todoData
var todoData = [
{id:1, task:'Take Breakfast'},
{id:2, task:'Read Book'},
{id:3, task:'Take Launch'},
{id:4, task:'Start Meeting'},
];

//set view engine
app.set("view engine"," Pug ")

app.get('/', function (req, res) {
res.render(' index ', { TodoList: todoData });


});

var server = app.listen(8000, function () {
    console.log('Node server is running..');
});
```

4. Update the **index.pug** file to list out **todoData** by using the following code:

```
doctype html
html
    head
        title Pug Todo List Page
    body
        h1 This page is produced by Pug engine to display todo List
        p Todo List
ul
        each list in TodoList
            li=list.task
```

5. To use custom error handling middleware to handle errors, we use the main middleware before the route:

```
app.use(function(err, req, res, next) {
  // Do logging and user-friendly error message display
  console.error(err);
// Using template engine
  res.render('500');
});
```

6. Run the following command on the command line:

```
node server
```

7. Open the browser and type **localhost:8000** in the address bar. You will obtain the following output:

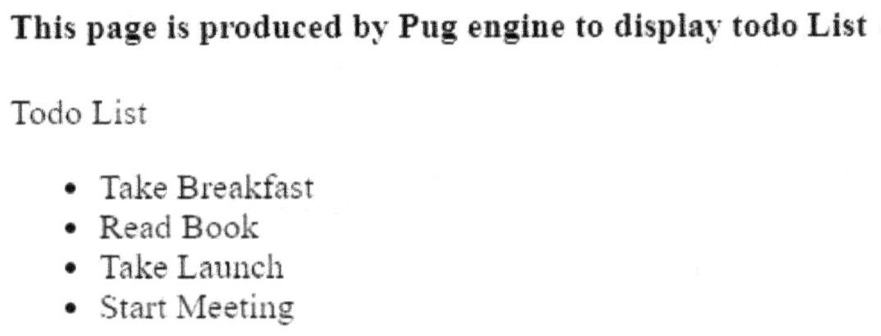

This page is produced by Pug engine to display todo List

Todo List

- Take Breakfast
- Read Book
- Take Launch
- Start Meeting

Figure 2.17: Using the Pug template engine

Note

To learn more about Pug syntax rules in detail, refer to this link: https://pugjs.org/api/getting-started.html.

Activity 5: Testing a Fully Functional RESTful API

In the previous chapter, we created a blogging application in which we established a database connection, created the schema and model, and wrote the controllers. In this activity, we'll aim to setup a functional API Express route, assemble all the components and test it to ensure that we have a fully functional RESTful API in action and that we can perform CRUD operations.

Before we attempt this activity, all previous activities must have been completed. For this activity, open the **Blogging Application** project folder in your IDE (Visual Studio Code) and create a subfolder called **config** as a directory for the **db** connection file.

> **Note:**
>
> The code files for this activity can be found here: http://bit.ly/2NiTZNI.

The following steps have to be performed to complete this activity:

1. Create a routes folder within the api folder and create an **articleListRoutes.js** file.

2. Open the **articleListRoutes.js** file and create a route function .

3. Import the controller into the route function.

4. Create route for get and post requests on **/articles**.

5. Create route for get, put, and delete requests on **/articles/:articleid**.

6. Install Express and the **bodyParser** module using the integrated command line.

7. Create a **server.js** file in the **Blogging Application/config** folder and then import the Express and **bodyParser** module.

8. Create the Express application using the **express()** function.

9. Define the connection port

10. Call the **bodyParser** middleware on the created express app.

11. Import the **db** connection.

12. Add CORS (Cross-Origin Resource Sharing) headers to support cross-site HTTP requests

13. Import the route.

14. Call the route on the Express application.

15. Listen to the Express server.

16. Run **server.js** inside the **configserver** folder to test the connection.

17. Open Postman to test the **API**.

18. Post a new article to **localhost:3000/articles** using the **POST** request.

19. Get the posted articles by id on **localhost:3000/articles/:id** using the **GET** request.

20. Get all posted articles by id on **localhost:3000/articles** using the **GET** request.

21. Update posted articles by id on **localhost:3000/articles/:id** using the **PUT** request.

22. Delete posted articles by id on **localhost:3000/articles/:id** using the **DELETE** request.

> **Note**
>
> The solution to this activity can be found on page 259.

Summary

This chapter got us started on the introduction to RESTful APIs and their design concepts. First, we defined what an API is and then expanded on REST. Thereafter, we looked into design practices that have been employed by established companies and described the guiding framework for web standards.

In the subsequent sections, we looked into how MongoDB Atlas is implemented with Node. We also performed an exercise on creating MongoDB Atlas server components, known as clusters, and connected them with applications. Later in this section, we established connections with applications using middleware such as the native MongoDB driver and Mongoose. We also described how schemas are created and defined with Mongoose. Finally, we performed an exercise on model creation using the default Mongoose method.

In the final sections of this chapter, we implemented various features in Express with Node. These included routing HTTP requests, configuring middleware, error handing, rendering HTML views, and registering a template engine. Finally, we tested a RESTful API.

In the next chapter, we will begin frontend development with the Angular CLI.

3

Beginning Frontend Development with Angular CLI

Learning Objectives

By the end of this chapter, you will be able to:

- Develop applications with the Angular CLI

- Describe the consumption of RESTful API services from the client side

- Implement core Angular features

- Create a robust frontend design

This chapter begins with the development of Angular CLI applications and then goes on to describe components, directives, services, and making HTTP requests in Angular by walking through several exercises and activities.

Introduction

In the previous chapter, we learned about the RESTful API and its design concepts, performed operations on MongoDB Atlas, and completed exercises on feature implementations in the Express framework for Node applications. The chapter concluded with activities aimed at implementing Node, MongoDB Atlas, and Express together to develop a RESTful API to perform CRUD operations.

This chapter will get you started on frontend development with the Angular CLI: a command-line interface developed by Angular to help developers jump-start frontend development. Later, you will implement features such as **components**, which are the basic building blocks of any Angular application. This chapter will describe the different directives that are available in Angular. Also, you will learn how to consume API services and create templates, reactive forms, perform routing, and so on.

Finally, you shall be putting together all the knowledge you gained in this chapter to develop a robust web application with a solid Angular frontend. The chapter activity will wrap up the development for our sample application by consuming the RESTful API we created in the previous chapter from the client side.

Getting Started with Angular CLI

The Angular CLI

CLI simply stands for command-line interface. Although some may refer to it as a command-line interpreter, it is actually a tool that is used to issue commands for a computer to perform specific tasks, such as creating new directories and files, listing all files in a directory, and so on. Many creators of application frameworks or environments such as **Angular**, **React**, **Vue**, and **Node**, to mention a few, have taken advantage of this tool to make development easier.

The Angular CLI is a command-line tool or environment that makes the creation of Angular projects, the management of files, and a variety of development tasks possible by just running some specific commands.

It is important to know that before we can create an Angular application with the Angular CLI environment, we must first have Node and **npm** installed and running. It is assumed that we already have them installed from the preceding chapter. The major steps in the creation of an Angular application are as follows:

1. Install the Angular CLI.
2. Create a new application.
3. Serve the application.

Installing the Angular CLI

Before we start, let's verify that our prerequisite tools (Node and **npm**) have been installed by running the following commands:

For Node: **node -v**

For **npm**: **npm -v**

The commands reveal details about the versions of the tools installed, as shown in the following diagram. At the time of developing this book, the minimum recommended versions are Node LTS version 8.11 and **npm** version 6:

```
PAUL@DESKTOP-QSA6PEV MINGW64 ~/Desktop
$ node -v
v8.11.3

PAUL@DESKTOP-QSA6PEV MINGW64 ~/Desktop
$ npm -v
5.6.0
```

Figure 3.1: Checking the installed versions of Node and npm

To install Angular CLI globally, we run the following command:

```
npm install -g @angular/cli
```

You will see the following output by running the preceding command:

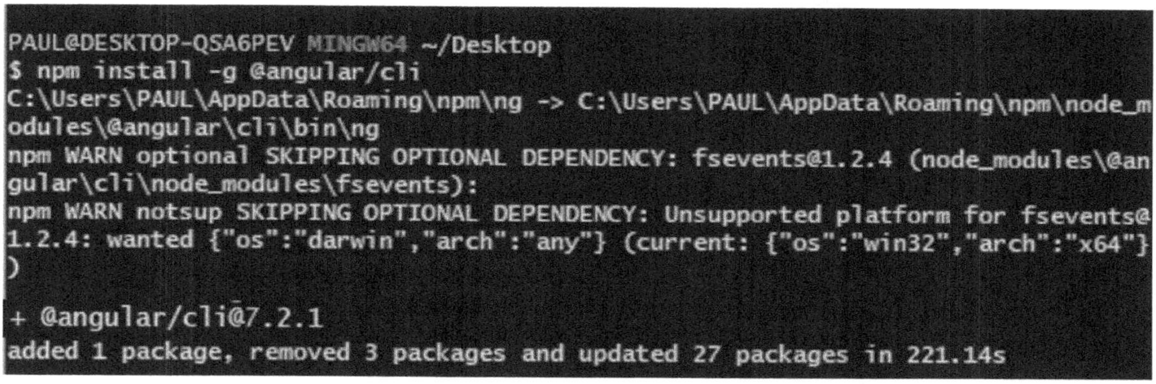

```
PAUL@DESKTOP-QSA6PEV MINGW64 ~/Desktop
$ npm install -g @angular/cli
C:\Users\PAUL\AppData\Roaming\npm\ng -> C:\Users\PAUL\AppData\Roaming\npm\node_m
odules\@angular\cli\bin\ng
npm WARN optional SKIPPING OPTIONAL DEPENDENCY: fsevents@1.2.4 (node_modules\@an
gular\cli\node_modules\fsevents):
npm WARN notsup SKIPPING OPTIONAL DEPENDENCY: Unsupported platform for fsevents@
1.2.4: wanted {"os":"darwin","arch":"any"} (current: {"os":"win32","arch":"x64"}
)

+ @angular/cli@7.2.1
added 1 package, removed 3 packages and updated 27 packages in 221.14s
```

Figure 3.2: Installing the Angular CLI

Now that Angular CLI has been installed, we will begin creating Angular applications.

Exercise 10: Creating and Running a New Application on the Angular CLI

The Angular CLI has made application development very easy as CLI commands help generate all the required files to build a basic web app. In this exercise, we will be creating and running an application using the Angular CLI. Open the CLI in the **chapter-3-exercises** directory and perform the following steps to create or generate a new default Angular application project:

> **Note**
>
> The code files for this exercise can be found here: http://bit.ly/2TdtIFg.

1. Create or generate a new Angular CLI application from the command line using the following command:

```
ng new my-new-app
```

Note that the necessary packages can also be installed as needed, using the **ng add <package-name>** command. However, for now, we will only use the default packages that have been auto generated by Angular CLI, as shown in the following output:

```
Paul@DESKTOP-678HNE1 MINGW32 ~/Desktop
$ ng new my-new-app
installing ng
    create .editorconfig
    create README.md
    create src\app\app.component.css
    create src\app\app.component.html
    create src\app\app.component.spec.ts
    create src\app\app.component.ts
    create src\app\app.module.ts
    create src\assets\.gitkeep
    create src\environments\environment.prod.ts
    create src\environments\environment.ts
    create src\favicon.ico
    create src\index.html
    create src\main.ts
    create src\polyfills.ts
    create src\styles.css
    create src\test.ts
    create src\tsconfig.app.json
    create src\tsconfig.spec.json
    create src\typings.d.ts
    create .angular-cli.json
    create e2e\app.e2e-spec.ts
```

Figure 3.3: Creating a new application

Now that the application has been created, the next thing we need to do is run the application on the server.

2. Serve or run the Angular CLI application by running the following command in the project directory:

```
cd my-new-app
ng serve -open
```

Note that **ng serve** builds the application and starts a web server.

The **serve** property is the architect target, whereas **@angular-devkit/build-angular:dev-server** is the prebuilt Angular application builder. On top of the Angular builder, we can run the targets of a specific project directly using **ng run** so that serving a target is performed by running **ng run angular-cli-workspace-example:serve**.

3. Run the following command in the CLI to open the default browser:

```
ng serve -open
```

-open or **-o** is a command to automatically open default browsers on **http://localhost:4200/** as soon as the application starts running, as shown in the following screenshot:

Figure 3.4: The default Angular application

> **Note**
>
> The Angular QuickStart method is deprecated. Therefore, the officially recommended method for getting started with Angular is using the Angular CLI. If you want to know more about Angular QuickStart, refer to this link: https://github.com/angular/quickstart.

Project File Review

By default, the Angular CLI produces a project and layout template. It is the foundation for both quick experiments and enterprise solutions. Basic information on various CLI commands can be retrieved from the `README.md` file in the Angular CLI repository, as shown here:

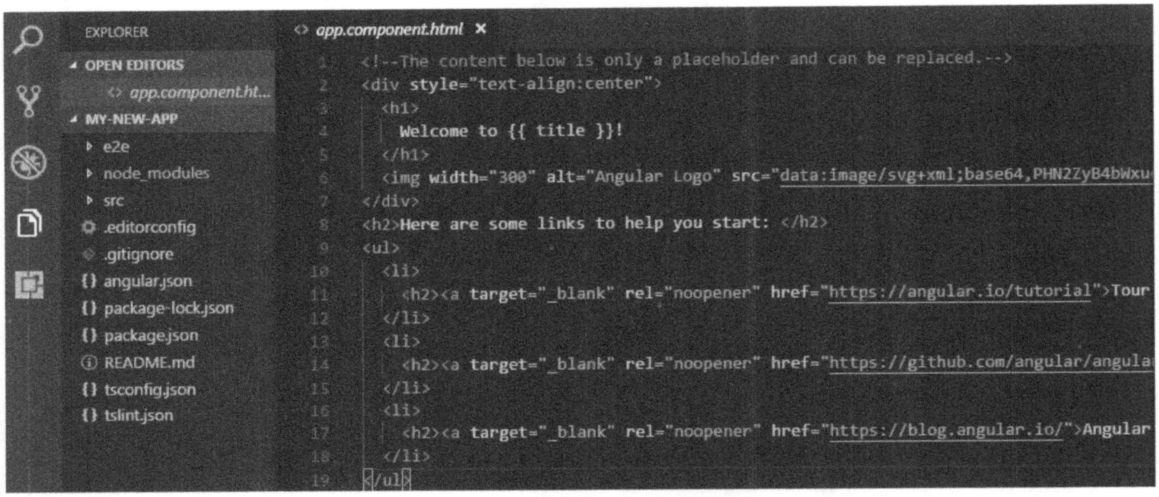

Figure 3.5: The Angular CLI project folder structure

Described here are the project directories, folders, and files:

e2e: This is where our end-to-end tests are kept. The main purpose of this is to make sure that our applications function correctly at a high level. Inside the folder, you will find the **src** folder housing two files: `app.e2e-spec.ts` and `app.po.ts`. Also, in the **e2e** directory, you'll find `protractor.conf.js` and `tsconfig.e2e.json`. All these files make end-to-end testing possible.

node_module: This directory is only for build tools. It houses installed **npm** packages that are listed in `package.json`.

src: This folder contains the application and the tooling files.

app: This folder contains the app root modules and app components. `app.module.ts` is a TypeScript file that defines the **AppModule**, whose function is to tell Angular how to assemble files. `app.component.ts` is also a Typescript file that defines our app-root component. The `app.component.html` file contains the HTML template for the app. The `app.component.css` file contains the CSS for our app.

assets: This is a folder that holds app resources such as fonts, images, media, and so on.

environment: This folder contains application configuration variables that are to be exported for various destination environments.

favicon.ico: This is an app icon that is displayed in the browser tab.

`index.html`: This is the main HTML template file that is presented to the site visitor. The CLI automatically handles other resources that need to be exported into it.

`main.ts`: This file compiles and bootstraps the application to run in the browser.

`polyfills.ts`: This file helps to normalize the different levels of support for web standards, as required for different browsers.

`styles.css`: This file is initially empty, and it is meant to hold global styles for the app.

`test.ts`: This is our unit test entry point.

`tsconfig.app.json`: This is a TypeScript compiler configuration for the Angular app.

`tsconfig.spec.json`: This is a TypeScript compiler configuration that's used for unit tests.

`karma.conf.js`: This file holds the unit test configuration for the Karma test runner.

`.editorconfig`: This is the configuration for the editor.

`.gitignore`: This is a `git` configuration file that ensures listed directories or files are not committed to source control.

`angular.json`: This file holds Angular CLI configuration, and enables you to add or remove files that are used for building the application.

`package.json`: This file holds the third-party packages that have been installed.

`tsconfig.json`: This file holds the configuration for the TypeScript compiler and is used by the IDE for tooling.

`tslint.json`: This file holds the linting configuration, which aims to ensure coding styles are consistent.

`README.md`: This is just a basic documentation file for your project.

In the next section, we will begin using components, directives, and services, and also perform an exercise on making HTTP requests.

Using Components, Directives, Services, and Making HTTP Requests in Angular

Now that we have started working with the Angular CLI and created our first Angular CLI application, it is time to start exploring the various features that make Angular a highly sought after framework on the web application development scene. We'll start with Angular **components**, the basic building blocks of any Angular application.

Angular Components

Everything in Angular is developed as a component; classes interact with different files that are embedded in components, which form a browser display. It can also be referred to as a kind of a directive with configuration that's suitable for an application structure that is component-based.

The architecture of an Angular application is a tree of **components** originating from one root component configured in the bootstrap property on your root `NgModule` (in the `app.module.ts` file).

Let's look at the file structure of an Angular root component that was created by default in the process of bootstrapping a new Angular application:

- `app.component.css`: This is the style sheet for the component
- `app.component.html`: This is the HTML template file for the component
- `app.component.spec.ts`: This is the testing file for the component
- `app.component.ts`: This is the TypeScript class for the component
- `app.module.ts`: This is the TypeScript module file for the application

The details of these component files will be discussed later in this section. Now that we have discussed Angular components briefly, we will perform an exercise on creating them.

Exercise 11: Creating Angular Components

In this exercise, we will create a `Hello World` component for the `my-new-app` application we created in the previous exercise. We can either do this manually or use the CLI `ng generate component hello-world` command. Before you begin those exercise, make sure that you first use the CLI command to create the `hello-world.component.html` in the `my-new-app` application located inside the **chapter-3-exercises** folder. Perform the following steps to complete the exercise:

> **Note**
>
> The code files for this exercise can be found here: http://bit.ly/2VbHfui.

1. Import the component from the Angular core library into the hello-world.component.ts file:

   ```
   import { Component, OnInit } from '@angular/core';
   ```

2. Insert a component decorator path in the `hello-world.component.ts` file that specifies the metadata of the component class using the following command:

   ```
   @Component({
     selector: 'app-hello-world',
     templateUrl: './hello-world.component.html',
     styleUrls: ['./hello-world.component.css']
   })
   ```

   The metadata consists of objects with different key-value pairs, such as the following:

   `templateUrl: './app.component.html'`, `selector`: `'app-root'`, and a `styleUrl:'[]./ app/component.css'`

   These objects are the major building blocks that need to be defined to successfully create and present the component to the DOM view. The template that describes a view or renders a component can be associated with components either directly with inline code, `template: '<div> {{title}} </div>'`, or with a reference: `templateUrl: './hello-world.component.html'`.

3. Create an exportable component class and assign a string 'Hello World' to title using the following code:

```
export class HelloWorldComponent implements OnInit {
title='Hello World'
  constructor() { }
  ngOnInit() {
  }
}
```

This class holds all the variables and methods being used by the components. The component can either be referred to from another component or reused by other components.

4. Update the app.module.ts file using the following code:

```
import { BrowserModule } from '@angular/platform-browser';
import { NgModule } from '@angular/core';

import { AppComponent } from './app.component';
import { HelloWorldComponent } from './hello-world/hello-world.component';

@NgModule({
  declarations: [
    AppComponent,
    HelloWorldComponent
  ],
  imports: [
    BrowserModule
  ],
  providers: [],
  bootstrap: [AppComponent]
})
export class AppModule { }
```

5. Update the component template using the following code:

```
{{title}}
```

6. Update the root component template by attaching the **hello world** component element tag:

```
<app-hello-world></app-hello-world>
```

7. Serve the application to view the output by running the following command on the CLI:

```
'ng serve -o'
```

You should obtain an output similar to the following:

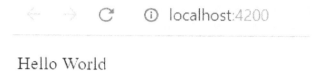

Figure 3.6: Creating a hello world component

As can be seen in the preceding output, we have successfully created our first Angular component.

> **Note**
>
> Many decorators are allowed in Angular. To get more information about different component directive options and their descriptions, refer to this link: https://angular.io/api/core/Component.

So far, we have learned how to start an Angular CLI project and learned how to create the building blocks of an Angular application, which are components. Next, we'll look into another concept in Angular, known as a directive.

Directives

A directive is a concept in Angular that allows you to attach attributes and behaviors to a DOM element. This concept is used to extend the power of HTML by giving it a new syntax. Each directive has a name, which can either be predefined in Angular, such as **ng-repeat**, or a name that's generated by the developer. Each directive determines where it can be used: in an element, attribute, class, or comment. We will focus more on predefined directives here. There are three types of directives: **component**, **structural**, and **attribute**. Let's look at each of these in detail.

Component directive: This is the most commonly used directive, known as a directive in a template. In this type of directive, you can use other directives, custom or built-in, in the `@Component` annotation, as shown here:

```
@Component({
    selector: "my-app"
    templateUrl: './app.component.html',
    styleUrls: ['./app.component.css']
    directives: [custom_directive_here]
})
use this directive in your view as:
<my-app></my-app>
```

From the previous snippet, the objects we have inside the `@Components` decorators are known as component directives and can be explained further. `selector: "string"` identifies and instantiates a directive in a template. `directives: [custom_directive_here]` defines a set of directive providers in the format, as follows:

- **Inputs**: This defines a set of data-bound input properties: `inputs: ['string'],`

- **Outputs**: This defines a set of event-bound output properties: `outputs: ['string'],`

Other directives are `providers`, `exportAs`, `queries`, `jit`, and `host`. Even though we have already made use of component directives in previous sections, we will be covering some other directives in detail in the following sections and exercises.

Structural directive: Structural directives are responsible for providing a DOM structure and for reshaping the HTML layout by adding or manipulating elements. Most structural directives are easily recognized by the `*` sign that precedes the directive. Examples of structural directives are `*ngIf`, `*ngFor`, and `*ngSwitch` (this includes a set of cooperating directives: `NgSwitch`, `NgSwitchCase`, and `NgSwitchDefault`). You can create a custom structural directive as well.

Attribute directive: This is a directive that attaches behavior to the DOM element.

Let's quickly run a few exercises to cement our understanding of how structural and attribute directives are implemented.

Exercise 12: Implementing a Structural Directive

In this exercise, we will implement a structural directive. We will be implementing the ***ngFor** directive in a component of an existing application (**my-new-app**, located in the **chapter-3-exercises** folder). Perform the following steps to complete the exercise:

> **Note**
>
> The code files for this exercise can be found here: http://bit.ly/2IBQKSu.

1. Create a **structural-dir** component in **my-new-app** using the following command:

   ```
   ng g component structural-dir the previous snippet, the objects we have
   inside
   ```

2. Declare a global variable named **courseTitles** in the component after the class class, in the aforementioned file, as shown in the following snippet:

   ```
   courseTitles = ['MEAN Stack', 'MEVN Stack', 'MERN Stack'];
   ```

3. Edit the content of the component template (**structural-dir.component.html**) with the following code:

   ```
   <div class="form-group" *ngFor="let course of courseTitles">
   {{course}}</div>
   ```

4. Update the root component HTML file with the following code:

   ```
   <app-structural-dir ></app- structural-dir >
   ```

5. Run the application using the following command:

   ```
   ng serve -o
   ```

   You will obtain the following output:

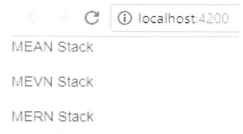

Figure 3.7: *ngFor output

As can be seen in the preceding output, we have successfully implemented the *ngFor structural directive.

In the next exercise, we will be implementing an attribute directive.

Exercise 13: Implementing an Attribute Directive

In this exercise, we will be implementing the [ngStyle] and [hidden] built-in attribute directives in a component of an existing application (my-new-app). Perform the following steps to complete the exercise:

> **Note**
>
> The code files for this exercise can be found here: http://bit.ly/2GExPnW.

1. Create an **attribute-dir.component.ts** file in the **app** folder by running the following command:

```
ng g component attribute-dir
```

2. Apply [ngStyle] and [hidden], which are attribute directives to H1 and H2 elements, respectively, in the component template (**attribute-dir.component.html**) using the following command:

```
<h1 [ngStyle]="myStyle"> Attribute directive </h1>
<h2 [hidden]="hide">Attribute directive 2 </h2>
```

3. Declare and assign a value to the variable named **myStyle** and hide it in the component class in **attribute-dir.components.ts** using the following code:

```
hide = true;

public myStyle={
    "color":"green"
  }
```

4. Update the root component HTML file with the following command:

```
<app-attribute-dir></app-attribute-dir>
```

5. Run the application using the following command:

```
ng serve -o
```

You will obtain the following output:

Attribute directive

Figure 3.8: Output with implemented attribute directives

In the preceding output, observe that the **H1** element is displayed in green and that the **H2** element is hidden.

Data Binding in Angular

Data binding is simply a mechanism that implements how data is presented by the application and how the application interacts with the data. Angular supports two-way data binding, which is a mechanism for coordinating and synchronizing data between the major parts of a template, such as the model and the view.

As the data model changes, the view (the HTML template) reflects this change and vice versa. These changes between both sections happen in real time (immediately) and automatically, which makes sure that the model and the view are updated at all times. The following examples show three forms of data binding markup:

- Form has a direction toward the DOM:

  ```
  {{value}}     i.e.    <li>{{people.name}}
  ```

- Form has a direction from the DOM:

  ```
  [property] = 'value' : i.e.     [hidden] = "submitted"
  ```

- Form has a direction both toward the DOM and from the DOM:

  ```
  (event) ="handler' i.e.      (click)="submitData
  [(ng.model)] = 'property' i.e.     [(ngModel)]="name"
  ```

Thus, we have described different types of directives in Angular and their implementations. We also described two-way data binding and its implementation. In the next section, we'll look into another concept of Angular, known as services.

Services

Services are just JavaScript functions and properties that can be reused by injecting them across application components. Services can be created either manually or by using the Angular CLI.

In the case of services, we have used the following pattern in different examples, when we had to inject services into constructors inside component classes. The steps involved are as follows:

- Define a service class

- Register with Injector

- Declare services as a dependency in components

> **Note**
>
> Many features of dependency injection in Angular, such as nested service dependencies and multiple service instances, can be read about and understood in the Angular documentation: https://angular.io/guide/dependency-injection-in-action.

In the following exercise, we will implement the aforementioned steps.

Exercise 14: Creating Angular Services Manually

In this exercise, we will create services manually for the **my-new-app** default Angular application. We will be creating these services in the **app** directory. Perform the following steps to complete the exercise:

> **Note**
>
> The code files for this exercise can be found here: http://bit.ly/2V95rxF.

1. Create a service file, **cars.service.ts**, in the app directory using the following command:

```
touch cars.service.ts
```

2. Import **Injectable** and create an injectable decoration with or without metadata using the following command:

```
import { Injectable } from '@angular/core';
@Injectable()
```

3. Create an exportable service class using the following command:

```
export class CarsService {
  constructor() { }
}
```

4. Hardcode an array object to serve as a record for cars in the class before the **constructor**:

```
public hondaCar = [
   {id: "1",model: "Accord", year: "2012"},
   {  id: "2",model: "Accord Hybrid",year: "2015"},
   {id: "3", model: "CR-V",year: "2013"    },
   {id: "4",model: "Civic",year: "2016"},
   {   id: "5", model: "Civic Hybrid",year: "2014"    }
]
```

5. Create a **get** method to retrieve each object from the record, as shown in the following code:

```
public getHondaCar(id: string): any {
  console.log(id);
  let car: any;
  for (let i = 0; i < this.hondaCar.length; i++) {
    console.log(this.hondaCar[i].id);
    if (id === this.hondaCar[i].id) {
      car = this.hondaCar[i];
      break;
    }
  }
  return car;
}
```

6. Import **Service** and **FormModule** into the app module (**app.module.ts**) and add them as a **provider** and an **import**, respectively:

```
import { CarsService } from './cars.service';
import { FormsModule } from '@angular/forms';
.............................. .
imports: [
    BrowserModule,
    FormsModule
  ],

providers: [CarsService],
```

7. Import **Service** into **app.component.ts** and inject it into the constructor:

```
import { CarsService } from './cars.service'
constructor(private carService:CarsService) { }
```

8. Declare a variable to hold a record object and object ID:

```
public hondaCarObj:any;
public carId:string;
```

9. Write a method to call the service:

```
public getHondaCarsDetail():void{
this.hondaCarObj = this.carService.getHondaCar(this.carId);
}
```

10. Update the HTML template part of the component to display the object as requested, using the following code:

```
<h1>Honda Cars</h1>
<div><label>Model  : </label> <strong *ngIf="hondaCarObj">{{hondaCarObj.
model}}</strong></div>
<div><label>Year   : </label> <strong *ngIf="hondaCarObj">{{hondaCarObj.
year}}</strong></div>
<input type="text" [(ngModel)]='carId'>
<button (click)="getHondaCarsDetail()">Get Honda Car</button>
```

11. Run the application using the following command and go to **localhost:4200** to view the output:

```
ng serve -open
```

The output is as follows:

Figure 3.9: Retrieving data using the service

For services requesting resources over HTTP servers, we have to use the **HttpClientModule**, which is made available by Angular. We will be discussing this in detail in the next section.

HTTP Requests Using Angular's HttpClient

HttpClientModule was introduced in Angular version 4.3 and is available in the **@angular/common/** package. The new **HttpClient** service can be used to begin HTTP requests and process the responses. This comes with several advantages makes handling requests easy. Some advantages are streamlined error handling, the ability to observe the API, typed request and response objects, testability features, and request and response interception.

The **XMLHttpRequest** interface is used by **HttpClient** to make HTTP requests. Most frontend applications communicate with backend services over the HTTP protocol. Modern browsers support two different APIs for making HTTP requests. To get started with **HttpClient** in an Angular project, you have to do the following:

- Import **HttpClientModule** into **app.module.ts** and update the import array using the following code:

```
import { HttpClientModule } from '@angular/common/http';

imports: [
    HttpClientModule
  ]
```

- Inject **HttpClientModule** inside a service:

```
import { HttpClient } from '@angular/common/http';
@Injectable()

export class sampleService {
  constructor(private http: HttpClient) { }
}
```

Working with JSON Data

One of the changes brought about by **HttpClientModule** is handling responses as JSON by default. Before **HttpClientModule** was introduced, we could handle responses using the **.json** extension, as shown in the following snippet:

```
this.data = this.http.get('https://api.data.com/data')
      .map(response => response.json())
      .subscribe(data => console.log(data));
```

But we can now do this in the following way:

```
this.http.get('https://api.github.com/users')
    .subscribe(data => console.log(data));
```

Type Checking Responses

TypeScript flags an error when a response type isn't the same as what is expected. When a method is declared as a particular type, the response is expected to be of the same type, as shown in the following snippet:

```
interface LoginResponse {
  accessToken: string;
  accessExpiration: number;
}
this.http.post<LoginResponse>('api/login', {
  login: 'foo',
  password: 'bar'
}).subscribe(data => {
  console.log(data.accessToken, data.accessExpiration);
});
```

Non-JSON Data Request

In situations where we're requesting non-JSON data, **HTTPClient** provides the **responseType** property to handle such responses, as seen in the following snippet:

```
this.http.get('...', { responseType: 'text' });
responseType?: 'arraybuffer' | 'blob' | 'json' | 'text'
```

Error Handling

What happens in a situation where the server couldn't be reached due to network unavailability or an error? Instead of returning a successful response, **HttpClientModule** returns an error object by adding a second callback, as seen in the following snippet:

```
.subscribe(
    (data: Config) => this.config = { ...data}, // success path
    error => this.error = error // error path
  );
```

Sending a Data Request to the Server

Apart from getting data from the server using a HTTP request, HTTP data mutation methods are also available to manipulate data on the server. The **HttpClient** methods for **POST**, **PUT**, and **DELETE** are **HttpClient.post()**, **HttpClient.put()**, and **HttpClient.delete()**, respectively.

Activity 6: Designing the Frontend and Components for the Blogging Application

Recall the blogging application project from the previous chapter, for which we created a RESTful API? We will be creating the frontend for the application. Specifically, we will be creating components and directives for the application. Once finished, our aim is to have a well-designed frontend and components for the blogging application.

> **Note**
>
> The code files for this activity can be found here: http://bit.ly/2SPq5Gs.

Make sure you have completed all the exercises and activities in both the previous and current chapter before attempting this activity. Create a **Blogging Application** project folder and open it in the IDE (Visual Studio Code). Perform the following steps to complete the activity:

1. Create a new Angular project, **blog**.
2. Import the bootstrap theme and its resources from https://goo.gl/VGTYra.
3. Update the automatically created `index.html` file of the application.
4. Create the `header` components.
5. Create the `title-header` component and update the HTML template with the theme's content.
6. Create the `blog-home` components.
7. Create the `footer` components.
8. Update the root component template.
9. Create the `view-post` components and update the HTML template.
10. Run `ng serve -o` to start the application.
11. Update the root component template to see the `view-post` page.

> **Note**
>
> The solution for this activity can be found on page 265.

Activity 7: Writing Services and Making HTTP Request Calls to an API

In the last activity, we designed the frontend and created components for the blogging application project. Now, we will be writing services and making HTTP request calls to APIs for the application. Specifically, we will be writing a service function to perform CRUD operations via HTTP request calls that are made to APIs. Once finished, our aim is to be able to view all blog posts collectively and individually.

Make sure you have completed all the exercises and activities in both the previous and current chapter before attempting this activity. Open the **Blogging Application** project folder in the IDE (Visual Studio Code).

Perform the following steps to complete the activity:

> **Note**
>
> The code files for this activity can be found here: http://bit.ly/2txtavx.

1. Create a service file (**article.service**) for blog post articles.
2. Update **app.module.ts** file by importing provider for **ArticleService**.
3. Write the interface class in a newly created posts.ts file..
4. Import the **Injectable**, **HttpClient**, **HttpHeaders**, **Post**, and **Observable** modules
5. Declare the **Url** variables and assign string values in the **ArticleService** class.
6. Import and inject **HttpClient**.
7. Write the CRUD service functions.
8. Update the **blog-home** components class file.
9. Update the **blog-home** components HTTP template file.
10. Update the **root** component.
11. Run **ng serve -o** on the command line to view the output.
12. Update the **view-post** components class file.
13. Update the **view-post** components HTTP template file.

14. Update the **root** component template file.

15. Run **ng serve -o** to start the application.

> **Note**
>
> The solution for this activity can be found on page 271.

Understanding Angular Forms and Routing

In the previous topic, we were able to look at Angular components, directives, services, and using HTTP to make requests in Angular. In this topic, we will be looking at Angular forms and routing. Specifically, we will describe Angular forms and their uses in Angular. We will discuss two ways of working with forms: **template-driven** and **model-driven forms**. Furthermore, we will learn about Angular's support for two-way data binding, change tracking, validation, and error handling. Later in this section, we'll look into routing and navigation between pages in Angular applications.

Angular Forms

In website development, a form is an essential element of a web application that allows users to input, validate, and process data before it is used in the program or sent to the database. Forms are also a very important part of business applications, and they are used in registering, logging in, submitting requests, and are used to perform countless data entry tasks. A good data entry experience makes it easy for users to effectively and efficiently perform tasks that involve data collection and manipulation.

A form is also a part of the HTML element group that contains numerous HTML element fields or spaces to enter data. Each field holds a field label, and the label gives the user an idea of the content that's contained in the field view area. For Angular, there are many built-in directives that enhance form elements and templates. These not only extend the primary function of a native HTML form template/element, but also make form implementation, usage, and validation very easy. For example, it saves the builder the time of writing several click or event-driven functions to validate form inputs and so on. There are two types of Angular forms:

- Template-driven

- Model-driven

We will look at each of these in detail in the following sections.

Template-Driven Forms

In a template-driven form, just as the name implies, most of the scripting is done in an HTML template. To enable template-driven forms, we need to explicitly import a module called **FormsModule** in our application and bootstrap the application dynamically because they are not available by default. For a better understanding, let's dive into creating a form application in a template-driven way.

Exercise 15: Creating a Form Using the Angular Template-Driven Method

In this exercise, we will be creating a form application named **packt-course-form** in the **chapter-3-exercises** folder using the template-driven method. Perform the following steps to complete the exercise:

> **Note**
>
> The code files for this exercise can be found here: http://bit.ly/2XfLcQM.

1. Create a new Angular project using the CLI in the **chapter-3-exercises** folder by using the following command:

   ```
   ng new packt-course-form
   ```

2. Create a model using the **ng generate class students** command and ensure that the model has a structure similar to the following snippet:

   ```
   src/app/students.ts

   export class Students {

       constructor(
       public id: number,
       public name: string,
       public courseTitle: string,
       public duration?: string
   ) { }
   }
   ```

3. Using the **ng generate component packt-form/PacktStudentForm** Angular CLI command, generate a new component named **PacktStudentForm** and implement the following:

   ```
   src/app/packt-form/packt-student-form.component.ts
   import { Component } from '@angular/core';
   import { Students }    from '../../students';
   ```

```
@Component({
  selector: 'app-packt-student-form',
  templateUrl: './packt-student-form.component.html',
  styleUrls: ['./packt-student-form.component.css']
})
export class PacktStudentFormComponent {

  courseTitles = ['MEAN Stack','MEVN Stack','MERN Stack'];

  model = new Students(1, 'Paul Adams', this.courseTitles[0], '6 days');

  submitted = false;

  onSubmit() { this.submitted = true; }
  newStudent() {
    this.model = new Students(42, '', '');
}}
```

4. Enable the template-driven forms from our root module defined in `app.module.ts`.

    To do this, we need to explicitly import a module called `FormsModule` in our application and add it to the list of `NgModule` decorators, as shown in the following code:

    src/app/app.module.ts

```
import { NgModule }      from '@angular/core';
import { BrowserModule } from '@angular/platform-browser';
import { FormsModule }   from '@angular/forms';

import { AppComponent }  from './app.component';
import { PacktStudentFormComponent } from './ packt-form/ packt-student-
form.component';

@NgModule({
  imports: [
    BrowserModule,
    FormsModule
  ],
  declarations: [
    AppComponent,
    PacktStudentFormComponent
```

```
    ],
    providers: [],
    bootstrap: [ AppComponent ]
})
export class AppModule { }
```

5. Update the template file (**packt-student-template-form.component.html**) by hosting the form component, as shown here:

File name **packt-student-template-form.component.html:**

```
<div class="container">
    <div [hidden]="submitted">
        <h1>Packt Course Form</h1>
        <form (ngSubmit)="onSubmit()" #studentForm="ngForm">
            <div class="form-group">
                <label for="name">Name</label>
                <input type="text" class="form-control" id="name" required
[(ngModel)]="model.name" name="name"
                #name="ngModel">
                <div [hidden]="name.valid || name.pristine" class="alert
alert-danger">
//[…]
    <div [hidden]="!submitted">
        <h2>You submitted the following:</h2>
        <div class="row">
            <div class="col-xs-3">Name</div>
            <div class="col-xs-9  pull-left">{{ model.name }}</div>
        </div>
        <div class="row">
            <div class="col-xs-3">Course Duration</div>
            <div class="col-xs-9 pull-left">{{ model.duration }}</div>
        </div>
        <div class="row">
            <div class="col-xs-3">Packt Course Title</div>
            <div class="col-xs-9 pull-left">{{ model.courseTitle }}</div>
        </div>
        <br>
        <button class="btn btn-primary" (click)="submitted=false">Edit</
button>
    </div>
</div>
```

Live link: http://bit.ly/2VoNmLV

6. Update the style sheet (**packt-student-template-form.component.css**) and the main application style sheet (**style.css**):

```
// packt-student-template-form.component.css
.ng-valid[required], .ng-valid.required  {
   border-left: 5px solid #42A948; /* green */
 }

 .ng-invalid:not(form)  {
   border-left: 5px solid #a94442; /* red */
 }
```

```
// style.css
/* You can add global styles to this file, and also import other style files
*/
@import url('https://unpkg.com/bootstrap@3.3.7/dist/css/bootstrap.min.
css');
```

7. Update the root template file (**app.component html**) by hosting the form component **src/app/app.component.html**, as shown here:

```
src/app/app.component.html
< app-packt-student-template-form ></ app-packt-student-template-form >
```

8. Launch the application by running the following snippet in the command-line terminal and go to the address **localhost:4200**:

```
ng serve --open
```

You will obtain the following output:

Figure 3.10: Template-driven form

Now that we have working code, let's break it down to see how the various features are implemented.

Two-way Data Binding

In the previous exercise, when you run the app, you discover that values have already been input into the field. Two-way data binding in Angular using **[(NgModel)]** makes it possible to display, listen, and update/extract input variable values at the same time. The **[NgModel]** syntax is used to bind a form to a model, as shown in the following snippet:

```
<input type="text" class="form-control" id="name" required
[(ngModel)]="model.name" name="name">

<div class="col-xs-9  pull-left">{{ model.name }}</div>
                <input type="text" class="form-control" id="name" required
[(ngModel)]="model.name" name="name" #name="ngModel">
```

The form input interface is as follows:

Paul ad

Paul ad|

Figure 3.11: Output of two-way data binding

Tracking Control State and Validity

ngModel not only performs two-way data binding–it also helps to track control state and the validity of form inputs. For example, it watches the form input to see whether it's been touched, the values have changed, or whether the value has become invalid. Special Angular CSS classes, which are presented as follows, make it possible to reflect the state when controls change:

State	Class if true	Class if false
The control has been visited	ng-touched	ng-untouched
The control's value has changed	ng-dirty	ng-pristine
The control's value is valid	ng-valid	ng-invalid

Figure 3.12: Control states

Also, we can see how **ng-pristine** is implemented in the following snippet to bind a hidden directive to a **div**:

```
<div class="form-group">
            <label for="name">Name</label>
            <input type="text" class="form-control" id="name" required
[(ngModel)]="model.name" name="name" #name="ngModel">
            <div [hidden]="name.valid || name.pristine" class="alert
alert-danger">
               Name is required
            </div>
        </div>
```

The resulting output of this snippet can be seen as follows:

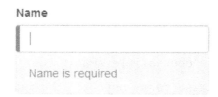

Figure 3.13: Validation using styling and messages

Template Reference Variable

Template-driven variables such as **#name** and **#courseTitle** make it possible for Angular to observe input tags for validation. They provide access to the input box's Angular control from within the template to reveal and conceal validation error messages when an input value is either valid or invalid. Error message visibility is controlled by binding the properties of a set variable to the **<div>** element's hidden property, as shown in the following code snippet:

```
<input type="text" class="form-control" id="name" required
[(ngModel)]="model.name" name="name"
                  #name="ngModel">

<div [hidden]="name.valid || name.pristine" class="alert alert-danger">
```

Using NgForm, ngSubmit, and NgFor

NgForm is a directive in Angular. Its main function is not only to govern the form, but also to add various features it possesses as supplements to the form element. It returns true if the validity of all other controls, such as name (attribute), **NgModel** directive, and so on, are true.

Let's see how it's used in the following snippet:

```
<form (ngSubmit)="onSubmit()" #studentForm="ngForm">

  ...---------------------------------------------------------

  -----------------------------------------------------------

    <button type="submit" class="btn btn-success" [disabled]="!studentForm.
form.valid">Submit</button>

</form>
```

ngSubmit is an event property that buttons with type properties such as the **submit** bind with the **onSubmit()** method in our component. You should also see from the preceding snippet that it's only triggered if the submit button is enabled, and that's dependent on the validity of **NgForm**.

NgFor is a directive for listing or displaying items in an array. It can also be used over an iterable object to repeat items, as shown in the following snippet:

```
        <div class="form-group">

          <label for="courseTitle">Packt Course Title</label>

          <select class="form-control" id="courseTitle" required
[(ngModel)]="model.courseTitle" name="courseTitle" #courseTitle="ngModel">

        <option *ngFor="let course of courseTitles"
[value]="course">{{course}}</option>
```

```
        </select>
                <div [hidden]="courseTitle.valid || courseTitle.pristine"
  class="alert alert-danger">
                    courseTitle is required
                </div>
            </div>
```

You will obtain the following output when the preceding snippet is run:

Figure 3.14: *ngFor directive output

Now that we've been introduced to the structure of what an Angular application entails in the preceding section, we will be delving into those features that make Angular great, as highlighted in the first chapter.

This section will briefly describe how to create, update, and implement a simple and advanced form control; we will also look into how reactive form values are validated.

Reactive/Model-Driven Forms

When it comes to handling forms whose values change over time, a model-driven approach or reactive form is used. Such forms are built around observable streams, in which input values are accessed synchronously. They are highly testable because data requests have a high probability of being predictable and consistent.

To have a better understanding, let's dive into creating a form application in the reactive/model-driven format.

Exercise 16: Creating a Simple Form Application Using the Reactive/Model-Driven Method

In this exercise, we will be creating a form using the Angular reactive or model-driven method, in the **packt-course-form** application that's located in the **chapter-3-exercises** folder. Perform the following steps to complete the exercise:

> **Note**
>
> The code files for this exercise can be found here: http://bit.ly/2GBuPce.

1. Generate a new component named **packt-simple-reactive-form** using the following code:

   ```
   ng generate component packt-simple-reactive-form
   ```

2. Register the reactive forms module in **app.module.ts** and add it to the import property:

   ```
   src/app/ app.module.ts
   import { ReactiveFormsModule } from '@angular/forms';
   ```

3. Import the new form control and form group into **app.component.ts**:

   ```
   import { FormGroup, FormControl } from '@angular/forms';
   ```

4. Generate a new form control and group control using the following code:

   ```
   name = new FormControl('');
   ....................................... .
   studentForm = new FormGroup({
   firstName: new FormControl(''),
   lastName: new FormControl(''),
   });
   ```

5. Register the control and form group in the template. It's important to know that **FormControl** gives control over an input field, while **FormGroup** gives control over the group of the control instance, as shown in the following snippet.

   Let's register a **formGroup** as follows:

   ```
   <form [formGroup] ="studentForm ">
   <label>
   ```

The following is the code for `firstName`:

```
<input type="text" formControlName="firstName">
</label>
<label>
```

The following is the code for `lastName`:

```
<input type="text" formControlName="lastName">
</label>
</form>
```

6. Update the root template file (`app.component.html`) by hosting the form component in **src/app/app.component.html**:

```
src/app/app.component.html
<app-packt-simple-reactive-form></app-packt-simple-reactive-form>
```

7. Launch the application by running the following snippet in the command-line terminal and go to the `localhost:4200` address:

```
ng serve --open
```

You will obtain the following output:

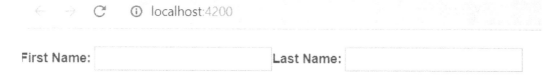

Figure 3.15: A simple reactive form

Validating Model-Driven Forms

The three most used methods for validating model-driven forms are using validators, rendering form controls with styling, and adding validation error messages. Each of these are discussed here.

Using Validators

Pre-built validators are already provided in the Angular Validators module to match the ones we can define via standard HTML5 attributes. These validators are required: **minlegth**, **maxlength**, and **pattern**. The implementations are as shown here:

```
import { FormGroup, FormControl, Validators } from '@angular/forms':

    myform = new FormGroup({
        name: new FormGroup({
            firstName: new FormControl('', Validators.required),
            lastName: new FormControl('', Validators.required),
        }),
        email: new FormControl('', [
            Validators.required,
            Validators.pattern("[^ @]*@[^ @]*")
        ]),
        password: new FormControl('', [
            Validators.minLength(8),
            Validators.required
        ]),
        language: new FormControl()
    });
}
```

Rendering Form Controls with Styling

This method works the same as that for the template-driven form. We have already discussed the various form control instances, which are Dirty/Pristine, Touched/Untouched, and Valid/Invalid, and these can be implemented as follows:

```
<div>Dirty? {{ myform.controls.email.dirty }}</div>,

<div>Touched? {{ myform.controls.email.touched }}</div>

<div>Valid? {{myform.controls.email.valid}}</div>
y
```

We can use the **ngClass** to give nicely styled feedback, as follows:

```
<div class="form-group" [ngClass]="{
  'has-danger': myform.controls.email.invalid && myform.controls.email.
dirty,
  'has-success': myform.controls.email.valid && myform.controls.email.
dirty
}">
```

Adding Validation Error Messages

We can apply the same method we used previously to conditionally show or hide an error message. This can be done as follows:

```
<div class="form-group">

  <label>Password</label>

  <input type="password"
         class="form-control"
         formControlName="password">

  <div class="form-control-feedback"
       *ngIf="password.invalid && password.dirty">

    Field is invalid

  </div>

</div>
```

Routing in Angular

The Angular router makes navigation from one view to another possible in applications. It adopts the browser navigation model to interpret a URL as an instruction to a client-generated view. Parameters can be passed to determine the specific content to present. Routers can be bound to page links, and the page opens as the user clicks the link. Activities are also logged to the browser's history to ensure back and forward button navigation functionalities.

Getting Started with the Router

It's necessary to know that the Angular router is not part of the Angular core. It's an optional feature that presents a component view, and it has its own library, which is **@angular/router**. So, to get started with using Angular router, let's go to the **index.html** file of the application; in the head tag, you'll see **<base href ='/'>**. It is the first child in the **<head>** tag, and tells the router how to compose navigation URLs. Then, we import this router module from its library into the app module, as shown in the following snippet:

```
import { RouterModule, Routes } from '@angular/router';
```

The following snippet shows an array of routes that have been configured for different view navigation:

```
const appRoutes: Routes = [
  { path: 'post/:id', component: PostDetailComponent },
  { path: 'posts', component: PostListComponent, data: { title: 'Post List' }
},
  { path: '', redirectTo: '/posts', pathMatch: 'full' },
  { path: '**', component: PageNotFoundComponent } ];
```

It is important to know that the router uses a first-match-wins strategy to match routes. So, the order of routers really matters. It should be designed in such a way that more specific routes should be placed above less specific routes. The following flow of design is advised:

- Routes with a static path
- Empty path route, for the default route
- Wildcard route

Now, let's talk about the route array defined in the app module. In a route such as **post/: id**, the ID is a token for a route parameter. For example, let's say we have a URL that is **/post/20**. This means it'll retrieve data for the post whose **id = 20**, and route to a different page.

The data property in a route is a place to store arbitrary data associated with the specific route, and it's accessible within each activated route. You can store variables such as page title, actions, and so on, and all the data that's stored can be retrieved dynamically. The empty path, ' ', represents the default path for the application, from the route defined previously; it means that if the route is empty, redirect to the post. The ****** path is a wildcard. This path is used to display a "**404 - Not Found**" page or redirect to another route if the path doesn't match any in the route. There is the **enableTracing** option configuration, which can be added as a second argument to the **RouterModule.forRoot()** method. This is mainly meant for debugging.

Router Outlets, Links, States, and Events

Router outlet

RouterOutlet is a tag that's placed in the host view's HTML. It uses the given configuration to match the URL to the route, as defined in the route array:

```
<router-outlet></router-outlet>
```

Router link

The router link makes navigation between pages possible. For example, let's assume we have a route whose path is set to **about-us** and we are currently on the home page of the application. The router link can be configured as follows:

```
  <nav>
 <a routerLink="/home" routerLinkActive="active">Home</a>
    <a routerLink="/about-us" routerLinkActive="non-active">About Us</a>
  </nav>
  <router-outlet></router-outlet>
```

Don't forget that we are still going to have **router-outlet** on the view to enable routing on the HTML view.

The **routerLinkActive** directive visually distinguishes the anchor for the currently selected **"active"** route by adding an active CSS class.

Router State

A tree of `ActivatedRoute` objects is built after successful navigation; this makes up the current state of the router, which is known as `RouterState`. Both router service properties (`ActivatedRoute` and `RouterState`) provide methods that enable up ward and down ward traversing for information retrieval from the tree elements (parent, child, and sibling node).

Router Events

These are events that are emitted at every stage of the routing process. Events such as `NavigationStart` are triggered when navigation starts. `RoutesRecognized` is triggered when the router parses the URL and the routes are recognized. `RouteConfigLoadStart` is triggered before the router lazy-loads a route configuration. Other events include `RouteConfigLoadEnd`, `NavigationEnd`, `NavigationCancel`, and `NavigationError`. Their meanings can easily be understood by the event names.

Activity 8: Creating a Form Application Using the Reactive/Model-Driven Method

Remember the template-driven form project that was used as an illustration in this section? We'll be developing the same form using a reactive/model-driven approach from the knowledge that we've gained in this section. Once finished, our aim is to have a reactive/model-driven form with the same functionality as the template-driven form in *Exercise 16, Creating a Form Using the Angular Template-Driven Method*, from the previous section.

To complete the activity, perform the following steps:

> **Note**
>
> The code files for this activity can be found here: http://bit.ly/2IuqzwN.

1. Create an Angular project with the name **reactive-form** and open the folder in Visual Studio Code.

2. Create a component and name it `packt-student-reactive-form`.

3. Register the reactive forms module in `app.module.ts` and add it to the import properties to activate the reactive form.

4. Import the `FormControl` and `FormGroup` modules into the reactive form component (`packt-student-reactive-form.component.ts`).

5. Declare and initialize the array in the reactive components class.

6. Create the `FormGroup` and `FormControl` variable instances.

7. Create functions to initialize and validate.

8. Register the control and form group in the HTML form template (`packt-student-reactive-form.component.html`) of the reactive component.

9. Add a **submitted** view to the template.

10. Update the components and the main app's style sheet (`packt-student-reactive-form.component.css` and `style.css`).

11. Update the root template file (`app.component.html file`) by hosting the form component `src/app/app.component.html`.

12. Launch the application and go to the address `localhost:4200`.

> **Note**
>
> The solution for this activity can be found on page 278.

Activity 9: Creating and Validating Different Forms Using the Template and Reactive-Driven Method

Continuing the frontend development of our blogging application, we will be creating and validating three different forms (**login**, **register**, and **create/edit**) that we will be making use of in the application as we progress. These forms will be reactive-driven. Once finished, our aim is to create reactive-driven forms for user login, and template-driven forms for user registration and for creating or editing the blog post.

Make sure you have completed all the exercises and activities in both the previous and current chapter before attempting this activity. Open the **Blogging Application** project folder in the IDE (Visual Studio Code) and perform the following steps:

> **Note**
>
> The code files for this activity can be found here: http://bit.ly/2BOfXmO.

1. Create the **User Login** form component.

2. Update the **User Login** form component class and update the HTML template to be reactive/model-driven.

3. Update the **app** component template and run **ng serve** to view the **User Login** form's output.

4. Create the **User Registration** form component and an exportable user class.

5. Update the **User Registration** form component class and update the HTML template to be template-driven.

6. Update the app component template and run **ng serve** to view the **User Registration** form output.

7. Create the **Post Create/Edit** form components.

8. Update the **Post Create/Edit** form component class and update the HTML template to be template-driven.

9. Update the **app** component template and run **ng serve** to view the **Post Create/ Edit** form output.

> **Note**
>
> The solution for this activity can be found on page 282.

Activity 10: Implementing a Router for the Blogging Application

Continuing the frontend development of our blogging application, we will be implementing an Angular router so that we are able to navigate between pages. Once finished, our aim is to navigate between pages and also, finally, to have a robust blogging application ready for deployment. Before attempting the activity, ensure that the previous activities and exercises have been completed.

Open the Angular **blog** project located in the **Blogging Application** project folder in the IDE (Visual Studio Code) and perform the following steps:

> **Note**
>
> The code files for this activity can be found here: http://bit.ly/2U25Pho.

1. Import **RouterModule** into the **app** module file (**app.module.ts**) and update the **import** property.

2. Configure the route in **app.module.ts**.

3. Add **router-outlet** to the **app.component.html** file.

4. Add the router link to the **blog-home** component.

5. Start the server and serve the Angular application using the CLI.

6. Open the browser and input **http://localhost:4200/blogin** in the URL address bar to view the router in action.

> **Note**
>
> The solution for this activity can be found on page 291.

Summary

In this chapter, we presented an introduction to the Angular CLI and highlighted the main steps involved in the creation of Angular applications. We began by creating and serving an Angular CLI application and performed exercises on creating and running new applications.

As the chapter progressed, we introduced using components, directives, and services, and making HTTP requests in Angular. We began with the building blocks of Angular applications (components). Thereafter, we described various directives and some of their implementations. We performed exercises on the creation and implementation of Angular services and described how Angular handles HTTP requests. The last section introduced us to Angular forms and routing. We began with the types of forms used in Angular and performed exercises on routing.

In the next chapter, we will introduce you to Node application security practices and the different forms of access authentication for Node applications.

The MEAN Stack Security

Learning Objectives

By the end of this chapter, you will be able to:

- Describe best practices for securing Node applications

- Create token-based authentication using JSON web tokens

- Implement session-based authentication using passport

- Apply authentication using a third-party application

This chapter presents best practices for securing Node applications in addition to several exercises and activities on creating JSON web tokens, authentication using passport, third-party authentication, many more GI.

Introduction

The previous chapter introduced us to frontend development with Angular. We learned how to jump-start frontend development using the Angular CLI and gainfully engaged with exercises and activities that taught us how to implement various features, such as directives, components, templates, reactive forms, and so on. In *Chapter 2, Developing RESTful APIs to Perform CRUD Operations*, we described RESTful APIs and their design concepts, and also developed an HTTP server for a Node application (backend development).

In this chapter, we will be continuing with the backend development; however, the focus will be on securing access to the use of APIs and securing Node applications in general. This chapter introduces Node application security practices and different forms of authentication. You will learn how to grant user access to the RESTful API that we developed in the previous chapter and perform user authentication on Node applications. This chapter also describes the structure and workings of **JSON web tokens** (**JWTs**). We will also implement token-based authentication using **JWT**. We will learn the different means of implementing authentication in Node using strategies provided by the **passport** middleware.

We will walk through exercises aimed at implementing different forms of authentication (**Facebook**, **Twitter**). Finally, the chapter will end with us performing activities that will take our blog application to the next level by securing the RESTful API and distinguishing guest and admin access.

Node Security and Best Practices

We will begin this section by describing how security is handled and implemented by Node. In this section, we will be skimming through the security practices that are required for Node applications.

Securing your Node Applications

Security has become increasingly important ever since Node became one of the leading platforms for backend application development. Security matters because, as a backend or Node.js developer, you will be exposed to handing huge amounts of sensitive data, especially in the cloud native era where most business are operating in the cloud. The following Node modules have been strictly developed to address the aforementioned points:

- **Helmet modules**
- **Input validations**
- **Regular expressions**

- **Security.txt**

- **Session management**

- **Cross-Site Request Forgery (CSRF)**

We will begin by describing the **Helmet** module.

Helmet Module

Helmet provides various HTTP headers that can be set to secure Express applications. Among the collection of 14 middleware provided by **Helmet**, a few are as follows, along with their uses:

- **X-Frame-Options** is used to mitigate clickjacking attacks

- **Strict-Transport-Security** is used to ensure that users are on HTTPS

- **X-XSS-Protection** is used to prevent reflected **cross-sectional scripting** (**XSS**) attacks

- **X-DNS-Prefetch-Control** is used to disable a browser's **domain name server** (**DNS**) prefetching

> **Note**
>
> There are more headers supported by Helmet. Refer to the following document for a complete list: https://helmetjs.github.io/docs/.

Helmet also prevents Node applications from common attacking techniques such as the following:

- **SQL Injection**: Whereby a partial or complete SQL query is injected via user input. It is advisable to use parameterized queries or prepared statements to guard against this kind of attack.

- **Command injection**: Whereby an OS command is run on the remote web server to obtain or steal objects or resources such as passwords.

Implementing Helmet

It is a best practice to use **Helmet** at an early stage in our middleware stack. This gives us the assurance that the HTTP headers are set. The following snippet shows how **Helmet** is implemented after being installed using the `npm install helmet -save` command:

```
const express = require('express')
const helmet = require('helmet')
const app = express()
app.use(helmet())
app.use(helmet.noCache())
app.use(helmet.frameguard())
```

Some middleware is normally enabled by default. It can be disabled if need be; for example, the x-frame option from **Helmet**, also known as `frameguard`, can be disabled using the following command:

```
app.use(helmet({
  frameguard: false
}))
```

Validating user input

The repercussions of poor input validation can be devastating. Implementing application security involves validating user inputs from dreadful attacks such as **SQL injection**, **XSS**, or **command injection**. One of the best libraries that helps to achieve this is **joi**. It is used to validate inputs and define schema for JavaScript objects. The **joi** library can be implemented with Mongoose as follows:

```
const Joi = require('joi'),
mongoose = require('mongoose')
const userSchema = mongoose.Schema({
      username: String,
      password: String,
          email: String,
          full_name: String,
          created: { type: Date, default: Date.now },
    });
    userSchema.methods.joiValidate = function(obj) {
```

```
        var Joi = require('joi');
        var schema = {
                username: Joi.types.String().min(6).max(30).required(),
                password: Joi.types.String().min(8).max(30).regex(/
[a-zA-Z0-9]{3,30}/).required(),
                email: Joi.types.String().email().required(),
                full_name: Joi.types.String().required(),
                created: Joi.types.Date(),
        }
        return Joi.validate(obj, schema);
    }
```

Imagine a situation where a visitor decides to sign up to your website with **l337_p@ndain** as their first name, for example. You need to define the limitations of what can be input and validate it against this set of rules. The **joi** library makes this possible, as schemas can be created for JavaScript objects to ensure the validation of key information to be stored. In this view, for input validation on SQL queries, it is advisable to always escape (**/**) a user's data before passing an input for an SQL query. For **Object** **Relational** **Mapping** (**ORM**), such as **Sequelize**, which uses parametrized (prepared) statements (that is, values are supplied at execution), you can encode the escape symbol, **/**, properly.

Regular Expression Security

Some attackers use **Regular** **Expression** (**Regex**) **Denial** **of** **Service** as an attacking technique. It involves exposing the **Regex** implementation to some specially crafted input that causes these inputs to function slowly. The main purpose of using a Regex is to manipulate text to get the required resources. However, when some Regex that contains groupings with repetitions or repetition/alternation with overlapping (that is, **(a+)+** , **([a-zA-Z]+)*** , **(a|aa)+**) is implemented, it makes the server vulnerable to attacks and can lead to the server being taken down. These expressions are called **Evil** **Regular** **Expressions**, and they can be detected using the safe-regex module. For example, **aaaaaaaaaaaaaaaaaaaaaaaaX** is a potential input that can cause the regular expression **(a+)+** to run very slowly.

Security.txt

Risk Society was a concept that was developed by independent risk researchers in the 1980s. This concept lists the book of action that a contemporary society undertakes in response to various types of risks. In the field of software development, often, developers may find that they are unable to effectively communicate to other stakeholders the various risks that might render applications vulnerable. With this in mind, **Security.txt** was proposed. **Security.txt** specifically deals with web development by proposing standards that enable websites to define security policies. Even though **Security.txt** is in a draft stage, its purpose is to help developers disclose security vulnerabilities.

> **Note**
>
> For more information, please refer to the following web page: https://tools.ietf.org/html/draft-foudil-securitytxt-00.

There is a module named **express-security.txt** that helps researchers report security bugs to the programmers. This module is implemented as follows:

```
const express = require('express')
const securityTxt = require('express-security.txt')
const app = express()
app.get('/security.txt', securityTxt({
  // your security address
  contact: 'email@example.com',
  // your pgp key
  encryption: 'encryption',
  // if you have a hall of fame for security resources, include the link
here
  acknowledgements: 'http://acknowledgements.example.com'
}))
```

Session Management

The importance of the secure use of cookies cannot be understated—most importantly, in a situation where web application is dynamic and there is a need to maintain state across a stateless protocol such as HTTP.

Some of the many attributes, each having a different meaning, that can be set for cookies, are described as follows:

- **Path**: In addition to the domain, the URL path that the cookie is valid for can be specified. If the domain and path match, then the cookie will be sent in the request.

- **Expires**: This attribute is used to set persistent cookies, since the cookie does not expire until the set date is exceeded.

- **Secure**: Inform the browser to only send the cookie when an HTTPS request is being sent.

- **httpOnly**: Cookies are not allowed to be accessed via JavaScript, thereby preventing an attack.

- **Domain**: This attribute is used to compare against the domain of the server in which the URL is being requested. If the domain matches or if it is a sub-domain, then the path attribute will be checked next.

In Node, there is a cookie module available for creating cookies. Also available is a wrapper-like cookie-session that can be implemented as follows:

```
var cookieSession = require('cookie-session');
var express = require('express');

var app = express();
 var expiryDate = new Date(Date.now() + 60 * 60 * 1000) // 1 hour
app.use(cookieSession({
  name: 'session',
  keys: [

    COOKIE_KEY1,
    COOKIE_KEY2
  ],
cookie: {
    secure: true,
    httpOnly: true,
    domain: 'siteexample.com',
    path: 'foo/bar',
    expires: expiryDate
  }

}));
```

```
app.use(function (req, res, next) {
  var n = req.session.views || 0;
  req.session.views = n++;
  res.end(n + ' views');
});

app.listen(3000);
```

The preceding snippet is an example of using cookie-session middleware. The first session is the import stage where the required modules are loaded. Thereafter, an Express application is created, and a cookie session is defined on the application using the attributes that we highlighted in the previous section. The last few lines of the snippet perform view manipulation with the sessions.

CSRF

CSRF executes unwanted actions (one-click attack or session riding), unauthorized commands, and state-changing requests on web applications to which a user is currently logged in. **csrf**, a Node module, is available to mitigate unwanted actions and can be implemented as follows:

```
var cookieParser = require('cookie-parser'); //

var csrf = require('csrf'); // csrf requires session middleware or cookie-parser to be initialized first.

var bodyParser = require('body-parser');

var express = require('express');


// setup route middlewares

var csrfProtection = csrf({ cookie: true });

var parseForm = bodyParser.urlencoded({ extended: false });


// create express app

var app = express();


// we need this because "cookie" is true in csrfProtection

app.use(cookieParser());


app.get('/form', csrfProtection, function(req, res) {
```

```
    // pass the csrfToken to the view
    res.render('send', { csrfToken: req.csrfToken() });
});


app.post('/process', parseForm, csrfProtection, function(req, res) {
    res.send('data is being processed');
});
```

While on the view layer you have to use the CSRF token like this:

```
<form action="/process" method="POST">
    <input type="hidden" name="_csrf" value="{{csrfToken}}">
    Favorite color: <input type="text" name="favoriteColor">
    <button type="submit">Submit</button>
</form>
```

In the preceding snippet, we first load the modules in the order in which they are required. Then, the **csrf** requires session middleware or cookie-parser to be initialized. Next, the middleware is loaded and the Express application is created. The **csrfProtection** implementation is done on the application route by passing **csrfToken** to the view. Finally, **crsfToken** is embedded into the form to be rendered.

Understanding Authentication and Authorization

In this section, we will be looking at two important processes: **Authentication** and **Authorization**. Authentication can be said to be the act of confirming the attributes of data against pre-described definitions. For example, a document may be used to authenticate or confirm the identity of a person or thing; digital certificates can also be used to confirm the identity of a website.

There are three types of authentication:

- Proof of identity
- Comparing an attribute known about an object to the object itself
- Documentation or external affirmations

The fact that a user has a username and password for an account does not mean authenticity is guaranteed. We say the user has been authenticated only when access based on those (username and password) user credentials is provided.

There are three factors that ensure authentication: the user's knowledge, ownership, and inheritance. These can be better explained as something that the user knows (that is, the user's password, their pattern, security questions answered, and so on), something the user has (ID card, security token, software token, biometrics, and so on), and something the user possesses (fingerprint, retina, and so on).

These authentication factors can be combined to reinforce the security level of online users into the following different authentication types:

- **Single-factor authentication**: One single component from any of the three categories of authentication is used to authenticate an individual's identity. This is the weakest type of authentication and is not recommended for financial or transactional services that warrant a high level of security.

- **Two-factor authentication**: Two components of authentication are used to authenticate an individual's identity. For example, in financial transactions, debit card information can serve as the ownership component while the PIN can serve as the knowledge component.

- **Three-factor authentication**: All components of authentication are employed. For example, entering a PIN (knowledge component) to unlock the user's phone (ownership) and then supplying an iris scan (inheritance) to finalize authentication. This is the strongest of the three types.

Authorization

Authorization is not authentication. Recall that authentication is the process of verifying that someone is who they claim to be. Authorization means you are permitted to do what you are trying to do. This does not mean authorization presupposes authentication. A guest could be authorized to a limited action set. For example, if a user wants to perform a mobile transfer from an application, after being successfully logged in (authenticated), the user then proceeds to transfer funds, and knowing that there is a balance of USD 10,000, the user still intends to transfer USD 20,000. The transaction will not go through because it won't be permitted (authorized), since the account balance is less than what the user was trying to transfer.

Node Application Authentication with JWTs

In terms of web applications, we have reached the stage where the application data doesn't only benefit you alone. It is often required to enable a third-party application access/usage of your backend applications and APIs to unleash the full potential of your application. For example, Twitter provides an API to grab its data (for an authenticated user, of course) and makes this usable for all third-party applications. Thus, there's always a reason to have a secure backend application or API.

Authentication simply means the action of proving or showing that something is true or valid. So, we can say that user authentication is the action of validating a user, while authorization is permitting or granting the user access to web resources, features, or pages. In the following section, we will be looking at how a user can be authenticated and authorized using a JSON Web Token.

The Structure of a JWT

JSON Web Tokens (JWTs) transmit restricted information that can be verified and trusted by means of a digital signature via JSON. JWT explicitly defines a compact and self-containing secure protocol for transmitting data. A JWT is made up of three components in the form of strings separated by a dot (.). These components are as follows:

- header
- signature
- payload

Header

The header is declared in the form of an object that consists of two properties: type declaration and the hashing algorithm. Object declaration can be seen in the following snippet:

```
{
    "typ": "JWT",
    "alg": "HS256"
}
```

The **typ** property will always be JWT, while the **alg** property could take any preferred hashing algorithm (**HMAC SHA256** is preferred in this case). Once these header objects are **base64** encoded, the output becomes the first part of JWT, as shown in the following code:

```
eyJ0eXAiOiJKV1QiLCJhbGciOiJIUzI1NiJ9
```

Payload

A payload is a JWT object and is known as a claim, where information about the token with information to be transmitted is held. The object also gives room for multiple claims, and this includes the following:

1. **Registered claim names**: These reserved names are claims that are not mandatory and are of the following types:

   `iss`: This holds the issuer of the token

   `sub`: This holds the subject of the token

   `aud`: This holds the information about the audience of the token

   `exp`: This defines the expiration (after the current date/time) in `NumericDate` value

   `nbf`: This defines the time before which the JWT should not be accepted for processing

   `iat`: This defines the time at which the JWT is issued

   `jti`: This is a unique identifier that is used to prevent the replay of JWT and is helpful for a one-time-use token

2. **Public claim names**: These are user-created or defined claims such as username, information, and so on.

3. **Private claim names**: These claims are defined based on the agreement between the consumer and the producer. It is advisable to use private claims with caution because they are subject to name collision (name clashing).

Let's consider an example payload that has two registered claims (`iss` and `exp`) and two public claims (author and company). The resulting snippet would be as follows:

```
{
    "iss": "meanstack courseware",
    "exp": 2000000,
    "author": "Paul Oluyege",
    "company": "Packt"
}
```

After going through **base64** encoding, the preceding snippet will result in the following:

eyJpc3MiOiJtZWFuc3RhY2sgY291cnNld2FyZSIsImV4cCI6MjAwMDAwM

CwiYXV0aG9yIjoiUGF1bCBPbHV5ZWdlIiwiY29tcGFueSI6InBhY3t0In0

The preceding output is the second part of our JWT.

Signature

The last part of a JWT is the signature. It is made up of a hash of the following components:

- Header
- Payload
- Secret

The aforementioned components can be hashed as follows:

```
var encodedString = base64UrlEncode(header) + "." + base64UrlEncode(payload);

HMACSHA256(encodedString, 'secret');
```

The variable named **secret** from the preceding snippet is the signature held by the server. This is the way that our server will be able to verify existing tokens and sign new ones.

The following snippet is used to obtain the signature:

```
14VeadfCPLa_XR2Swfu8WI8ZvnU03lnlQN7P1Rea2mk
```

Now, after putting all this (header, payload and signature) together, we have our full JSON Web Token, as shown in the following snippet:

```
eyJ0eXAiOiJKV1QiLCJhbGciOiJIUzI1NiJ9.
eyJpc3MiOiJtZWFuc3RhY2sgY291cnNld2FyZSIsImV4cCI6MjAwMDAwMCwiYXV0a
G9yIjoiUGF1bCBPbHV5ZWdlIiwiY29tcGFueSI6InBhY2t0In0.14VeadfCPLa_
XR2Swfu8WI8ZvnU03lnlQN7P1Rea2mk
```

The following diagram summarizes the structure of a JWT:

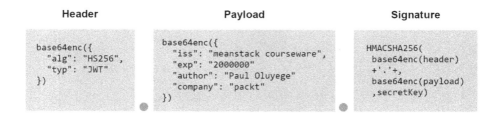

Figure 4.1: A standard JWT structure

How JWTs Work

In token-based authentication, you do not have to store information on the server or in a session. This means that the application can scale without worrying about where a user is logged in. Once we have authenticated with our information and we have our token, we are able to do many things with this token, as can be seen in the following diagram:

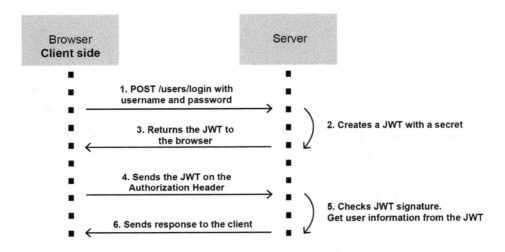

Figure 4.2: Client–Server token-based authentication

Access is requested by a user after submitting credentials (username and password). The credentials are validated by the application and a signed token is also provided to the client. The client side stores that token and sends in the HTTP header to ensure stateless HTTP requests. The server-side application does not accept requests from all domains using the access-control-allow-origin principle: * verifies the token and responds with data. Note that even a single request needs a token. However, only the information that we allowed with that specific token will be accessible.

Exercise 17: Creating a Token-Based User Authentication System for a Node Application

In this exercise, we will be creating a token-based user authentication system for a Node application. To complete this exercise, you must have completed the exercises and activities from the previous chapters. To get started, create a new folder in a known directory and name it **jwt**, and then install the most recent versions of the following packages: **express**, **body-parser**, **mongoose**, and **bcryptjs.** You can do this by running **npm install express body-parser mongoose bcryptjs -save** . Perform the following steps to complete the exercise:

> **Note**
>
> The code files for this exercise can be found here: http://bit.ly/2Is9rYA.

1. Create a **package.json** file using the following code:

    ```
    npm init
    ```

2. Install express and body-parser using the CLI by running the following code:

    ```
    npm install express body-parser
    ```

3. Create a **server.js** file using **touch** and import **express** and **body-parser**:

    ```
    touch server.js
    const express = require("express");
    const bodyParser = require("body-parser");
    ```

4. Create an Express application, assign the port number, and use the **body-parser** middleware on the Express application by using the following code:

    ```
    const app = express();
    const port =  4000
    app.use(bodyParser.urlencoded({ extended: true }));
    app.use(bodyParser.json());
    ```

5. Create a **config** folder using the following code:

    ```
    mkdir config
    ```

6. Create a database file named **db.js** in the **config** folder directory using the following code:

    ```
    touch db.js
    ```

We will create the database connection in the next few steps. Install mongoose from the CLI using the following code:

```
npm install mongoose
```

7. Export the **mongoose** module using the following code:

```
const mongoose = require("mongoose");
```

8. Declare and assign values to the **mongodb atlas** connection parameter, as shown here:

```
var uri = "mongodb+srv://username:password@cluster0-0wi3e.mongodb.net/
test?retryWrites=true";
  const options = {
    reconnectTries: Number.MAX_VALUE,
    poolSize: 10
  };
```

9. Connect to the database by typing in the following code:

```
mongoose.connect(uri, options).then(
    () => {
      console.log("Database connection established!");
    },
    err => {
      console.log("Error connecting Database instance due to: ", err);
    }
  );
```

10. Create an **api** directory using the following code:

```
mkdir api
```

11. Create three subfolders named **controllers**, **models**, and **routes** in the **api** directory using the following code:

```
mkdir - controllers && mkdir - models && mkdir - routes
```

12. Create the **userModel.js** model file inside the model directory using the following code:

```
-- touch userModel.js,
```

13. Install bcryptjs from the CLI using the following code:

```
npm install bcryptjs
```

14. Export **brcyptjs** and **mongoose** by typing in the following code:

```
const mongoose = require("mongoose"),
bcrypt = require('bcryptjs'),
```

15. Declare a **mongoose** schema using the following code:

```
const Schema = mongoose.Schema;
```

16. Create a **UserSchema** using the following code:

```
const UserSchema = new Schema({
  fullName: {
    type: String,
    trim: true,
    required: true
  },
  email: {
    type:String,
    unique:true,
    lowercase:true,
    trim:true,
    required:true
  } ,
  hash_password: {
    type:String,
    required:true
  },
  createdOn: {
    type: Date,
    default: Date.now
  }
});
```

17. Create a method to check the password's validity using the following code:

```
UserSchema.methods.comparePassword = function(password){
  return bcrypt.compareSync(password, this.hash_password);
}
```

18. Create a **mongoose-model** from the schema using the following code:

```
mongoose.model("User", UserSchema);
```

19. Create controller file called **userController.js** inside the **controller** directory using the following code:

```
-- touch userController.js ,
```

20. Import **mongoose**, **jsonweboken**, and **bcryptjs** using the following code:

```
const mongoose = require('mongoose'),
    jwt = require('jsonwebtoken'),
    bcrypt = require('bcryptjs'),
Import user model
const User = mongoose.model('User');
```

21. Create controller logic for registering new users with the following code:

```
exports.register = (req, res) => {
    let newUser = new User(req.body); // a new user as an instance of the
User model
    newUser.hash_password = bcrypt.hashSync(req.body.password, 10); //
Hash the password using bcrypt.hashSync function

    newUser.save((err, user) => { // Call save function and return
responses

        if (err) {
            res.status(500).send({ message: err });
        }
        user.hash_password = undefined;
        res.status(201).json(user);
    });
};
```

22. Create controller logic to sign users in with the following code:

```
exports.signIn = (req, res) => {
    User.findOne({// User findOne method on User to check if user email
supplied exist
        email: req.body.email
    }, (err, user) => {
        if (err) throw err; // return  err if query was not successful,

        if (!user) {
            res.status(401).json({ message: 'User not found.
Authentication unsuccessful. ' });// if user not found, return a message
        } else if (user) {
```

```
            if (!user.comparePassword(req.body.password)) {
                res.status(401).json({ message: . Wrong password.
'Authentication unsuccessful ' });
// if password is worng, return a message
            } else {
                res.json({ token: jwt.sign({ email: user.email, fullName:
user.fullName, _id: user._id }, 'RESTFULAPIs') }); // if user is found,
return a token that is created using user details and some properties
            }
        }
    });
};
```

23. Create a controller logic to verify whether a user is logged in using the following code:

```
exports.loginRequired = (req, res, next) => {
    if (req.user) { // Check if user already exist
        next(); // If user exist, call next() function

        } else { // If user doesn't exist, return a message as 'Unauthorized
user!'
            res.status(401).json({ message: 'Unauthorized user!' });
        }
};
```

24. Create a route file inside the **routes** directory and name it **route.js**:

```
-- touch route.js
```

25. Create a function as an exportable module that takes in **app** using the following code:

```
module.exports = function(app) {
};
```

26. Declare **userHandler** and assign a controller to it:

```
module.exports = function(app) {
  var userHandler = require('../controllers/userController');
};
```

27. Create a route and pass **userHandler** using the following code:

```
module.exports = function(app) {
  var userHandler = require('../controllers/userController');

  app
  .route("/auth/register")
  .post(userHandler.register);

  app
  .route("/auth/sign_in")
  .post(userHandler.signIn);

  app
  .route("/")
  .get(userHandler.loginRequired);
};
```

28. Import **userModel**, **jsonwebtoken**, and **database** into **server.js** using the following code:

```
require("./config/db");
var User = require('./api/models/userModel'),
 jsonwebtoken = require("jsonwebtoken");
```

29. Add Express middleware before the route using the following code:

```
app.use((req, res, next) => {
    if (req.headers && req.headers.authorization && req.headers.
authorization.split('')[0] === 'JWT') {
        jsonwebtoken.verify(req.headers.authorization.split('')[1],
'RESTfulAPIs', (err, decode) => {
                if (err) req.user = undefined;
                req.user = decode;
                next();
            });
    } else {
        req.user = undefined;
        next();
    }
});
```

30. Add API endpoints using the following code:

```
var routes = require('./api/routes/route'); //importing route
routes(app);
```

31. Listen to the server using the following code:

```
app.listen(port, () => {
    console.log('Server running at http://localhost:${port}');
});
```

32. Run the server on the CLI using **node server** and open Postman for testing in the following order:
    Test for login (/) by typing **http:localhost:4000/** in the address bar. You will get the following output:

Figure 4.3: Screenshot for the login (/) test

Test for registration (**/auth/register**) by typing **http:localhost:4000/auth/register** in the address bar. You will get the following output:

Figure 4.4: Screenshot for the registration test

Test for sign-in (**/auth/sign_in**) by typing **http:localhost:4000/auth/sign_in** in the address bar. You will obtain the following output:

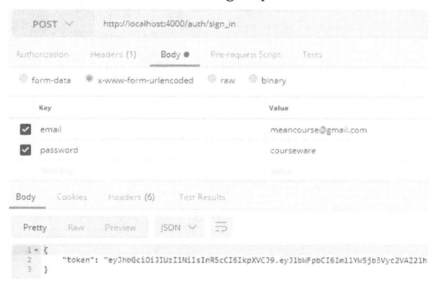

Figure 4.5: Screenshot for the sign-in test

Test for (/) login with the required route by typing **http:localhost:4000/** on the address bar. You will obtain the following output:

Figure 4.6: Screenshot for login with the required route

Activity 11: Securing the RESTful API

You have been tasked with securing the RESTful API that we built in the previous exercise. Our aim is to enable the admin to create, update, and delete data. Ensure that all previous exercises and activities have been completed. Also, use any IDE of your choice and open the **Blogging Application** project and the **server** sub-folder.

Perform the following steps to complete the activity:

> **Note**
>
> The code files for this activity can be found here: http://bit.ly/2IBLo9Q

1. Create an admin user model by creating a file named **userModel.js** inside the **api** folder.

2. Create an admin user controller.

3. Update the route file.

4. Update the **server.js** file.

5. Run the server using **node server** on the CLI and open Postman for testing.

6. Register a new user on **localhost:3000/auth/register**.

7. Attempt the login required path and post request on **localhost:3000/articles**.

8. Attempt user login by typing in **localhost:3000/auth/sign_in** in the address bar.

9. Set the authentication key on the header and input the value in the JWT token format.

10. Attempt the login required path and post request on **localhost:3000/articles**.

> **Note**
>
> The solution for this exercise can be found on page 295.

Node Application Authentication with Passport

This topic will take us further into the authentication process in the Node application. We will be learning how passport, an extremely flexible and modular authentication middleware, is used to authenticate requests for Node.

Getting Started with Passport

Any Express-based web application can easily make use of passport without having to bother with integration and implementation issues. Passport implementation is so simple that it does not obstruct the flow of any Express web-based application. Just as we said in the introduction, passport uses modularity to help ensure that its code is clean, maintainable, and easy to integrate with applications. It also possess over 300 sets of strategies that support authentication using the traditional method, involving a username and password and third-party applications such as **Instagram**, **Gmail**, **GitHub**, **Facebook**, and many others. To use passport for authentication, you must configure the following:

- Authentication strategies

- Application middleware

- Sessions (optional)

Passport's Features

The following are some of the features of passport:

- Over 500+ authentication strategies are available to pick and use, which makes it possible to implement custom strategies.

- It features single sign-on with OpenID, which is a safe, fast, and an easy way to log in to web sites. Also, OAuth provides a simple way to publish and interact with protected data. It's also a safe and secure way of providing access.

- It allows you to easily handle success and failure using flash messages to display status information to the user.

- It supports persistent sessions; that is, the client can still access the backend server for information as long as the client is still in the session window or period.

- It has dynamic scope and permissions.

- It does not mount routes in the application.

- It has a lightweight code base.

Passport Authentication Strategy

Strategy in passport is an authentication mechanism that is packaged as individual modules. The main purpose of the passport authentication strategy is to address the peculiarity or uniqueness that exists in the authentication requirement of various applications. Therefore, passport makes it possible for applications to choose which strategies to use, without creating unnecessary dependencies.

The local strategy is the passport-supported authentication mechanism. It allows developers to implement username and password authentication. Another strategy is **OAuth**, is also known as a **delegated authentication protocol**, which is mainly used by social platforms. It allows users to register on web applications using an external provider, without the need to input their username and password. Lastly, there's the custom strategy, OpenID. OpenID is provided by passport to implement federated authentication, where one-time signup gives access to multiple systems. Developers might decide to define their own custom logic for authentication. Unless it's meant for public distribution, you do not really need to create your own strategy; you can use the passport-custom strategy, OpenID, which allows you to build this logic.

To implement any of the strategies that we have discussed, you'll need to install them like any other module and configure them to use the database model of your choice.

Implementing Local Strategy

The first step is installing the local strategy module. After the module installation, the next step is to configure the strategy to be used before asking passport to authenticate a request. The **use()** function supplies an Express application with strategies and their configuration. For example, the following snippet uses **LocalStrategy** for **username/password** authentication:

```
var passport = require('passport')
  , LocalStrategy = require('passport-local').Strategy;

passport.use(new LocalStrategy(
  function(username, password, done) {
    User.findOne({ username: username }, function (err, user) {
      if (err) { return done(err); }
      if (!user) {
        return done(null, false, { message: 'Incorrect username.' });
      }
      if (!user.validPassword(password)) {
        return done(null, false, { message: 'Incorrect password.' });
      }
      return done(null, user);
    });
  }
));
```

The preceding snippet implements LocalStrategy for user authentication. The **User.findOne** function returns a callback to help verify the user that possesses a set of credentials. If the credentials are valid, the verify callback is invoked to supply a passport for the user that is authenticated, and the passport invokes **done** (as true), as seen in the following snippet:

```
return done(null, user);
```

In a situation where the credentials are not valid, **done** will be invoked as **false** and an additional message can also be supplied to specify the reason for the failure. For example, if the password is not correct, passport will invoke **done** as **false**, as seen in the following snippet:

```
return done(null, false, { message: 'password not correct!.' });
```

Finally, if there is an exception, that is, a database connection could not be established, **err** will be invoked, as shown here:

```
return done(err);
```

This approach makes passport database agnostic; that is, the application can choose where to store information without relying solely on the assumptions imposed by the authentication layer. In **LocalStrategy**, the login credentials are **username** and **password** by default; however, if you wish to change these, provisions have been made, as seen in the following snippet:

```
passport.use(new LocalStrategy({

    usernameField: 'email',

    passwordField: 'passwd'

  },

  function(username, password, done) {

    // ...

  }

));
```

Implementing OAuth

OAuth, a delegated authentication mechanism that we briefly described earlier is a standard protocol that guides and allows authorization for APIs to access web, desktop, or mobile applications. OAuth can be implemented using the generic OAuth (**OAuth 1.0** and **OAuth 2.0**) authentication format, which gives room to specify parameters based on the service provider in use. For example, a Facebook authentication can be implemented using OAuth, as seen in the following snippet:

```
npm install passport-oauth

var passport = require('passport')
  , OAuthStrategy = require('passport-oauth').OAuthStrategy;

passport.use('provider', new OAuthStrategy({

    requestTokenURL: 'https://www.provider.com/oauth/request_token',

    accessTokenURL: 'https://www.provider.com/oauth/access_token',

    userAuthorizationURL: 'https://www.provider.com/oauth/authorize',

    consumerKey: '123-456-789',

    consumerSecret: 'shhh-its-a-secret'

    callbackURL: 'https://www.example.com/auth/provider/callback'

  },
```

```
  function(token, tokenSecret, profile, done) {
    User.findOrCreate(..., function(err, user) {
      done(err, user);
    });
  }
));
```

From the callback in the preceding snippet, we can see that the arguments that are accepted are **token**, **tokenSecret**, **profile** (these are the access tokens), and their corresponding **secret**, along with user profile information provided by the service provider. Passport normalizes profile information for easy implementation; this is because each service provider tends to have different ways of encoding this information.

> **Note**
>
> Go to http://www.passportjs.org/docs/profile/ to find out more about the common fields that are available in the normalized profile argument.

Authenticating Requests with Passport

passport.authenticate() is used to authenticate a request. The **authenticate()** function serves as a convenient routing middleware for an Express application. Several parameters that can be passed into authentications are as follows:

- strategy
- callback functions
- redirects
- flash messages
- custom callbacks

The implementation of the preceding parameters can be seen in the following snippet:

```
app.post('/login',
    passport.authenticate('local', /* strategy */
        {
            session: false, /* To disable session by default */
            successRedirect: '/', /* called if authentication is successful,
```

```
overrites redirect callback */
            failureRedirect: '/login', /* called if authentication failed,
overrites redirect callback */
            failureFlash: true, /* flash message of authentication fails */
            successFlash: 'Welcome' /* flash message of authentication passes
*/
        }),
    function (req, res) { /* if this function get called, authentication was
successful */
        /* res.user contains the authenticated user */
        res.redirect('/users' + req.user.username)
    },
);
```

Note that custom callbacks are used to handle success or failure if the built-in options are not sufficient for handling an authentication request. In the following snippet, **authenticate()** was not used as route middleware; it was called from within the route handler, thereby giving the callback access to the **req** and **res** objects through closure:

```
app.get('/login', function (req, res, next) {
    passport.authenticate('local', function (err, user, info) {
        if (err) { return next(err); }
        if (!user) { return res.redirect('/login') }
        req.console.logIn(user, function (err) {
            if (err) { return next(err); }
            return res.redirect('/users/' + user.username);
        });
    })(req, res, next);
});
```

In a situation where an application is an Express-based application, passport must be initialized as middleware using **passport.initialize()**. Also, in an application that implements persistent login sessions, **passport.session()** middleware must also be used, as seen in the following snippet:

```
var session = require("express-session"),
    bodyParser = require("body-parser");
```

```
app.use(express.static("public"));

app.use(session({ secret: "cats" }));

app.use(bodyParser.urlencoded({ extended: false }));

app.use(passport.initialize());

app.use(passport.session());
```

Sessions

For applications that use sessions, on first authentication, the credentials will be sent to the users' browsers and a session will be established and maintained via a cookie that's set in the user's browser, for subsequent requests, and as long as the session is still valid, the request will not contain credentials, but rather the unique cookie that identifies the session. Passport support for login sessions is obtained by serializing and de-serializing user instances to and from the session as shown in the following:

```
passport.serializeUser(function(user, done) {
  done(null, user.id);
});

passport.deserializeUser(function(id, done) {
  User.findById(id, function(err, user) {
    done(err, user);
  });
});
```

As seen in the preceding snippet, the amount of data stored within the session is small because only the user ID is serialized to the session, Also, when subsequent requests are received, this ID is used to find the user, which will be restored to **req.user**.

The application supplies serialization and deserialization logic and also chooses an appropriate database and/or object mapper to avoid application layer imposition.

Exercise 18: Creating a User-Authenticating System in a Node Application Using Passport's LocalStrategy

In this exercise, we will create a user authentication system in Node using **LocalStrategy**, which is a passport middleware. Ensure that all previous exercises and activities have been completed. To get started, create a new folder in a known directory, name it **passport-local**, and install the most recent versions of the following packages: **express**, **body-parser**, **mongoose**, **bcryptjs**, and **passport-local**. You can do this by running `npm install express body-parser mongoose bcryptjs passport-local express-session cookieParser morgan flash -save` on the CLI. Perform the following steps to complete the exercise:

> **Note**
>
> The code files for this exercise can be found here: http://bit.ly/2SigWkq.

1. Create a **package.json** file using the following code:

    ```
    npm init
    ```

2. Create a **server.js** using **touch** on the CLI (**touch server.js**) and import **express** and **body-parser** using the following command:

    ```
    const express = require("express");
    const bodyParser = require("body-parser");
    ```

3. Create an Express application, assign a port number, and use **body-parser** on the Express application:

    ```
    const app = express();
    const port = process.env.PORT || 4000;
    app.use(bodyParser.urlencoded({ extended: true }));
    app.use(bodyParser.json());
    ```

4. Create a **config** folder using the following code:

    ```
    mkdir config
    ```

5. Create a database file called **db.js** in the **config** folder using the following code:

    ```
    touch db.js
    ```

6. Export **mongoose** using the following code:

    ```
    const mongoose = require("mongoose");
    ```

7. Assign values to the **mongodb atlas** connection parameter using the following code:

```
var uri = "mongodb+srv://username:password@cluster0-0wi3e.mongodb.net/
test?retryWrites=true";
  const options = {
    reconnectTries: Number.MAX_VALUE,
    poolSize: 10
  };
```

8. Connect to the database using the following code:

```
mongoose.connect(uri, options).then(
  () => {
    console.log("Database connection established!");
  },
  err => {
    console.log("Error connecting Database instance due to: ", err);
  }
);
```

9. Create an **api** directory and then create three sub-folders called **controllers**, **models**, and **routes** using the following code:

```
mkdir api
mkdir controllers && mkdir  models && mkdir  routes
```

10. Create the **userModel.js** model file inside the **controller** directory using the following command:

```
touch userModel.js
```

11. Export **bryptjs** and **mongoose** using the following code:

```
const mongoose = require("mongoose"),
bcrypt = require('bcryptjs'),
```

12. Declare a **Mongoose.schema** using the following code:

```
const Schema = mongoose.Schema;
```

13. Create a **UserSchema** using the following code:

```
const UserSchema = new Schema({
  fullName: {
    type: String,
    trim: true,
    required: true
  },
```

```
      email: {
        type:String,
        unique:true,
        lowercase:true,
        trim:true,
        required:true
      } ,
      hash_password: {
        type:String,
        required:true
      },
      createdOn: {
        type: Date,
        default: Date.now
      }
    });
```

14. Create a method to check the password's validity using the following code:

```
    UserSchema.methods.comparePassword = function(password){
      return bcrypt.compareSync(password, this.hash_password);
    }
```

15. Create a **mongoose.model** from the schema using the following code:

```
    mongoose.model("User", UserSchema);
```

16. Create a passport file called **passport.js** inside the **config** directory using the following code:

```
    touch passport.js
```

17. Import **mongoose**, **passport-local**, and **bcryptjs**:

```
    const bcrypt = require('bcryptjs');
    const LocalStrategy = require("passport-local").Strategy;
    const mongoose = require('mongoose'),
```

18. Import the user model using the following code:

```
    const User = mongoose.model('User');
```

19. Create an function exposed to our **app** using `module.exports`, as shown here:

```
module.exports = function (passport) {
//serialize the user for the session
    passport.serializeUser(function (user, done) {
        done(null, user.id);
    });
```

20. Deserialize the user using the following code:

```
passport.deserializeUser(function (id, done) {
    User.findById(id, function (err, user) {
        done(err, user);
    });
});
```

21. Create a local strategy authentication for signup using the following code:

File name: passport.js

```
passport.use('local-signup', new LocalStrategy({
        // by default, local strategy uses username and password, we will
override with email
        usernameField: 'email',
        passwordField: 'password',
        passReqToCallback: true // allows us to pass back the entire
request to the callback
    },
//[...]
                    // save the user
                    newUser.save(function (err) {
                        if (err)
                            throw err;
                        return done(null, newUser);
                    });
                }

        });

    }));
```

Live link: http://bit.ly/2EgWnjk

22. Create a local strategy function for login using the following code:

```
passport.use('local-login', new LocalStrategy({
        usernameField: 'email',
        passwordField: 'password',
        passReqToCallback: true //
    },
        function (req, email, password, done) {
            User.findOne({
                email: email
            }, function (err, user) {
                // This is how you handle error
                if (err) return done(err);
                // When user is not found
                if (!user) return done(null, false, req.
flash('loginMessage', 'No user found.'));
// req.flash is the way to set flashdata using connect-flash
                // When password is not correct
                if (!user.comparePassword(req.body.password)) return
done(null, false, req.flash('loginMessage', 'Oops! Wrong password.'));
    // When all things are good, we return the user
                return done(null, user);
            });
        })
    )
```

In the following steps, we will hash the password using the **bcrypt.hashSync** function:

23. Call the **save** function and return the responses using the following code:

```
exports.register = (req, res) => {
    let newUser = new User(req.body);
    newUser.hash_password = bcrypt.hashSync(req.body.password, 10);
    newUser.save((err, user) => {
        if (err) {
            res.status(500).send({ message: err });
        }
        user.hash_password = undefined;
        res.status(201).json(user);
    });
};
```

24. Create a view folder with four embedded JavaScript templates in its directory, namely, **index.ejs**, **login.ejs**, **signup.ejs**, and **profile.ejs**. For **index.ejs**, use the following snippet:

File name: index.ejs

```
<!doctype html>
<html>
<head>
    <title> Passport Local strategy - Authentication
</title>
//[…]
                <a href="/login" class="btn btn-default"><span class="fa
fa-user"></span> Local Login</a>
                <a href="/signup" class="btn btn-default"><span class="fa
fa-user"></span> Local Signup</a>
            </div>
        </div>
</body>
</html>
```

Live link: http://bit.ly/2VnkvYA

Use the following snippet for **login.ejs**:

File name: login.ejs

```
<!-- views/login.ejs -->
<!doctype html>
<html>
<head>
    <title>Node Authentication</title>
    <link rel="stylesheet" href="//netdna.bootstrapcdn.com/
bootstrap/3.0.2/css/bootstrap.min.css"> <!-- load bootstrap css -->
    <link rel="stylesheet" href="//netdna.bootstrapcdn.com/font-
awesome/4.0.3/css/font-awesome.min.css"> <!-- load fontawesome -->
    <style>
            body           { padding-top:80px; }
    </style>
</head>
<body>
//[…]
```

```
                        <p>Need an account? <a href="/signup">Signup</a></p>
                        <p>Or go <a href="/">home</a>.</p>
                </div>
        </div>
    </body>
</html>
```

Live link: http://bit.ly/2TpoyXb

Use the following snippet for `signup.ejs`:

File name: signup.ejs

```
    <!doctype html>
    <html>
    <head>
            <title>Node Authentication</title>
            <link rel="stylesheet" href="//netdna.bootstrapcdn.com/
    bootstrap/3.0.2/css/bootstrap.min.css"> <!-- load bootstrap css -->
            <link rel="stylesheet" href="//netdna.bootstrapcdn.com/font-
    awesome/4.0.3/css/font-awesome.min.css"> <!-- load fontawesome -->
            <style>
                    body         { padding-top:80px; }
            </style>
    </head>
    <body>
    //[…]
    </body>
    </html>
```

Live link: http://bit.ly/2T2xaDy

Use the following snippet for `profile.ejs`:

File name: profile.ejs

```
    <!doctype html>
    <html>
    <head>
            <title>Node Authentication</title>
            <link rel="stylesheet" href="//netdna.bootstrapcdn.com/
    bootstrap/3.0.2/css/bootstrap.min.css">
```

```
    <link rel="stylesheet" href="//netdna.bootstrapcdn.com/font-
awesome/4.0.3/css/font-awesome.min.css">
    <style>
//[…]
                                        <strong>id</strong>: <%= user.id
%><br>
                                        <strong>Full</strong>: <%= user.
fullName %><br>
                                        <strong>email</strong>: <%= user.
email %><br>
                                        <strong>password</strong>: <%= user.
hash_password %>
                        </p>
                </div>
        </div>
```

Live link: http://bit.ly/2tDDF0j

---

25. Create a route file inside the routes directory and name it **route.js** using the following code:

    ```
    touch route.js
    ```

26. Create an exposed function as an exportable module that takes in **app** and **passport** using the following code:

File name: http://bit.ly/2Ubjgvd

```
module.exports = function(app){

    // HOME PAGE (with login links)
    app.get('/', function (req, res) {
        res.render('index.ejs'); // load the index.ejs file
    });
    // LOGIN
    // show the login form
    app.get('/login', function (req, res) {
        // render the page and pass in any flash data if it exists
        res.render('login.ejs', { message: req.flash('loginMessage') });
    });
//[…]

    // if they aren't redirect them to the home page
```

```
        res.redirect('/');
    }
```

Live link: http://bit.ly/2Ubjgvd

27. Update the **server.js** file using the following code:

```
// Import
bcrypt = require('bcryptjs'),
session  = require('express-session'),
cookieParser = require('cookie-parser'),
morgan = require('morgan'),
flash     = require('connect-flash');
```

28. Import the database using the following code:

```
// db instance connection
require("./config/db");

// update an express application
app.use(morgan('dev')); // log every request to the console
app.use(cookieParser()); // read cookies (needed for auth)
app.set('view engine', 'ejs'); // set up ejs for templating
app.use(session({
     secret: 'paulouyegepackt',
     resave: true,
     saveUninitialized: true
 } )); // session secret");
```

29. Implement local authentication with passport using the following code:

```
const passport = require("passport");
app.use(passport.initialize());
app.use(passport.session());
app.use(flash());

require('./config/passport')(passport);
```

30. Update the API endpoint using the following code:

```
var routes = require('./api/routes/route'); //importing route
routes(app,passport);
```

31. Listen to the server using the following code:

```
app.listen(port, () => {
    console.log('Server running at http://localhost:${port}');
});
```

32. Run the server (**node server**) on the CLI and open Postman for testing in the following order:

Test for login (**/**) by typing **localhost:4000** in the address bar. You will obtain the following output:

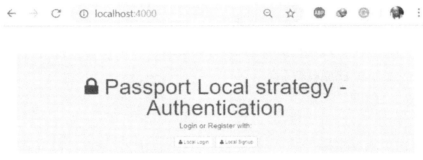

Figure 4.7: Output for login (/) test

Test for signup by typing **localhost:4000/signup** in the address bar and fill in the credentials. You will obtain the following output:

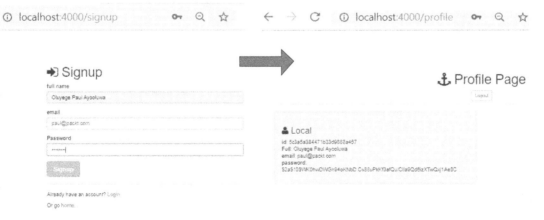

Figure 4.8: Output for the signup test

Test for login by typing **localhost:4000/login** in the address bar. You will obtain the following output:

Figure 4.9: Successful login

Implementing Facebook and Twitter Strategies

Implementation complexities might be a challenge while dealing with OAuth. To overcome this challenge, passport provides a provider-specific strategy, which can be used instead of the generic OAuth strategies we described previously. The implementation does not really differ from OAuth – only a few changes and a provider strategy differ, as seen in the following snippet:

```
var passport = require('passport')
  , ProviderStrategy = require('passport-provider').Strategy;


passport.use(new ProviderStrategy({
    clientID: PROVIDER_APP_ID,
    clientSecret: PROVIDER_APP_SECRET,
    callbackURL: "http://www.example.com/auth/provider/callback"
  },
  function(accessToken, refreshToken, profile, done) {
    User.findOrCreate(..., function(err, user) {
      if (err) { return done(err); }
      done(null, user);
    });
  }
));
```

In the preceding snippet, replace **Provider** with the name of any provider you want to implement. For example, if you want to use Facebook, the snippet becomes the following:

```
FacebookStrategy = require('passport-facebook').Strategy;

passport.use(new FacebookStrategy({
    clientID: FACEBOOK_APP_ID,
    clientSecret: FACEBOOK_APP_SECRET,
    callbackURL: "http://www.example.com/auth/facebook/callback"
  },
```

For Twitter, the snippet will be as follows:

```
TwitterStrategy = require('passport-twitter').Strategy;
```

Note that the **clientID**, **clientSecret**, and **callbackURL** properties hold the application connection strings provided by the service provider; these might vary depending on the provider. The callback function, from line eight, remains the same – the only varying parameters are the arguments, which might vary depending on the provider.

Creating Routes and Granting Permissions

There are two routes involved with the Facebook strategy. The first (**'auth/facebook'**) redirects the user to Facebook and the second (**'/auth/facebook/callback'**) redirects the user back to the application, as seen in the following snippet:

```
app.get('/auth/facebook', passport.authenticate('facebook'));

app.get('/auth/facebook/callback',
    passport.authenticate('facebook', { successRedirect: '/',
                                        failureRedirect: '/login' }));
```

In situations where the application is permissions-bound, a scope setting can be provided to handle it, be it single or multiple permissions (this can be specified as an array), as seen in the following snippet:

```
app.get('/auth/facebook',
    passport.authenticate('facebook', { scope: 'read_stream' })
);
//multiple permissions
app.get('/auth/facebook',
```

```
    passport.authenticate('facebook', { scope: ['read_stream', 'publish_
  actions'] })
  );
```

Exercise 19: Creating a User-Authenticating System in Node Using the Facebook Strategy

In this exercise, we will create a user authentication system in Node by using the **passport-facebook** strategy. Ensure that all previous exercises and activities have been completed. To get started, create a new folder in a known directory, name it **passport-facebook**, and install the most recent versions of the following packages   : **express body-parser**, **mongoose**, **bcryptjs**, and **passport-facebook**. You can do this by running **npm install express body-parser mongoose passport-facebook -save**. Perform the following steps to complete the exercise:

> **Note**
>
> The code files for this exercise can be found here: http://bit.ly/2T2Zs01.

1. Create a **package.json** file using the following code:

   ```
   npm init
   ```

2. Create a **server.js** file and import **express** and **body-parser** using the following code:

   ```
   touch server.js
   const express = require("express");
   const bodyParser = require("body-parser");
   ```

3. Create an Express application, assign the port number, and use the **body-parser** middleware on the Express application using the following code:

   ```
   const app = express();
   const port = process.env.PORT || 4000;
   app.use(bodyParser.urlencoded({ extended: true }));
   app.use(bodyParser.json());
   ```

4. Create a **config** folder using the following code:

   ```
   mkdir config
   ```

5. Create a database file named **db.js** in the **config** folder directory using the following code:

```
touch db.js
```

6. Export Mongoose using the following code:

```
const mongoose = require("mongoose");
```

7. Assign values to the **mongodb atlas** connection parameter, as shown here:

```
var uri = "mongodb+srv://username:password@cluster0-0wi3e.mongodb.net/
test?retryWrites=true";

const options = {
  reconnectTries: Number.MAX_VALUE,
  poolSize: 10
};
```

8. Connect to the database using the following code:

```
mongoose.connect(uri, options).then(
  () => {
    console.log("Database connection established!");
  },
  err => {
    console.log("Error connecting Database instance due to: ", err);
  }
);
```

9. Create an **api** directory using the following code:

```
mkdir api
```

10. Create three subfolders in the **api** directory, named **controllers**, **models**, and **routes** using the following code:

```
mkdir - controllers && mkdir - models && mkdir - routes
```

11. Create the model file inside the controller directory named **userModel.js**:

```
touch userModel.js
```

12. Import Mongoose using the following code:

```
const mongoose = require("mongoose"),
```

13. Declare a Mongoose schema using the following code:

```
const Schema = mongoose.Schema;
```

14. Create a user schema using the following code:

```
const UserSchema = new Schema({
facebook          : {
    fullName      : String,
    email         : String,
    createdOn: {
      type: Date,
      default: Date.now
    },
  },
});
```

15. Create a Mongoose model from the schema using the following code:

```
mongoose.model("User", UserSchema);
```

16. Create a passport file inside the **config** directory named **paqssport.js** using the following code:

```
touch passport.js
```

17. Import **mongoose** and **passport-facebook** using the following code:

```
const FacebookStrategy = require("passport-facebook").Strategy;
const mongoose = require('mongoose'),
```

18. Import the **User** model using the following code:

```
const User = mongoose.model('User');
```

19. Create an exposed function to our **app** using **module.exports**, as shown here:

```
module.exports = function (passport) {}
serialize the user for the session
    passport.serializeUser(function (user, done) {
        done(null, user.id);
    });

  deserialize the user
    passport.deserializeUser(function (id, done) {
        User.findById(id, function (err, user) {
            done(err, user);
        });
```

```
  });
```

In the following steps, we will create **FacebookStrategy** authentication:

20. Use **passport** on the application, as shown here:

```
passport.use('facebook', new FacebookStrategy({
clientID: 'XXXXXXXXX',
clientSecret: 'YYYYYYYYYYYYYYYY',
callbackURL: " http://localhost:4000/auth/facebook/callback",
profileFields:['id','displayName','emails']
},

    function (accessToken, refreshToken, profile, done)
{    let newUser            = new User();
    // set the user's facebook credentials
    newUser.facebook.email    = profile.emails[0].value,
    newUser.facebook.fullName = profile.displayName,

    User.findOne({email:newUser.facebook.email }, function(err, user) {
      if(!user) {
        newUser.save(function(err, newUser) {
          if(err) return done(err);
          done(null,newUser);
        });
      } else {
        done(null, user);
      }
    });
  }
));
  }
```

21. Create a **route** file inside the routes directory:

```
touch route.js
```

22. Create an exposed function as an exportable module that takes in **app** and **passport** using the following code:

```
module.exports = function(app,passport)  {
app.get('/auth/facebook',
  passport.authenticate('facebook', {scope:"email"}));
```

```
app.get('/auth/facebook/callback',
  passport.authenticate('facebook', { failureRedirect: '/error' }),
  function(req, res) {
    res.redirect('/success');
  });
}
```

23. Update the **server.js** file, as shown here:

```
// db instance connection
require("./config/db"); app.get('/success', (req, res) => res.send("You
have successfully logged in"));
app.get('/error', (req, res) => res.send("error logging in"));
```

24. Import and initialize passport using the following code:

```
const passport = require("passport");
app.use(passport.initialize());
app.use(passport.session());

require('./config/passport')(passport);
```

25. Update the API endpoint using the following code:

```
var routes = require('./api/routes/route'); //importing route
routes(app,passport);
```

26. Listen to the server using the following code:

```
app.listen(port, () => {
    console.log('Server running at http://localhost:${port}');
});
```

27. Run the server (**node server**) and open a browser for testing in the following order:

Test for authorization by typing **localhost:4000/auth/facebook** in the browser and fill in the necessary credentials. You will obtain the following output:

Figure 4.10: Successful authorization attempt

Activity 12: Creating a Login Page to Allow Authentication with Twitter Using Passport Strategies

You have been tasked with creating a login page to allow authentication with Twitter using passport strategies. Our aim is that, once finished, we should be able to access a restricted route and have user information stored in the database. Ensure that all exercises and activities have been completed in this chapter before attempting this activity. You can use any IDE of your choice. Finally, create a project called **Social Logins** before beginning the activity.

Perform the following steps to complete the activity:

> **Note**
>
> The activity requires credentials such as consumerKey and consumerSecret, which can be obtained by creating an app on twitter. Please refer to the following documentation to create an app: https://developer.twitter.com. The code files for this activity can be found here: http://bit.ly/2U0iSQl

1. Create a **package.json** file and install **express body-parser**, **mongoose**, **passport-twitter**, and **passport**.

2. Create a **server.js** (using **touch server.js** on the CLI) file and import **express** and **body-parser**.

3. Create an Express application, assign a port number, and use the **body-parser** middleware on the Express application.

4. Create a **config** folder.

5. Create a database by first creating a file named **db.js** (using **touch db.js** on the CLI) in the **config** folder directory.

6. Create an **api** directory and three subfolders named **controllers**, **models**, and **routes**.

7. Create a model file inside the **controller** directory (using **touch userModel.js** on the CLI) and then create the schema and mode.

8. Create a passport file inside the **config** directory (using **touch passport.js**) and then create a Twitter strategy.

9. Create a route file inside the **routes** directory (using `touch route.js`) and then create an exposed function as an exportable module that takes in `app` and `passport`.

10. Update the `server.js` file.

11. Import and initialize Passport.

12. Update the API endpoints.

13. Run the server (using `node server` on the CLI), open a browser, and test this by typing `localhost:4000/auth/twitter` in the browser address bar.

> **Note**
>
> The solution to this activity can be found on page 302.

Summary

This chapter introduced Node security practices and the different forms of access authentication for Node applications and APIs. We described different methods for authenticating and authorizing users to access resources from the frontend and backend using JWT and passport.

The first section introduced us to Node security and best practices for securing applications. We also described modules, features, and measures such as **Helmet**, **input validations**, **regular expressions**, **security.txt**, **session management**, and **cross-site request forgery** for implementing and ensuring security. That section ended with an introduction to authorization and authentication. The next section covered the authentication of Node applications using JWT. JWT's structure was demystified and explained with comprehensive exercises. The chapter ended with us describing and implementing passport strategies such as **Facebook**, **local**, **JWT**, and **Twitter** to authenticate the security login sessions of Node applications.

In the next chapter, we will be describing declarables, bootstrapping, and modularity in Angular. Furthermore, we will be creating custom structural and attribute directives, in addition to bootstrapping an Angular application.

5

Angular Declarables, Bootstrapping, and Modularity

Learning Objectives

By the end of this chapter, you will be able to:

- Describe declarables such as pipes and directives
- Create custom structural and attribute directives
- Create, define, and subscribe to observables
- Bootstrap an Angular application
- Implement modules in Angular

This chapter presents an overview of declarables, bootstrapping, and modularity in Angular, in addition to exercises and activities on these topics.

Introduction

The previous chapter introduced us to Node application security practices and different forms of authentication for Node applications. We learned, with the aid of exercises and activities, how to grant user access to a RESTful API and perform user authentication on Node by implementing token-based authentication using JWT. We also implemented passport middleware authentication using local and social application strategies.

In this chapter, we will go over an introduction to Angular declarables, which includes **pipes** and **custom directives**, and we'll also describe the concept of **observables**. You will learn about various forms of inbuilt pipes, such as **Uppercase**, **AsyncPipe**, **percentPipe**, and so on. You will create both custom pipes and directives and describe their usage in the DOM. We'll then describe observables and <u>**reactive**</u> <u>**extensions**</u> (<u>**RxJs**</u>), and how they are implemented in Angular applications.

Later in this chapter, you'll learn the details of Angular application bootstrapping and modularity in its code base. You'll also learn how **feature** modules and **lazy-loading** modules are used. At the end of each section, you will be presented with exercises and activities to ensure a comprehensive understanding of the content.

Using Inbuilt Pipes, Custom Pipes, Custom Directives, and Observables

Angular Pipes

Pipes were initially referred to as a **filter** in Angular 1. They are used mainly for data transformation in HTML templates. The purpose of this feature is to reduce the complexity of tasks such as streaming data over a WebSocket, which involves getting data, transforming it, and then displaying it to users. Input data is converted into a desired output through the use of pipes.

For example, if we need a currency output of USD 1,000,000 and we have 1000000 as the data variable, then how do we achieve our output using the inbuilt pipe for currency in Angular?

We can achieve this by using a pipe with the | (pipe character) syntax in the template, as shown in the following snippet:

```
{{ 1000000 | currency : 'USD' }}
```

From the preceding code, we can see that the number 1000000 is converted into a currency string to be displayed in the template. The output is USD 1,000,000.

The output is fine-tuned by providing an optional parameter. The parameter values are separated with colons in a situation wherein pipe accepts multiple parameters. There is also a process known as **pipe chaining**, which provides us with the ability to use two inbuilt pipes simultaneously, as shown in the following snippet:

```
{{ 1000000 | currency: 'USD' | lowercase }},
```

The output will be USD 1,000,000. The types of pipe available in Angular are as follows:

- **Inbuilt**
- **Custom**

We will briefly describe them in the following sections.

Inbuilt Pipes

As the name implies, inbuilt pipes are provided by Angular and are all available to be used in any template without writing any classes or declaring any variables. Inbuilt pipes include the following:

1. **Uppercase Pipe**: The uppercase pipe transforms any string into uppercase, as implemented here:

    ```
    <p>{{ 'meanstack' | uppercase }}</p>  // output :  MEANSTACK
    ```

2. **Currency Pipe**: As we discussed previously, it's used to format currencies. The first argument or parameter denotes the currency type, such as "EUR", "CAD", "USD," and so on. The implementation is as follows:

    ```
    {{ 1234.56 | currency:'USD' }}    //output :   $1,234.56.
    ```

    If, instead of the abbreviation of USD, we want the currency symbol as output, a second, or more, parameters can be passed. The following list presents the available parameter currency pipes:

    currencyCode: The input is a string such as a currency code, for example, USD. The default value is undefined.

    display: The input is string or Boolean, which can be any of the following:

    code: Shows the code (such as USD)

    symbol (default): Shows the symbol (such as $)

    symbol-narrow: This is used in cases where there are two symbols for a given currency.

digitsInfo: The parameters can be **minIntegerDigits** (the minimum number of integer digits before the decimal point, and the default value is 1), **minFractionDigits** (also used for the minimum number of digits after the decimal point with 0 as the default value), and **maxFractionDigits** (the maximum number of digits after the decimal point with 3 as the default value).

3. **Date Pipe**: This pipe is used on dates to transform and format the date type value. The argument is a format string, as shown in the following snippet:

```
<p>{{ dateVal | date: 'shortTime' }}</p>
<p>{{ dateVal | date: 'fullDate' }}</p> //
<p>{{ dateVal | date: 'd/M/y' }}</p>
```

dateVal is the date type and an instance of the **newDate()** method.

4. **Decimal Pipe**: This pipe is used to transform decimal numbers, as implemented in the following code:

```
<p>{{ 3.14159265 | number: '3.1-2' }}</p>
<p>{{ 3.14159265 | number: '1.4-4' }}</p>
```

In the preceding snippet, the first argument is a format string of the **form {minIntegerDigits}. {minFractionDigits}-{maxFractionDigits}**. The output of this is shown as follows:

003.14

3.1416

Figure 5.1: Decimal pipe output

5. **JSON Pipe**: This is used to transform a JavaScript object into a JSON string. The implementation is as follows:

```
<p>{{ jsonVal | json }}</p> ,
```

jsonVal is an object that can be, for example, declared as **{ a: 1, b: { c: 2 }}**.

6. **LowerCase Pipe**: This pipe is used to transform strings to lowercase, as shown in the following code:

```
<p>{{ 'ASIM' | lowercase }}</p> //output: asim
```

7. **Percent Pipe**: This pipe is used on numbers and formats them as percentages, as shown in the following snippet:

```
<p>{{ 0.123456 | percent }}</p>
<p>{{ 0.123456 | percent: '2.1-2' }}</p>
<p>{{ 0.123456 | percent : "3.4-4" }}</p>
```

In the preceding snippet, the first argument is in the form of `{minIntegerDigits}` `{minFractionDigits}-{maxFractionDigits}`, and the output is as follows:

12%

12.35%

012.3456%

Figure 5.2: Decimal pipe output

8. **Slice Pipe**: This pipe returns a slice of an array. The first and second arguments are the first and end indexes, respectively. Negative indexes can be used to indicate an offset from the end. An example is shown in the following snippet:

```
<p>{{ [3,1,2,4,5,6] | slice:1:2 }}</p>
<p>{{ [3,1,2,4,5,6] | slice:3 }}</p>
<p>{{ [3,1,2,4,5,6] | slice:3:-1 }}</p>
```

The preceding snippet will typically generate the following output:

1

4,5,6

4,5

Figure 5.3: Slice pipe output

9. **Async Pipe**: This pipe accepts an observable or a promise and renders the output without having to call them or subscribe. An **async** pipe class and template is shown in the following snippet:

```
//class
class AsyncPipeComponent {
  promiseData: string;
  constructor() {
            this.getPromise().then(v => this.promiseData = v); (3)
  }
//template
{{ promiseData | async }}
```

Custom Pipes

In addition to inbuilt pipes, Angular allows you to create and define custom pipes. For example, if you wanted to create a custom pipe that takes a string and reverses the order of the letters, you would have to perform the following steps:

1. Create a pipe class file either manually or using the following command-line code:

   ```
   ng g pipe reverse-str.pipe.ts
   ```

2. Import the **Pipe** and **PipeTransform** classes from Angular:

   ```
   import { Pipe, PipeTransform } from '@angular/core';
   ```

3. Give the pipe a name in the **Pipe** decorator:

   ```
   @Pipe({name: 'reverseStr'})
   ```

4. Write an exportable class that implements the **PipeTransform** class:

   ```
   export class ReverseStr implements PipeTransform {
     transform(value: string): string {
       let newStr: string = "";
       for (var i = value.length - 1; i >= 0; i--) {
         newStr += value.charAt(i);
       }
       return newStr;
     }
   }
   include the custom pipe as a declaration in your app module
   import { BrowserModule } from '@angular/platform-browser';
   import { FormsModule } from '@angular/forms';
   //[…]
     providers: [],
     bootstrap: [AppComponent]
   })
   export class AppModule { }
   ```

5. Use the custom pipe in the app template

   ```
   {{ 'inioluwa'| reverseStr }}
   ```

Custom Directive

In addition to inbuilt directives, Angular allows you to create and define custom directives. Therefore, in this section, we will learn how to create both structural and attribute custom directives. However, before creating them, we will briefly describe them.

Structural and Attribute Custom Directives

Structural directives are directives that manipulate the DOM structure. These can create, destroy, or recreate DOM elements based on certain conditions. Attribute directives manipulate DOM attributes. Typical examples include applying conditional styles and classes to elements, changing the behavior of an element on the basis of changing the property, and hiding and showing elements conditionally.

The steps involved in creating and implementing custom attribute directives are as follows:

1. Call the directive (prefixed with a namespace) and attach it to the HTML element:

   Implementation:

   ```
   <div class="card card-block" cardHover>...</div>
   ```

2. Create and import directives. Annotate a class with the **@Directive** decorator:

   Implementation:

   ```
   import { Directive } from '@angular/core';
           ..........
           @Directive({
             selector:"[cardHover]"
           })
           class CardHoverDirective { }
   ```

Note that the attribute selector is wrapped with [ ], unlike the case of components, which are wrapped with { }. To associate a selector with any element, we can write the selector as .cardHover:

Implementation:

```
import { Directive } from '@angular/core';
........
@Directive({
  selector:".cardHover"
})
class CardHoverDirective { }
------------html -------------
<div class="card card-block cardHover">...</div>
```

3. Wrap the name of the attribute with [ ]; that is, [cardHover], to associate the directive to an element, which has a certain attribute.

4. Inject an instance of **ElementRef** into its directive constructor. It's important to know that **ElementRef** gives the directive direct access to the DOM element to which it's attached:

Implementation:

```
import { ElementRef } from '@angular/core';
class CardHoverDirective {
  constructor(private el: ElementRef) {
  }
}
```

To change the background color of our card to gray, we can use the following code:

```
el.nativeElement.style.backgroundColor = "gray";
```

5. Inject **Renderer** for multiplatform rendering:

Implementation:

```
import { Renderer } from '@angular/core';
-----
class CardHoverDirective {
  constructor(private el: ElementRef,
              private renderer: Renderer) {
    renderer.setElementStyle(el.nativeElement, 'backgroundColor', 'gray');
  }
}
```

Now that we have learned how to create both custom pipes and directives, we will be working on some exercises to validate our understanding of this topic in the next section.

Exercise 20: Creating a Custom Structure Directive that Functions as an Inbuilt *ngIf

In this exercise, we will be creating a custom structure directive that functions as a built-in ***ngIf**. To complete this exercise, you must have completed the exercises in the previous chapters. To get started, create a new folder in a known directory and name it **chapter-5-exercises**. Perform the following steps to complete this exercise:

> **Note**
>
> The code files for this exercise can be found here: http://bit.ly/2GEUL6u.

1. Create a new Angular CLI application with the name **customs**.

2. Create directives using the following CLI command:

```
ng generate directive if/if
```

3. Import the **Directive** class into the **app** module using the following command:

```
import { IfDirective } from './if/if.directive';

@NgModule({
  declarations: [
........................
    IfDirective
  ],
........................ ..
})
export class AppModule { }
```

4. Import **Directive**, **Input**, **TemplateRef**, and **ViewContainerRef** from the Angular core and define the directive decorator using the following code:

```
import { Directive, Input, TemplateRef, ViewContainerRef } from '@angular/
core';

@Directive({ selector: '[myIf]' })
```

5. Inject **TemplateRef** and **ViewContainerRef** into the constructor, as shown here:

```
private templateRef: TemplateRef<any>,
    private viewContainer: ViewContainerRef
```

6. Write a function to add and remove the template to DOM, as shown in the following code:

```
@Input() set myIf(shouldAdd: boolean) {
    if (shouldAdd) {
      // If condition is true add template to DOM
      this.viewContainer.createEmbeddedView(this.templateRef);
    } else {
     // Else remove template from DOM
      this.viewContainer.clear();
    }
   }
```

7. Call **Directive** (prefixed with a namespace) and attach it to the HTML element, as shown here:

```
<div *myIf="true">
    Inside if
</div>
```

8. Run **ng serve** on the CLI and open a browser on **localhost:4200**. You will obtain the following output:

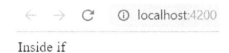

Inside if

Figure 5.4: Custom structure directive for inbuilt *ngIF

We have now created and implemented a structural directive in Angular. In the next exercise, we will be creating custom attribute directives.

Exercise 21: Creating a Custom Attribute Directive that Underlines Text by Listening to the Mouse Hover Effect

In this exercise, we will create a custom attribute directive that underlines any text by listening to the mouse hover effect. To complete this exercise, you must have completed the exercises in the previous chapters. To get started, open the project named **customs** located in the **chapter-5-exercises** folder, and then perform the following steps:

> **Note**
>
> The code files for this exercise can be found here: http://bit.ly/2Iv0NZq.

1. Create a directive using the following CLI command:

   ```
   ng generate directive underline/Underline
   ```

2. Import the **Directive** class into an app module using the following code:

   ```
   import { UnderlineDirective } from './underline/underline.directive';

   @NgModule({
     declarations: [
   ........................
       UnderlineDirective
     ],
   .................... . .
   })
   export class AppModule { }
   ```

3. Import **Directive**, **Input**, **ElementRef**, and **Renderer** from the Angular core and define the **@Directive** decorator using the following code:

   ```
   import { Directive, Input, HostListener ElementRef, Renderer } from '@
   angular/core';
   @Directive({ selector: '[myUnderline]' })
   ```

4. Inject **ElementRef** and **Renderer** into the constructor, as shown in the following code:

   ```
   constructor(public el: ElementRef, public renderer: Renderer) {}
   ```

5. Add **Event** listeners for the element hosting the directive, as shown in the following snippet:

```
@HostListener('mouseenter') onMouseEnter() {
    this.hover(true);
}
@HostListener('mouseleave') onMouseLeave() {
    this.hover(false);
}
```

6. Write an event method to be called on **mouse enter** and on **mouse leave** events:

```
hover(shouldUnderline: boolean){
    if(shouldUnderline){
    this.renderer.setElementStyle(this.el.nativeElement, 'text-
decoration', 'underline');
    } else {this.renderer.setElementStyle(this.el.nativeElement,
'text-decoration', 'none');
    }
}
```

7. Call **Directive** (prefixed with a namespace) and attach it to the **app.component.html** element, as shown here:

```
<p> <span myUnderline>Hover to underline</span> </p>
```

8. Run **ng serve** and open a browser on **localhost:4200** to view the following output:

Hover to underline

Figure 5.5: Custom attribute directive that underlines text

As can be seen in the preceding output, we have created a custom attribute directive.

Observables

Observables help pass messages between the data creator (publisher) and data subscriber in an application. They have a significant advantage compared to other techniques for managing incoming data from the backend (asynchronous data), and in handling events and delivering multiple values of any type depending on the content. Owing to the aforementioned advantages, Angular uses **Reactive Extensions** (**RxJS**), which is a third-party library that's used to implement observables.

Observables are declarable. They are called on functions that publish values, and then, immediately, a subscriber subscribes to these values. The function then executes and the subscriber unsubscribes once the execution has completed.

Creating, Defining, and Subscribing to Observables

The observable interface is implemented by the three handlers that define three types of notifications sent by an observable: **next**, **error**, and **complete**. The **next** handler is the required handler for each delivered value. It is either called zero or multiple times after execution. The **error** handler is an optional handler for an error notification, which halts the execution of the observable instance. The **complete** handler is also an optional handler for the **execution-complete** notification. Delayed values can continue to be delivered to the **next** handler after execution is complete.

Recall that instances begin publishing values when the subscriber is actively using the **subscribe()** method, that is, when the **subscribe()** method of the instance is being called, thereby passing an observer object to receive notifications. The following snippet shows the implementation of an observable:

```
// Create simple observable that emits three values
const myObservable = of (1, 2, 3,4,5,6,7);


// Create observer object
const myObserver = {
  next: y => console.log ('a next value received by Obersver: ' + y),
  error: err => console.error('an error gotten by Observer: ' + err),
  complete: () => console.log ('complete notification is received by Oberseer'),
};


// Execute with the observer object
myObservable.subscribe(myObserver);
```

```
// Observer got a next value: 1

.................................................

// Observer got a complete notification
```

> **Note**
>
> To learn more about observable implementation such as multicasting, which is about running multiples subscribers in a single implementation, refer to the following guide: https://angular.io/guide/observables.

> **Note**
>
> To read more about the practical use of observables, refer to the following guide: https://angular.io/guide/practical-observable-usage.

The RxJs Library and Observables in Angular

Angular uses **RxJS**, a third-party library, to implement observables, as stated in the beginning of this section. **RxJs** makes a callback or an asynchronous program easy to use. **RxJs** provides several utility functions that are used on streams for filtering, iterating through values, and for composing multiple streams. Apart from utility functions, there are a number of functions that can be used to create observables from events, timers, promises, and so on. We will briefly describe the implementation of those functions that are used to create observables here.

Creating Observables from Timers or Counters

We import an interval from **RxJs** and an observable is created, as described in the following snippet:

```
const secondsCounter = interval(20000); /* Create an observables */
secondsCounter.subscribe(n => /* Subscribe to begin publishing values*/
  console.log('It's been ${n} seconds since subscribing!'));


for Promises, fromPromise function is imported from RxJs, and an observable
is created as follows
const data = fromPromise(fetch('/api/endpoint'));


data.subscribe({   /* Subscribe to begin listening for async result*/
```

```
next(response) { console.log(response); },
error(err) { console.error('Error: ' + err); },
complete() { console.log('Completed'); }
});
```

> **Note**
>
> For more information on the implementation of operations that use observables, refer to the following documentation: https://angular.io/guide/observables-in-angular.

Activity 13: Communicating Between Two Components Using Observable

You have been tasked with creating two components, **app-header** and **app-content**. When a user logs in from each component, the state in the component must be synchronized; that is, if the user logs in/logs out from the **app-header**, the **app-content** gets notified. Ensure that all previous exercises and activities have been completed. Also, create a new folder called **observable** and create an Angular project with the name **observe** inside the folder. Perform the following steps to complete this activity:

> **Note**
>
> The code files for this activity can be found here: http://bit.ly/2BQSnpn.

1. Create the **app-header** component using the CLI.

2. Create the **app-content** component using the CLI.

3. Create the user model and interface in **user.model.ts**.

4. Create and update the user service.

5. Define the user and inject **service** in the **app-header.component.ts** class.

6. Define the user and inject **service** in the **app-content.component.ts** class.

7. Write **ngOnInit()**, **login()**, **signup()**, and **logout()** methods for the **app-header.component.ts** class.

8. Write **ngOnInit()**, **login()**, **signup()**, and **logout()** methods for **app-content.component.ts** class.

9. Update the **app-header.component.html** template.

10. Update the **app-content.component.html** template.

11. Update the styles for both components (**app-header** and **app-content**).

12. Update the **app.component.html** template.

13. Run **ng serve** on the CLI and open the browser at **localhost:4200**.

> **Note**
>
> The solution for this activity can be found on page 306.

Angular Bootstrapping and Modularity

Bootstrapping an Angular Application

Bootstrapping in Angular is referred to as the process of initializing the Angular application during setup. The initialization process involves reading the HTML within the root and compiling it in an internal representation. This initializing process takes place in the **app.module.js** file (a pre-existing file in default Angular projects) in Angular. In the file, there is an **NgModule** decorator (this exists by default) that describes how the application's parts fit together. To understand bootstrapping, we will look at the implementation on the default Angular CLI application. First, let's open the **appModule** and view its components, as shown in the following snippet:

```
import { BrowserModule } from '@angular/platform-browser';
import { NgModule } from '@angular/core';
import { AppComponent } from './app.component';


/* the AppModule class with the @NgModule decorator */
@NgModule({
  declarations: [
    AppComponent
  ],
  imports: [
    BrowserModule,
  ],
  providers: [],
  bootstrap: [AppComponent]
```

```
})
export class AppModule { }
```

From the preceding snippet, we can deduce that the `NgModule` decorator that describes and initializes properties consists of the following:

- **Declarations**

- **Imports**

- **Providers**

- **Bootstrap**

We shall describe all the aforementioned components in the following sections. We will begin with **declarations**.

Declarations

The module's `declarations` array tells Angular which components belong to that module. As you create more components, you need to add them to declarations. The array holds the declarables (components, directives, and pipes) that belong to the module. Whenever any declarable (for example, a component) is created, it must be declared in the array or an error will be returned by Angular. If any declarable is declared twice, an error will be emitted by the compiler. The steps involved in implementing a declarable are as follows:

1. Export it from the file where it has been written

2. Import it into the `app.module.ts` file

3. Declare it in the `@NgModule` declarations array

Let's see what a declarations array looks like by using the following snippet:

```
declarations: [
Component,
  Pipe,
  Directive
],
```

Imports

The module's **import** array appears only in the **@NgModule** metadata object. It tells Angular about other **NgModules** that the module needs to function properly. Modules that are commonly used are **BrowserModule**, **FormsModule**, and **HttpClientModule** because they export components, directives, and pipes that the component templates in the module refer to. A component template can refer to another component, directive, or pipe when the referenced class is declared in this module or whether the class was imported from another module.

Providers

The **provider** array is where you list the services that the app requires. The listed services in the **provider** array are made available app-wide. You can also scope them when using the feature modules and the lazy loading modules.

Bootstrap

The process of bootstrapping involves the insertion of the components contained in the **bootstrap** array of **NgModule.bootstrap** into the browser DOM. The root **AppComponent** is the entry component that is created by default during the process of bootstrapping, which happens immediately when an application launches.

In most cases, applications have a single root component in the bootstrap array list. The bootstrap array is meant to trigger the creation of other components that fill out that tree based on the root components.

Angular Modularity

Modules in Angular are defined in the form of **NgModules**. Modules help to organize an application and extend its functions using external libraries. **NgModules** provide an application with the ability to share functions and reuse code across the application, which in turn helps reduce the actual size of it. Some of the most frequently used libraries, such as **HttpClientModule**, and **RouterModule,** are available as **NgModules**. They provide applications with the ability to use HTTP Services and routing in Angular, respectively. There are also some popular third-party applications, such as **Ionic** and **AngularFire2**.

Every Angular app has at least one module, which is the root module that is bootstrapped to launch the application. As the app's complexity increases, the root module is broken down into feature modules that represent collections of related functionalities. The features modules are then imported into the root module.

JavaScript Modules and NgModules

We have used the **export** statement on some JavaScript classes or methods so that we can use them externally. These are simply the JavaScript modules, as shown here:

```
export class AppComponent { ... }
```

When you need to access a class from another, we need to import it, as shown here:

```
import { AppComponent } from './app.component';
```

NgModules

NgModules are classes that are decorated with **@NgModule**. The presence of **@NgModule** and its metadata differentiates it from regular JavaScript modules. The **AppModule** that's generated from the Angular CLI uses both JavaScript modules and **NgModule** ,as shown in the following code:

```
/* These are JavaScript import statements. */
import { BrowserModule } from '@angular/platform-browser';
import { NgModule } from '@angular/core';
import { AppComponent } from './app.component';


/* The @NgModule decorator. */
@NgModule({
  declarations: [
    AppComponent
  ],
  imports: [      /* These are NgModule imports. */
    BrowserModule
  ],
  providers: [],
  bootstrap: [AppComponent]
})
export class AppModule { }
```

Feature Modules

A feature module delivers a well-integrated set of functionalities that is focused and is distinguished primarily by its intent and purpose. For example, a feature module can be created for business facilities (forms, HTTP, and routing), business domain, and user workflow collection of related utilities. The five types of feature module that are available in Angular are as follows:

Domain feature: This type of feature module is used to deliver a user experience regarding a particle application domain. They are characterized by the following points:

- They consist of mainly declarations and are only imported once by a more superior feature module

- They have top components that act as the root features, supporting other descendants (sub-components)

- They rarely have providers, but when they do, they become available for use if the provider keeps rendering the service

- They might be imported for the root `AppModule` of a small application that lacks routing

Routed feature: This type of feature module is used by router navigation. An example of this is lazy loaded modules; they are also defined as routed feature modules. Routed feature modules are characterized by the following points:

- Routed feature components never appear in the template of an external component; therefore, they don't export anything.

- They rarely have providers, but when they do, they become available to use as long as the provider keeps rendering a service (that is, the routed module life span becomes dependent on the provider's life span).

- They are not meant to be imported by any module to avoid eager load (a query for one type of entity also loads related entities as part of the query).

We are going to talk more about the lazy-loading module in the next section.

Routing: This type of module provides routing configuration for another module. It separates routing configuration from the main module. These modules are characterized by the following points:

- They do not have their own declarations; that is, they don't have declare components, pipes, or directives.

- They can only be imported by the module's companion module.

- They add guard and resolver service providers to the module's providers.

- The module should use the "**Routing**" suffix, which is a name parallel to the name of its companion module.

- They define the route and add the router's configuration to the module's import.

Service: This module has been implemented more than once in the previous sections. It is one of the most frequently used modules. An example of a service module is **HttpClientModule,** as we explained in the previous section. It provides utility services such as data access and specially formatted data describing events, requests, and replies. They are characterized by the following points:

- They only consist of providers and are not declarable

- A service module should only be imported by the application root

- Services in one module are available to all modules

A service must be isolated from the other modules so that it can be imported only once. As an example, you can have a **UserModule** that consists of many services imported into it. All these services will be available app-wide whenever the **UserModule** is imported.

Widget: This type of module is used whenever there is a need to use the declarable in an external module. Widgets are characterized by the following points:

- They can be imported into any module whose component's template needs it

- They consist entirely of exported declarations

- They rarely have providers

For example, you can have a **UIModule** that has many components declared inside it and every time you need to use one or all its exported elements, you import only **UIModule. core.**

Entry Components

An entry component is any component that Angular loads in a peremptory manner and is not referenced in any template. Entry components can be loaded in two ways:

Bootstrapping inside NgModule: The following is an example of specifying a bootstrapped component, **AppComponent,** in a basic **app.module.ts**:

```
@NgModule({
  declarations: [
    AppComponent
```

```
  ],
  imports: [
    BrowserModule,
    FormsModule,
    HttpClientModule,
    AppRoutingModule
  ],
  providers: [],
  bootstrap: [AppComponent] // bootstrapped entry component
})
```

Angular loads a root **AppComponent** dynamically because it's listed by type in **@NgModule**. **bootstrap**.

Including it in a route definition: This can be seen in the following snippet:

```
const routes: Routes = [
  {
    path: '',
    component: CustomerListComponent
  }
];
```

A route definition refers to a component by its type with **component: CustomerListComponent**. All router components must be entry components. This will require you to add the component in two places: **router** and **entryComponents**. The compiler is smart enough to recognize that this is a router definition, and it automatically adds the router component in **entryComponents**.

Service Provider Scope

In the previous chapter, we generated services using the **ng generate** CLI command in the root project directory. To have a good understanding of service scope, let's have a brief recap by generating a user service using the following command:

```
ng generate service User
```

After the service is generated, we have a **UserService** skeleton, **src/app/user.service. ts,** as shown in the following code:

```
import { Injectable } from '@angular/core';

@Injectable({
  providedIn: 'root',
})

export class UserService {

}
```

You can now inject **UserService** anywhere into your application. When CLI commands are used to generate a service, by default, you have the **@injectable** decorator configured with a **providedIn** property set **with 'root'**. This specifies that the service will be provided in the root injector, thereby making it available app-wide. Unless a service is meant to be consumed by a specific **@NgModule**, the root is recommended for the **providedIn** property. Beginning with Angular 6, it is the preferred method for creating a singleton service. It's done by setting **providedIn** to **root** on the service's **@ Injectable** decorator, as seen in the preceding snippet.

The following snippets show two alternative ways of implementing services in a module:

1. Using injectables (as discussed earlier):

    ```
    import { Injectable } from '@angular/core';
    import { UserModule } from './user.module';
    @Injectable({
      providedIn: AdminModule,
    })
    export class UserService {
    }
    ```

2. Using **NgModule**:

    ```
    import { NgModule } from '@angular/core';
    import { UserService } from './user.service';
    @NgModule({
      providers: [UserService],
    })
    export class UserModule {
    }
    ```

Limiting Provider Scope with Components and the Lazy-Loading Module

We already know that when a service is injected into the root application, it becomes available to all modules in the application. However, what if we want to limit the service to a specific component only? Or, what if we want to lazy load our application?

If we want to limit the services to a specific component only, there is a **providers** array property that can be set, as shown here:

```
@Component({
/* . . . */
  providers: [UserService]
})
```

When this is set, the service is only made accessible to the components alone since the component provider and **NgModule** providers are independent of each other.

In lazy loading, instead of loading all resources for every page of an app, you load what is needed at a specific time when it is really needed. Therefore, we can say lazy modules are modules that use lazy loading. This comes with a lot of advantages, with one of the greatest being performance. For example, on your e-commerce website, where you have a page that users rarely visit, and the page is meant to load **'new products'**. The logic can be split to not load resources for the page unless it is visited. This will make your application start faster because there will be one module less to load until someone visits that page.

Exercise 22: Creating a Shared Module for a Custom Attribute Directive

In this exercise, we will be creating a shared module for a custom attribute directive that displays text in HTML templates. To complete this exercise, you must have completed all the exercises in the previous chapters. To get started, open the project named **customs** located in the **chapter-5-exercises** folder, and then perform the following steps:

> **Note**
>
> The code files for this exercise can be found here: http://bit.ly/2E5BK9A.

1. Create a directives file using the CLI, as shown here:

   ```
   ng generate directive text/ShareText
   ```

2. Create a **shared.module.ts** file (using the CLI) as shown here:

```
ng generate module shared/shared
```

3. Input the following code in the file to import the directive class:

```
import { NgModule } from '@angular/core';
import { CommonModule } from '@angular/common';
import { ShareTextDirective } from '../text/share-text.directive';

@NgModule({
  declarations: [ShareTextDirective],
  imports: [
    CommonModule
  ],
  exports: [
    ShareTextDirective     ]
})

export class SharedModule { }
```

4. Import the **SharedModule** into our **AppModule**:

```
import { NgModule } from '@angular/core';
import { BrowserModule } from '@angular/platform-browser';
import { AppComponent } from './app.component';
// Load SharedModule
import { SharedModule } from './shared/shared.module';
@NgModule({
  // Import SharedModule
    imports: [BrowserModule, SharedModule],
    declarations: [AppComponent],
    bootstrap: [AppComponent]
})
export class AppModule{}
```

5. Import **Directive**, **ElementRef**, and **OnInit** from the Angular core and define the **@ Directive** decorator in the directive file, as shown here:

```
import { Directive, ElementRef, OnInit } from '@angular/core';
@Directive({
 selector: '[input-box]'
 })
```

6. Inject **ElementRef** and **Renderer** into the constructor, as shown here:

```
constructor(private elementRef: ElementRef) {
}
```

7. Write the **OnInit** method to attach the text to **innerHTML**:

```
ngOnInit() {
    this.elementRef.nativeElement.innerHTML ='<h1>Welcome to Packt
MEANStack Courseware Class</h1>';
    }
```

8. Call the **Directive** (prefixed with a namespace) and attach it to the **app.component. html** element:

```
<div input-box></div>
```

9. Run **ng serve** and open the browser at **localhost:4200** to view the output, as shown here:

Welcome to Packt MEANStack Courseware Class

Figure 5.6: Shared module output

As can be seen from the preceding output, we have created a shared module for a custom attribute directive.

Exercise 23: Creating a Lazy-Loaded Module

In this exercise, we will be creating a lazy-loaded module for a simple application. To complete this exercise, you must have completed all the exercises in the previous chapters. To get started, create an Angular project named **student** in the **chapter-5-exercises** folder, and then perform the following steps:

> **Note**
>
> The code files for this exercise can be found here: http://bit.ly/2BIHhm7.

1. Create a new app (**student**) with routing using the following CLI command:

```
ng new student --routing
```

   Note that the **--routing** flag generates a file called **app-routing.module.ts**, which is one of the files you need for setting up lazy loading for your feature module.

2. Create a **students** feature module with routing:

```
ng generate module students  --routing
```

3. Add a **student-list** component to the feature module:

```
ng generate component students/student-list
```

4. Create a **home** component:

```
ng generate component home
```

5. Create a book feature module (**courses**) with routing:

```
ng generate module courses -routing
```

6. Add a **course-list** component to the feature module:

```
ng generate component courses/course-list
```

7. Update the routes array in the **AppRoutingModule** with the following code:

```
src/app/app-routing.module.ts
import { NgModule } from "@angular/core";
import { RouterModule, Routes } from "@angular/router";
import { HomeComponent } from "./home/home.component";

const routes: Routes = [
  {
    path: 'students',
    loadChildren: './students/students.module#StudentsModule'
  },
  {
    path: 'courses',
    loadChildren: './courses/courses.module#CoursesModule'
  },

  {
    path: '',
    component: HomeComponent,
  }
];
```

```
@NgModule({
  imports: [RouterModule.forRoot(routes)],
  exports: [RouterModule],
  providers: []
})
export class AppRoutingModule {}
```

8. Configure the feature module's routes in **students-routing.module.ts**.

   First, import the component at the top of the file with the other JavaScript import statements, and then add the route to **StudentListComponent,** as shown in the following code:

```
import { NgModule } from '@angular/core';
import { Routes, RouterModule } from '@angular/router';
import { StudentListComponent } from './student-list/student-list.
component';

const routes: Routes = [
  {
    path: '',
    component: StudentListComponent
  }
];

@NgModule({
  imports: [RouterModule.forChild(routes)],
  exports: [RouterModule]
})
export class StudentsRoutingModule { }
```

9. Configure the **Routes** array for the **courses-routing.module.ts,** as shown in the following code:

```
import { NgModule } from '@angular/core';
import { Routes, RouterModule } from '@angular/router';
import { CourseListComponent } from './course-list/course-list.component';
const routes: Routes = [
  {
    path: '',
    component: CourseListComponent
  }
];
```

```
@NgModule({
  imports: [RouterModule.forChild(routes)],
  exports: [RouterModule]
})
export class CoursesRoutingModule { }
```

10. Update the **app.component.html** template with the following code:

```
<h1>
  {{title}}
</h1>


<button routerLink="">Home</button>
<button routerLink="/students">Students</button>
<button routerLink="/courses">Courses</button>


<router-outlet></router-outlet>
```

11. Go to **localhost:4200** in the browser. You will obtain the following output:

Figure 5.7: Output for the home page

Click on the **Students** tab. You will obtain the following output:

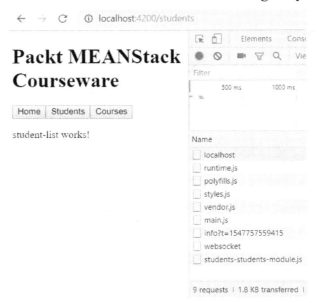

Figure 5.8: Output for the Students tab

Click on the **Books** tab. You will obtain the following output:

Figure 5.9: Output for the Books tab

Activity 14: Creating a Lazy-Loaded Application

You have been tasked with creating a lazy-loaded page for a user list. When the user list is created, and upon the clicking of any user item, the app should navigate to the user detail page (call it the **user-detail** component). The user details page must be dynamic; that is, the URL should contain the **user id** while navigating to the user detail page. There should be a back button on the user detail page so that the end user can go back to the user-listing page. The properties to show on the user details page are as follows: **Picture**, **First Name**, **Last Name**, **Email**, and **Phone**. Before you begin, ensure that all the previous exercises and activities have been completed. Also, create a new folder called **lazy-loaded**. Perform the following steps to complete this activity:

> **Note**
>
> The JSON-server library will be used to mock the API server. The data for this purpose can be found here: https://api.myjson.com/bins/10v4ns. The code files for this activity can be found here: http://bit.ly/2NDvb2N

1. Create an Angular project with the name **users**.

2. Create a **users-list** feature module with routing.

3. Add a **user-list component** to the feature module.

4. Create a **users-details** feature module with routing.

5. Add a **user-detail** component to the feature module.

6. Globally install **json-server** on your system using **npm** or **yam**.

7. Create a new JSON file named **db.json** and fill it with data from https://api.myjson.com/bins/10v4ns. Then, launch this file on the **json-server**.

8. Add a **user-list** service.

9. Update the routes array in **AppRoutingModule** .

10. Configure the feature module's routes in **users-list-routing.module.ts** by first importing the component at the top of the file with the other JavaScript import statements, and then add the route to **UserListComponent**.

11. Configure the feature modules for **users-detail-routing.module.ts**.

12. Create the user model and update it.

13. Write the service functions.

14. Update and inject **service** into **users-list.component.ts**.

15. Update and inject **service** into **users-details.component.ts**.

16. Style the **user-list** component.

17. Style the **users-details** components.

18. Update the **app.component.html** template.

19. Go to **localhost:4200** and then test for **/userslist** and **/userslist/1**.

> **Note**
>
> The solution for this activity can be found on page 310.

Summary

This chapter got us started on the use of Angular's inbuilt pipes, such as **upper case**, **date decimals**, **percent**, **async**, and so on. We later created custom pipes and directives via exercises and activities. We wrapped up this section by looking at the implementation of observables and the **RxJs** library.

We then described Angular **bootstrapping** and **modularity**. We first initialized an Angular application using **NgModule** decorator properties such as **declarations**, **imports**, **providers**, and **bootstrap**. We later described the difference between **NgModule** and JavaScript modules in application development. We continued by describing the feature modules available, such as **domain**, **routed**, **service**, and **widget**. The concept of the entry component service provider scope was described as well. We ended this chapter with an activity on creating a lazy loaded application.

In the next and final chapter of this book, we will be performing unit and e2e testing, in addition to animating and optimizing Angular elements.

Testing and Optimizing Angular Applications

Learning Objectives

By the end of this chapter, you will be able to:

- Animate an Angular element

- Optimize Angular applications

- Perform unit testing on an Angular application

- Implement end-to-end (e2e) testing on an Angular application

This chapter presents the basics of Angular animations in addition to an introduction on optimizing and testing Angular applications.

Introduction

In the previous chapter, we implemented the Angular animation module. That chapter described the various animation functions available in Angular, in addition to the methods for animating an element and a route transition.

In this chapter, we will be addressing the final objective of this book, testing and optimizing Angular applications. Additionally, you will learn about some features in Angular 7, along with concepts such as storing constants, Angular router, and more. Later in the chapter, you will also learn the various ways of optimizing Angular applications in terms of performance.

This chapter will get you started on performing unit and e2e tests, which are the two main testing procedures for Angular applications. You will also have a glimpse of continuous integration in Angular projects. At the end of each part, you will gain practical experience with exercises and activities that are tailored to the goals and objectives of this book.

Angular Animations and the Latest Angular Features

Animations have several uses; in the case of web applications, they are a powerful tool to enhance user experience. For example, when page transitions are animated, navigation through an application becomes easier. Developers and designers have realized that a clear knowledge of how an application functions can actually be communicated using animations. Therefore, in this section, you'll learn how to make use of the animation module provided by Angular in your application.

Getting Started with the Animation Module

The Angular animation module provides motion and interactive effects on an application's HTML elements by changing styles or transforming the user interface from one state to another state. Animations not only improve the performance of an application, but also user experience, thereby improving application ease of use. Animations can also help to call users' attention to where needed.

To get started using the Animation module, the first thing to do is to import the **BrowserAnimationsModule** into the app root module, as can be seen in the following snippet:

```
import { NgModule } from '@angular/core';

import { BrowserModule } from '@angular/platform-browser';

import { BrowserAnimationsModule } from '@angular/platform-browser/
animations';

@NgModule({
```

```
imports: [ BrowserModule, BrowserAnimationsModule ],
declarations: [ ], bootstrap: [ ]
})
export class AppModule { }
```

Animation Functions

@angular/animations and **@angular/platform-browser** are the main Angular modules for animations. The former comprises several animation functions that can be imported into component files, while the latter supports the delivery of apps on different supported browsers. Some of the most used functions are as follows:

trigger(): This function is the container for all other animation function calls. Its major task is to kick off the animation. It uses an array syntax, and a trigger name is declared as the first argument. The implementation is as follows:

```
animations: [
    trigger('openClose', [
      // ...
      state('open', style({
        height: '200px',
        opacity: 1,
        backgroundColor: 'yellow'
      }))
  ]),
  ]
```

style():This function controls the visual appearance of the HTML. It uses an object array as its syntax and defines the styles to use in the animations.

state(): This function defines the set of CSS styles that is to be applied to a component or element. The function also ensures a successful transition to a given state, as shown in the following snippet:

```
animations: [
trigger('openClose', [
state('open', style({
        height: '200px',
        opacity: 1,
        backgroundColor: 'yellow'
```

```
    })),
    state('closed', style({
      height: '100px',
      opacity: 0.5,
      backgroundColor: 'green'
    }))
  ]),
]
```

transition(): This function uses an array syntax to define the animation sequence between two named states. The implementation is as follows:

```
animations: [
    trigger('openClose', [
      // ...
      transition('open => closed', [
        animate('1s')
      ]),
      transition('closed => open', [
        animate('0.5s')
      ]),
    ]),
  ],
```

animate(): The function defines the specific time at which the transition will occur. It also defines the values for delay and easing (though optional) and can define style function calls within itself.

keyframes(): This function is used with the **animate()** function and uses an array syntax to permit successional change between styles within a given time interval. Styles can be defined within this function.

Some other functions available are **group()**, **query()**, **sequence()**, **stagger()**, **animation()**, **useAnimation()**, and **animateChild()**.

> **Note**
>
> More details about these functions can be found at https://angular.io/api/animations.

Animating an Element

Let's quickly see how we can animate an element using the functions we previously explained. Assuming we have an Angular app generated using the CLI, the following points can be implemented.

Importing animation functions into component files

We import a function whenever it is defined in any module and is to be used by components. In the following example, we will be importing the animation functions from **@angular/core** and **@angular/animations**:

```
import { Component, HostBinding } from '@angular/core';
import {
    trigger,
    state,
    style,
    animate,
    transition
} from '@angular/animations';
```

Adding the animation metadata property

The **@Component()** decorator holds the metadata property of the components. For the purpose of animations, we declare an **animation [trigger ()]** array property. This is a container for all other animation function calls. The implementation is as follows:

```
@Component({
    selector: 'app-root',
    templateUrl: 'app.component.html',
    styleUrls: ['app.component.css'],
    animations: [
```

```
      // animation triggers go here
  ]
})
```

Defining the state and styles

After implementing trigger definitions, we next define the different states of an animation in a transition process using a state function. As discussed earlier, each state has a different styling; for example, if we define two states as open and closed, then the open state could define the color style property as yellow, while the closed state defines the same property as green. The implementation is shown in the following snippet:

```
// ...
state('open', style({
  height: '200px',
  opacity: 1,
  backgroundColor: 'yellow'
})),
state('closed', style({
  height: '100px',
  opacity: 0.5,
  backgroundColor: 'green'
})),
```

Defining the transition and timing

A transition creates an impression of motion. Multiple styles can be set, but without instant illusory motion during the animation process, the element transforms with no visible indicator that a change is occurring, which in turn makes changes abrupt. Therefore, defining an animation transition help indicate the changes that occur over a period from one state to another. As explained earlier, the transition function accepts two parameters:

- Direction between the transition states

- An animated function that defines duration for the transition, delay, and easing (controls how animation accelerates and decelerates during its runtime) of the transition

Let's see how this plays out in the following example:

```
transition('open => closed', [
  animate('1s 300ms ease-in')
]),
transition('closed => open', [
  animate(''0.5s 100ms ease-out'')
]),
```

Triggering the animation

The trigger function does more than be a container: it tells the animation when to start, defines the states and transitions, and then gives the animation a name that is attached to the trigger element in the template.

We shall continue from the preceding snippet, name the trigger **startEnd**, and attach a trigger element, which is a button. The button being the trigger describes the open state, closed state, and transition timing between states, as shown in the following code:

```
animations: [
 trigger(startEnd,
 [ // ...
 ]) ]
```

The following snippet presents a typical definition of an animation in the

component.ts file:

```
import { Component, OnInit,HostBinding } from '@angular/core';
import {trigger,state,style,animate,transition} from '@angular/animations';


@Component({
  selector: 'app-animate',
  animations: [
    trigger('startEnd', [
      state('start', style({
      backgroundColor: 'green',
      width: '100px',
      height: '100px'
```

```
      })),
      state('end', style({
        backgroundColor: 'red',
        width: '50px',
        height: '50px'
      })),
      transition('start => end', [
        animate('1.5s')
      ]),
      transition('end => start', [
        animate('1s')
      ]),
    ]),
  ],
  templateUrl: './animate.component.html',
  styleUrls: ['./animate.component.css']
})
export class AnimateComponent {

  constructor() { }

  hasStarted = 'start';

  toggle() {
    this.hasStarted = this.hasStarted === 'start' ? 'end' : 'start';
  }
}
```

Attaching defined animations to the HTML template

The defined animation trigger is attached to an element in the component's template. This is done as shown in the following snippet:

```
<button (click)="toggle()">Change Size</button>
<br />
<div [@startEnd]=hasStarted></div>
<br />
```

Observe that the trigger name is wrapped in square brackets, [ ], and preceded by the @ symbol. The following screenshot is the output when the preceding code snippets are run:

Figure 6.1: A sample animation

Animating Route Transitions

We have looked into routing in previous sections; recall that routing enables navigation between different routes. The user experience can be greatly improved by enhancing route transition with animations and providing an animation sequence when switching between routes. Here are the steps involved in animating a route transition:

1. Import the routing module into the app module.

2. Create a routing configuration.

3. Add a router outlet to components in the DOM.

4. Define the animation.

Now let's see how we can animate page transition by performing an exercise on creating an animated route transition.

Exercise 24: Creating an Animated Route Transition between Two Pages

In this exercise, we will be animating a route transition between two pages. In order to complete the exercise, you must have completed the exercises in the previous chapters. To get started, create a new folder in a known directory and name it **chapter-6-exercises**, and then perform the following steps:

> **Note**
>
> The code files for this exercise can be found here: http://bit.ly/2GZ9xEv.

1. Create a new project using the CLI command shown here:

   ```
   ng new animate
   ```

2. Create a component named **about** with the following code:

   ```
   ng generate component about
   ```

3. Create a component named **home** with the following code:

   ```
   ng generate component home
   ```

4. Import the animation module (**BrowserAnimationsModule**) into the **app.module.ts** file using the following code:

   ```
   import { BrowserAnimationsModule } from '@angular/platform-browser/
   animations';
   import { BrowserModule } from '@angular/platform-browser';
   ................ . .
   imports: [
       BrowserModule,
       BrowserAnimationsModule
     ],
   ```

5. Create a routing configuration and define the route in the **app.module.ts** file using the following code:

   ```
   const appRoutes : Routes =
   [ { path: ' ', pathMatch: 'full', redirectTo: '/home', data: {animation:
   'HomeComponent'} },
     { path: 'about', component: AboutComponent, data: {animation:
   'AboutComponent'} },
     { path: 'home', component: HomeComponent, data: {animation:
   'HomeComponent'} } ]
   ```

6. Import the routing module into **app.module.ts** using the following code:

```
imports:   [
......................................... .
RouterModule.forRoot([router]);
]
```

7. Add a router outlet to the root component (**app.component.ts**) in the **AppComponent** class using the following code:

```
prepareRoute(outlet: RouterOutlet) {
   return outlet && outlet.activatedRouteData && outlet.
activatedRouteData['animation'];
}
```

8. Create a **ts** class file for the animation with the following code:

```
touch animation.ts
```

9. Import the animation functions into **animate.ts**:

```
import {trigger,state,style,animate,transition,query,animateChild,group}
from '@angular/animations';
```

10. Define the animations as shown in the following code:

```
export const slideInAnimation =
  trigger('routeAnimations', [
    transition('HomeComponent <=> AboutComponent', [
      style({ position: 'relative' }),
      query(':enter, :leave', [
        style({
          position: 'absolute',
          top: 0,
          left: 0,
          width: '100%'
        })
      ]),
//[..]
      query(':enter', animateChild()),
    ])

  ]);
```

11. Update the **app.component.html** template as follows:

```
<div [@routeAnimations]="prepareRoute(outlet)"
style="height:300px;width:100%;color:black;">
    <a routerLink="about"> About </a>
    <a routerLink="/home"> Home </a>
  <router-outlet #outlet="outlet"></router-outlet>
</div>
```

12. Run **ng serve -o** and observe the page transition in the browser by typing **localhost:4200/about** in the address bar. You will get the following output:

Figure 6.2: Output for animating route transitions between pages

As can be seen from the preceding output, we have successfully created and tested a page transition animation. Let's complete an activity to test our skills on animating route transitions.

Activity 15: Animating the Route Transition Between the Blog Post Page and the View Post Page of the Blogging Application

You have been tasked with animating the route transition between the **Blog Post** page and the **View Post** page of the **Blogging Application**. When the user navigates between the two pages, the transition should be animated. Ensure that all previous exercises and activities have been completed. Open the **Blogging Application** folder and perform the following steps to complete the activity:

> **Note**
>
> The code files for this activity can be found here: http://bit.ly/2VfAVlL.

1. Import the routing module into the **app.routing.module** file.

2. Create an **animation.ts** file using **touch**, and then import the animation classes and define the animation properties.

3. Update the animated route in the lazy loading **ap.route.module.tsrouting** configuration.

4. Import the animation and router outlet of the root component class.

5. Update the root component template file.

6. Run the application, and then test and observe the page transition.

> **Note**
>
> The solution for this activity can be found on page 318.

Other Angular Features

In this section, we shall be looking briefly into some new features that have just been released in Angular 7.

CLI Commands and Prompts

One of the most prominent features added to Angular in version 6 was the ability to easily update your old packages using the newly introduced CLI commands such as **ng add** and **ng update**. Also present is the ability to create native web elements using **Angular Elements**, and much more.

The CLI prompt introduced in the most recent version, 7, gives Angular the ability to prompt developers when you run commands such as **ng add** and **ng update**, with the aim to help developers discover built-in features such as **SCSS** support and routing. A list of typical prompts is shown in the following code:

```
"routing": {
  "type": "boolean",
  "description": "Generates a routing module.",
  "default": false,
  "x-prompt": "Would you like to add Angular routing?"
},
```

Angular Budget

This feature was also recently added to Angular; it enables a developer to actually set the threshold in the application configuration file (**angular.json**). This ensures the app stays within the defined size. In this view, for the default budget configuration, the maximum error size is raised to 5 MB, and an error warning is initiated when 2 MB is exceeded. The implementation of this feature is shown in the following code:

```
"budgets": [{
  "type": "initial",
  "maximumWarning": "2mb",
  "maximumError": "5mb"
}]
```

The Component Development Kit (CDK) for Angular

The CDK is a set of tools that implement a common interaction pattern with un-opinionated presentation. It helps developers with high-quality predefined behaviors for components by providing robust, well-tested tools to add common interaction patterns with minimal effort; it can help you build what you need in less time, with less code, and fewer bugs. The CDK consists of two categories: common behaviors and components.

The common behaviors are the tools for implementing the common application features presented in the following list:

- Accessibility
- Bi-directionality
- Drag and drop
- Layout
- Observers
- Overlay
- Platform
- Portal
- Scrolling
- Text field

Storing and Defining Constants in Angular

Storing constants such as **apiUrl** as an API URL in Angular apps can be achieved in two different ways by default. These constants can be stored in the development environment's constant storage file, **environment.ts**, where we will define constants for the development environment. They can also be stored in the production environment constant storage file, **environment.prod.ts**, where we define constants for the production environment. These two files are located in a folder named **environments** residing in the **src** directory.

Let's see an example of how we can store constants:

```
export const environment = {
  production: false,
  apiUrl: 'http://localhost:3000/movies'
};
```

The preceding snippet can be found in the **environment.ts** file. We can observe that a new constant called **apiUrl** with the local URL is being defined. Let's assume that the API has been deployed. So, we will add that URL to the **apiUrl** constant inside the **environment.prod.ts** file, as shown in the following code:

```
export const environment = {
  production: true,
  apiUrl: "https://apiurladdress.com"
}
```

Recall that we dealt with node API authentication in the previous chapter. This was done in the backend. In this section, we shall be describing different ways by which frontend routes can be authenticated and protected.

Angular Authentication Guard

Authenticating routes is an important task to embark on when we want to prevent users from having access to some pages, routes, or areas in our application. The Angular router module provides a **Navigation** guard, which is a feature that helps to solve the problem. Angular makes four different guard types available for route protection:

- **CanActivate**: This type of guard decides whether a route can be activated.
- **CanActivateChild**: This type of guard decides whether children routes of a route can be activated.
- **CanDeactivate**: This type of guard decides whether a route can be deactivated.

- **CanLoad**: This type of guard decides whether a module can be loaded lazily.

- **Resolve**: This guard is employed to retrieve dynamic data.

Depending on what we want to do, we might need to implement any one of these guards. In some cases, we may have to implement all of them.

For example, to implement **CanActivate** for a JWT, we can base our routing-access decision on properties, such as expiration time, roles, and so on, that make up the token. The implementation for all token properties is listed in the following steps:

1. If route decision is based on the expiration time, then install and load the **JwtHelperService** class from **angular2-jwt**:

    ```
    npm install --save @auth0/angular-jwt
    ```

2. If route decision is based on the role assigned to a user, then install and load the **decode** class from **jwt-decode** using the following command:

    ```
    npm install --save jwt-decode
    ```

3. Create a method in your authentication service to check whether a user is authenticated, as shown in the following snippet:

    ```
    import { Injectable } from '@angular/core';
    import { JwtHelperService } from '@auth0/angular-jwt';
    @Injectable()
    export class AuthService {
      constructor(public jwtHelper: JwtHelperService) {}
      public isAuthenticated(): boolean {
        const token = localStorage.getItem('token');

        return !this.jwtHelper.isTokenExpired(token); // Check whether the
    token is expired and return
        // true or false
      }
    }
    ```

4. Create a new service that implements the route guard. In the following snippet, we assume that both expiry date and the role assigned to a user is employed to validate the route access:

    ```
    import { Injectable } from '@angular/core';
    import { Router, CanActivate,  ActivatedRouteSnapshot } from '@angular/
    router';
    import { AuthService } from './auth.service';
    import decode from 'jwt-decode'
    ```

```
@Injectable()
export class ExpiryRoleGuardService implements CanActivate {
  constructor(public auth: AuthService, public router: Router) {}
    canActivate(route: ActivatedRouteSnapshot): boolean {

    const expectedRole = route.data.expectedRole; //expected route passed
from route config o data property
    const token = localStorage.getItem('token');
        const tokenPayload = decode(token); // decode the token to get its
payload

    if (
      !this.auth.isAuthenticated() ||
      tokenPayload.role !== expectedRole
    ) {
      this.router.navigate(['login']);
      return false;
    }
    return true;
  }
```

5. Apply the guard to any routes you wish to protect using the following snippet:

```
import { Routes, CanActivate } from '@angular/router';
import { ProfileComponent } from './profile/profile.component';
import {
  ExpiryRoleGuardService as ExpiryDateRoleGuard
} from './auth/auth-guard.service';
import { ]
export const ROUTES: Routes = [
  { path: '', component: HomeComponent },
  {
    path: 'profile',
    component: ProfileComponent,
    canActivate: [ExpiryDateRoleGuard] ,
    data: {
      expectedRole: 'admin'
    }
  },
  {
    path: 'admin',
    component: AdminComponent,
    canActivate: [ExpiryDateRoleGuard],
```

```
        data: {
          expectedRole: 'admin'
        }
      },
      { path: '**', redirectTo: '' }
    ];
```

Note that the preceding implementation is for both expired token and user role. However, these can also be implemented separately. Having seen example snippets on storing and defining constants, we will be performing an activity to cement our understanding of this Angular functionality.

Activity 16: Implementing Router Guard, Constant Storage, and Updating the Application Functions of the Blogging Application

You have been tasked with implementing router guard, constant storage, and updating the blogging application components and services. Ensure that all previous exercises and activities have been completed. Open the **Blogging Application** folder and perform the following steps to complete the activity:

> **Note**
>
> The code files for this activity can be found here: http://bit.ly/2NjgLo0.

1. Define a constant for **AuthService** and **ArticleService** in the **environment.ts** file with local URL's.

2. Import and declare the environment in the **auth.service.ts** file.

3. Import the **BehaviorSubject** class in the **auth.service.ts** file.

4. Declare **user** as an instance of the **BehaviorSubject** class and then observe using the Angular **asObservable()** method.

5. Write an authentication function in the **auth.service.ts** file to check if any tokens exist.

6. Update the **login**, **register**, and **logout** functions with the constant variable and then observe the behavioral variable.

7. Create a new **auth-guard.service.ts** service file to implement the router guard.

8. Apply the router guard service to the **app.routing.module.ts** route file.

9. Import and declare the environment in the **article.service.ts** file.

10. Declare the token and header in the **article.service.ts** file.

11. Update the functions in the **article.service.ts** file with constant variables and headers.

12. Update the **blog-home** component class (**blog-home.component.ts**), template (**blog-home.component.html**), and style (**blog-home.component.css**).

13. Update the **view-post** component class (**view-post.component.ts**) and the template (**view-post.component.html**).

14. Update the **login** component class (**login.component.ts**) and the template (**login.component.html**).

15. Update the **register** component class (**register.component.ts**) and the template (**register.component.html**).

16. Update the **create** component class (**create.component.ts**) and the template (**create.component.html**).

17. Update the **edit** component class (**edit.component.ts**) and the template (**edit.component.html**).

18. Run **ng serve** to test the route **'/blog'** before and after logging in.

> **Note**
>
> The solution for this activity can be found on page 320.

Optimizing Angular Applications

A lot of product developers/managers have an "if it works, don't fix it" mentality. They might not see reason why a software product should be optimized until a negative impact is obvious. But as a professional, it is your job to make sure that your product works efficiently even though optimization is complex. In this section, we shall be looking at the different means of improving Angular application development performance at load time (when the application is loading) and runtime (when the application is in use).

Measuring Load Time Performance

Before you begin optimization, you must run some performance analysis tests, for example, to check the load time, especially on different platforms. Testing is also essential because you cannot improve something if you don't measure it first. Google, for example, has been a top provider of optimization services such as **Lighthouse** and **PageSpeed Insights**, used to analyze and optimize your website manually or automatically. In the following exercise, we will be analyzing the performance of the author's personal website using **PageSpeed**.

Exercise 25: Web Application Performance Analysis Using PageSpeed

In this exercise, we are going to use the PageSpeed tool to analyze the author's personal website (www.pauloluyege.com). In order to complete the exercise, you must have completed the exercises in previous chapters. To get started, perform the following steps:

1. Visit the **PageSpeed** web address: https://developers.google.com/speed/ pagespeed/insights/. You will be taken to the home page:

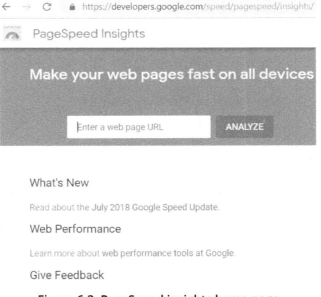

Figure 6.3: PageSpeed insights home page

2. Input the web address of the site to test and analyze, as shown in the following screenshot:

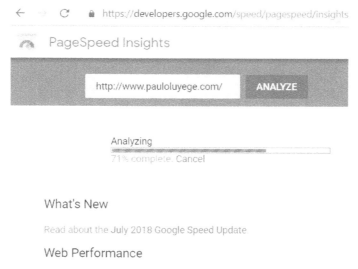

Figure 6.4: Analyzing the website

3. View the performance of web application (desktop version) by clicking the **DESKTOP** tab. An example screenshot is shown here:

Figure 6.5: Performance test result on desktop

4. View performance of the web application (mobile version) by clicking the **MOBILE** tab. An example screenshot is shown here:

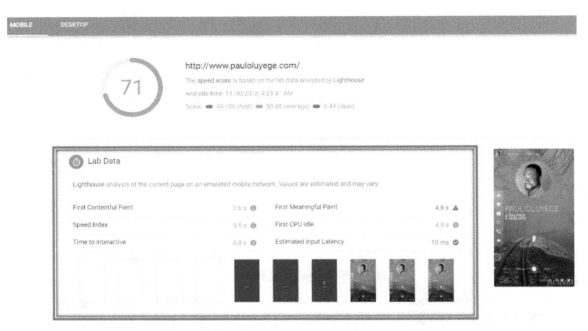

Figure 6.6: Performance test result on mobile

From the metrics shown in the result, you can identify the faster site and thus estimate on which site users will experience better performance. Therefore, even if you can make a website feel faster, actually knowing you're making the right changes is crucial.

Web application performance can be factored into two categories: load time performance and runtime performance. In the next section, we shall be looking at looking at methods and techniques in which Angular application load times can be improved and optimized.

Optimizing Angular Application Load Time Performance

Load time performance can be referred to as **the time it takes web pages to be downloaded and the entire content displayed in the browser window**.

When we talk about the load time as a web performance metric, we are talking about the features that have a direct impact on the user's engagement, as seen in the previous section, where we used **PageSpeed** to analyze a website. It indicates how long it takes for a page to fully load in the browser after a user clicks a link or makes a request.

The speed at which a page (web application) loads is dependent on some of the factors listed here:

- Hosting server
- Amount of bandwidth in transit
- Web page design
- Number, type, and weight of elements on the page
- User location, device, and browser type

In this section, we shall focus on the practices for optimizing a web application developed using Angular CLI. These practices aim to do the following:

1. **Making sure that application build size is small**: One of the methods to ensure a small build application is to eliminate dead code. Dead code elimination can also be referred to as tree-shaking. It has to do with preventing unused import and export modules from being included in the bundle during the build process. The Angular CLI enables tree-shaking to be implemented in webpack by default, thereby significantly reducing the code size of the application, and the less code we send over the wire, the more performant the application will be.

2. **Uglification**: This process is implemented in Angular by webpack using the `uglify` plugin. The uglification process help achieve a smaller build after the code has been subjected to transformation processes such as removal of comments, white spaces, and so on. The process is performed in Angular CLI by specifying the `prod` flag.

3. **Minification**: Angular 6 made aggressive minification easier by implementing a closure compiler, which is a bundling optimizer for JavaScript modules. This is used for almost all Google web applications to generate smaller bundles and for dead code elimination.

4. **Rendering**: Also recently introduced by Angular is a render engine called **Ivy**. The aim of this is to mainly improve speed and reduce code size by using **gzip** files, thereby making the app smaller in size and compilation faster. As of the release of Angular 7, the engine can only be used by enabling it manually.

5. **Compressing images and removing unused resources and packages**: Reducing image size without losing quality and removing unused resources (images, font, packages, and so on) are a couple of the best techniques for improving the build time, because bytes transferred over the network are saved. JPEG and PNG images can be compressed without losing much quality using extensions such as **TinyPNG**.

6. **Updated reactive extensions for JavaScript**: Using the updated version of RxJs (6) also reduces the final build size because unnecessary code will be removed.

7. **Updated webpack**: Using the updated version of Webpack can result in smaller builds and reduced development time. It has been proven that an updated webpack can be up to 60%-98% faster when compared to an earlier version.

8. **Using CLI flags**: The use of Angular CLI flags such as `prod` and `build-optimizer` is advised. The `prod` flag helps enable various build optimizations discussed earlier, such as **uglify**, thereby leading to smaller builds. The build optimizer disables the vendor chunk, thereby resulting in smaller code.

9. **Angular and Angular CLI Updates**: One of the alternative ways to improve the load time of an Angular application is to ensure that the Angular framework and CLI are regularly updated.

10. **Third-party package updates**: Third-party packages are also advised to be regularly updated because this gives the benefits of new features, security, performance optimizations, and bug fixes.

11. **Lazy-loading pages**: Angular CLI provides the lazy-loading mechanism, which ensures that only pages and modules required or needed at a particular moment are loaded. The basic principle of using lazy loading is "don't load something that you don't need", and thus implementing this mechanism on application routes can reduce initial load time.

12. **Compiling code offline**: The **ahead-of-Time** (**AOT**) compiler, which complies before (during the build stage) the code is run, reduces much of the processing overhead on the client browser. To enable **AOT**, you have to specify the **aot** flag. However, note that with the `prod` flag in use, the **aot** flag is not required.

13. **Cache-control header**: The cache-control header specifies the directives for caching mechanisms in both requests and responses. This header controls the conditions under which the response is cached, the identity of who catches the response, and the time needed for the network round trip for the resources that are cached.

14. **Progressive web application**: A **progressive web application** (**PWA**) gives offline capabilities to the application. It makes the application to load much faster and gives a near-native app experience, thereby greatly improving the overall perceived performance by the user.

Optimizing Angular Application Runtime Performance

Runtime performance refers to how your page performs when it is running. It is a crucial process in delivering high-performing apps. To create highly responsive interfaces, we need to address runtime performance, and to attain great runtime application performance, user input response and rendering must be less than 17 milliseconds. Achieving this creates a smooth and seamless experience, and in turn increases user confidence in your application.

In this section, we shall be looking at various ways of improving the runtime of Angular applications. Now first, let's highlight some tools available for analyzing the runtime performance of a web application.

DevTool CPU profile: This tool provides insights into the function that requires the maximum time to run.

Web tracing framework: This is an open source program that can be run on the browser to provide data insights.

> **Note**
>
> For more information on how to use the Chrome DevTools Performance panel and Web tracing framework to analyze runtime performance, refer to the following: https://developers.google.com/web/tools/chrome-devtools/evaluate-performance/ and https://github.com/google/tracing-framework.

Before runtime performance optimization: It is recommended by Angular that before trying out any runtime performance optimizations, you must first carry out a profiling test using a tool known as the **profiler**, which allows you to measure the time it takes for the change detection mechanism to run in the current page.

Runtime performances optimization techniques: Angular applications can be optimized by tuning the change detection mechanism.

Change detection: This mechanism automatically detects changes in the DOM. Therefore, to achieve the goal of optimization, we have to limit the rate at which the change detection is triggered, so that the amount of DOM changes is reduced. Angular applications are designed work optimally under heavy load by default. However, developers often perform arithmetic computation in the DOM, such as some recoding an Excel sheet with functions in the browser or loading components displaying thousands of records, thereby increasing the number of change detection cycles that are triggered. To manage these, you can employ the following:

- `enableProdMode`
- `trackBy` in `ngFor`
- `OnPush`
- An attribute decorator

enableProdMode : In development mode, change detection runs twice (by default) every time there's a change. When this happens, application slows down. It is therefore advised to go into production mode before deploying the application. To enable the production mode, you need to run `enableProdMode`. This prevents the change detection mechanism to run twice every time there's a change. This results in generating a DOM with less attributes, which in turn makes it lighter.

trackBy in ngFor: Earlier in this book, we stated that **ngFor** is an in-built directive. Let's see once again how it's used to display collections in a list:

```
<ul>
  <li *ngFor="let customer of customers">{{ customer.name }}</li>
</ul>
```

Assuming you want to add a new customer to the collection, a DOM node will be added; if the customer collection list is updated with new objects or refreshed with the addition of an object, the entire DOM list will be destroyed and recreated. It is normal to destroy and recreate when updating collections with new objects; however, when refreshing with an additional object, it is advisable to do so. There is no need to destroy and recreate the DOM since we are fetching the same object again. For instance, when results are being fetched from a server, the references are different but the same content is recreated. This impedes application performance. Therefore, a question arises: how can this be managed and optimized?

There is a property called **trackBy** provided by Angular to track objects by IDs and not references. The **trackBy** property expects a method and is used as shown:

```
<ul>

  <li *ngFor=" let customer of customers trackBy: customerById">{{ customer.
name }}</li>

</ul>



customerById(index: number, customer: CustomerModel) {

  return customer.id;

}
```

As seen in the preceding snippet, the current index and the current entity are the arguments passed into **custormerByid** with this method. DOM nodes are present only if the customer ID changes. This implementation is very cheap and doesn't have any cons; therefore, it is advised not to be hesitant in using it.

OnPush

OnPush is a change strategy offered by Angular to be defined on any component. When **OnPush** is employed, component templates will be checked for the following cases:

- If the reference of one of the inputs of the component changes

- If a component's event handler was triggered

Let's assume we have three components, A, B, and C, and all are, in one way or the other, interconnected.

We can deduce that all components are checked every time a change is detected in the application. This is a waste of time because we know that if A doesn't change, then B and C don't need to be checked. How do we solve this?

This issue can be solved using **OnPush**. Let's add a **changeDetection** attribute in the **@ Component** decorator as shown in the following snippet:

```
@Component({

  selector: 'a-comp',

  template: '….',

  changeDetection: ChangeDetectionStrategy.OnPush

})

export class AComponent {

  @Input() src: string;
```

```
check() {
  console.log( A component checked');
}
}
```

The result of the preceding snippet is that you will observe only components that are needed.

We can also add change detection to B as shown in the following:

```
@Component({
  selector: 'b-comp',
  template: '
    <p>{{ check() }}</p>
    <c-comp [src]="getBImageUrl()"></c-comp>
  ',
  changeDetection: ChangeDetectionStrategy.OnPush
})
export class BComponent {
  @Input() BModel: BModel;

  check() {
    console.log('b component checked');
  }

  getBImageUrl() {
    return 'images/b-${this.bModel.color}-running.gif';
  }
}
```

The Attribute decorator

The **@Attibute()** decorator can be used instead of **@Input()** in a component. By default, Angular assumes the value passed into an input can change at any time, thereby triggering the change detection for every change. However, some input values can actually be initialized only once, thus making it unnecessary to use the default setting. For example, let's assume we have a button component and aim to define its aspect such as primary, warning, danger, or success by passing a type. If were using an **@ Input()** decorator, the code will appear as the following:

```
import { Component, Input } from '@angular/core';


@Component({
  selector: 'btn',
  template: '
    <button type="button" class="btn btn-{{ bType }}">
      <ng-content></ng-content>
    </button>'
})
export class BtnComponent {

  @Input() bType;
}
  The template :
< btn bType ="primary">Hello!</ btn >
< btn bType ="success">Success</ btn >
```

From the template, we can see that the string value of the input is a constant, so it is better to use the **@Attribute** decorator instead, as shown in the following:

```
import { Attribute, Component } from '@angular/core';


@Component({
  selector: 'btn',
  template: '
    <button type="button" class="btn btn-{{ btnType }}">
      <ng-content></ng-content>
```

```
      </button>'
})


export class BtnComponent {


  constructor(@Attribute('bType') public bType: string) {}

}
```

Now that we have described various methods and strategies for optimization, we will be performing an exercise to implement change detection.

Exercise 26: Checking the Change Detection Cycle of an Angular Application

In this exercise, we will be analyzing the runtime performance of an Angular application by checking the change detection cycle. You must have completed the exercises in previous chapters. We will choose the app named **student** created in the previous exercise. To complete the exercise, perform the following steps:

> **Note**
>
> The code files for this exercise can be found here: http://bit.ly/2EoHVHr.

1. Open the **main.ts** file in the **student** folder and replace the application bootstrapping code with the following:

```
import { enableProdMode } from '@angular/core';
import { platformBrowserDynamic } from '@angular/platform-browser-
dynamic';
import { ApplicationRef } from '@angular/core';
import { AppModule } from './app/app.module';
import { environment } from './environments/environment';
import { enableDebugTools } from "@angular/platform-browser"

if (environment.production) {
  enableProdMode();
}

platformBrowserDynamic().bootstrapModule(AppModule)
  .then(modRef => {
    const appRef = modRef.injector.get(ApplicationRef);
    const compRef = appRef.components[0];
```

```
    // allows to run 'ng.profiler.timeChangeDetection();'
    enableDebugTools(compRef);
  })
  .catch(err => console.log(err));
```

2. Go to your browser console and run the following code:

```
ng.profiler.timeChangeDetection()
```

You will observe the change detection cycles it ran and the time per cycle. Try this more than once and compare the results. The recommended result is expected to be at least 5 cycles, lasting at least 500 ms. An example output of the detection cycles screen is shown here:

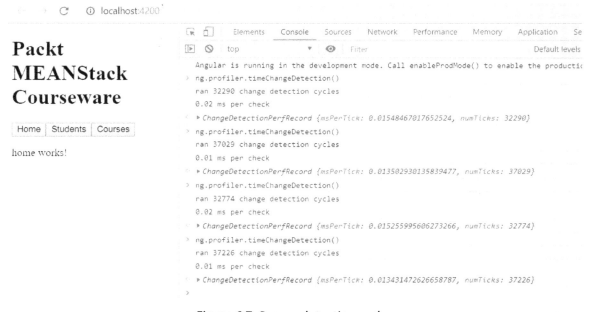

Figure 6.7: Screen detection cycles

In the preceding output, you can clearly see the number of change detection cycles that were run, in addition to the duration per check.

3. Run `ng.profiler.timeChangeDetection({ record: true })` in the browser console to record the CPU profile during these checks. You will obtain an output similar to the following:

Figure 6.8: Detection cycles screen while recording the CPU profile

From figures 6.7 and 6.8, we can say that we have successfully implemented the change detection method and thus analyzed the runtime performance of the website. Next, we will describe testing Angular applications.

Testing Angular Applications

In this section, we will be learning about Angular application testing. Tests are the best way to prevent software defects. As more features are being added and application complexity increases, updating code and checking the browser manually will no longer be easy, sustainable, error free, and will become expensive. Therefore, recent versions of Angular provide a module called `HttpClientTestingModule` to make testing very easy to perform.

There are two type of tests in Angular: unit testing and e2e testing (also known as functional testing). Unit testing can also be referred to as isolated testing, because it involves testing a small, isolated piece of code. The other type, e2e testing, involves testing the complete functionality of an application in a way that is close to real-life application use (just like a user would interact with it in real life).

Getting Started with Unit Testing

Unit testing an Angular application could involve writing a small isolated piece of pure JavaScript functions and classes and calling them to compare expected and actual results. However, this process can can be exhausting; therefore, there are libraries and frameworks that reduce the complexity and the time required to write test scripts . In this section, we shall be looking at the two such tools: **Jasmine** and **Karma**.

Jasmine

Jasmine is a testing framework. It supports a software practice that describes tests in a human-readable format so that non-technical people can understand what is being tested. This practice is known as **behavior-driven development (BDD)**.

Let's see how BDD testing with Jasmine plays out in this example:

```
function welcome() {
  return 'Welcome to MEANStack class!';
}
```

A Jasmine test spec for the `welcome()` function will appear as shown in the following:

```
describe('Welcome to MEANStack class!', () => {
  it('is says welcome to class, () => {
    expect(welcome())
        .toEqual('Welcome to MEANStack class!');
  });
});
```

From the preceding snippet, we notice that some function calls are used. These are described as follows:

- **describe()**: It is a **suits** function that is used for grouping interrelated specs.

- **it()**: This is a **spec** function that takes a title and a function containing one or more expectations.

- **expect()**: This is an assertion function to evaluate true or false. It is used for building expectations.

- `.toEqual()`: This is one of the matcher functions provided by Jasmine and is used to compare the expected and the actual results.

> **Note**
>
> There are many other functions defined by the Jasmine; you can refer to the following for a complete list: https://jasmine.github.io/2.0/introduction.html.

Running Jasmine Tests

There are two ways of running Jasmine in Angular applications: the manual technique, which involves creating a HTML file and including the required Jasmine JavaScript and CSS files, and the other technique is by using the built-in Angular CLI testing configuration. Both techniques need to be run. Manually running Jasmine tests can be exhausting and tiresome, because it involves refreshing the browser periodically after we edit some code. To solve this issue, a tool known as Karma

is used.

This tool listens to or monitors the changes in the development tool and automatically runs Jasmine tests inside browsers. All of this is done from the command line. It also displays the results of the tests on the browser interface.

> **Note**
>
> With the Angular CLI, you don't need know the detailed configuration of Karma, because it already handles the configuration as long as Jasmine is used. Our focus in this book shall mainly be on the Angular CLI application testing technique.

Unit Testing an Angular CLI Application

By default, when creating Angular projects using Angular CLI, everything you need to test using Jasmine and Karma is automatically downloaded and installed. Also, whenever we use the CLI to create declarables such as components, pipes, directives, and non-declarables such as services, the CLI automatically creates a simple Jasmine spec file with the same name as the main code file but ending in `.spec.ts`. You can run **test** on CLI to run the test.

Testing Components

To test a component, we will use some common setup utilities such as **TestBed**, **Async**, **ComponentFixture**, and **FakeAsync**. **TestBed** can be compared to **@NgModule** as it helps to configure dependencies for our test. **TestBed.configureTestingModule** is called to pass the test configuration and resolve dependencies, whereas **TestBed** loads the corresponding dependencies so they are available during your tests. The **async** utility is used when dependencies involve asynchronous handling. It wraps a test function in an asynchronous test zone. The **FakeAysnc** utility is similar to **async**, but it accepts a parameter, which is the time in milliseconds. The purpose of this is to move time forward because **FakeAysnc** doesn't execute in a synchronous order, unlike **async**. **FakeAsync** waits to execute until the tasks inside the asynchronous zone is executed.

The **ComponentFixture** utility has a method for testing and debugging components. The **isStable** method checks whether a component is stable and has completed an **async** task while the **destroy** method destroys a component in order to free up memory. By default, Angular generates a test file alongside other component files. For example, assuming we have already generated an Angular CLI application, we can perform the following steps:

1. Generate components using the **ng generate component testPage** command in the CLI.

2. Go to the **testPage** folder and locate a file named **test-page.component.spec.ts**, which is the spec file for components, and run the following:

```
import { async, ComponentFixture, TestBed } from '@angular/core/testing';

import { TestPageComponent } from './test-page.component';

//[...]

  xit('should create', () => {
    expect(component).toBeTruthy();
  });
});
```

3. Run **ng test** to launch the Karma test runner (as seen in figure 6.12) and observe four test were successfully passed: three from **AppComponent** and one from **TestPageComponent**. Figure 6.11 shows the output for the tests that are run:

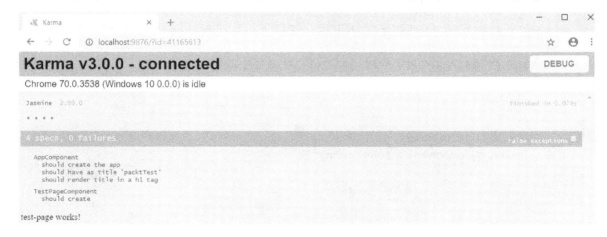

```
Paul@Software-Engineering-Lead MINGW64 ~/Desktop/PACKT/packtTest (master)
$ ng test
20 11 2018 20:07:38.661:WARN [karma]: No captured browser, open http://localhost
:9876/
20 11 2018 20:07:38.667:INFO [karma]: Karma v3.0.0 server started at http://0.0.
0.0:9876/
20 11 2018 20:07:38.668:INFO [launcher]: Launching browser Chrome with unlimited
 concurrency
20 11 2018 20:07:38.671:INFO [launcher]: Starting browser Chrome
20 11 2018 20:07:47.935:WARN [karma]: No captured browser, open http://localhost
:9876/
20 11 2018 20:07:49.197:INFO [Chrome 70.0.3538 (Windows 10 0.0.0)]: Connected on
 socket qcUWRg9eCniGwBAQAAAA with id 41165613
Chrome 70.0.3538 (Windows 10 0.0.0): Executed 1 of 4 SUCCESS (0 secs / 1.158 sec
Chrome 70.0.3538 (Windows 10 0.0.0): Executed 2 of 4 SUCCESS (0 secs / 1.707 sec
Chrome 70.0.3538 (Windows 10 0.0.0): Executed 3 of 4 SUCCESS (0 secs / 1.725 sec
Chrome 70.0.3538 (Windows 10 0.0.0): Executed 4 of 4 SUCCESS (0 secs / 1.862 sec
Chrome 70.0.3538 (Windows 10 0.0.0): Executed 4 of 4 SUCCESS (1.898 secs / 1.862
 secs)
TOTAL: 4 SUCCESS
TOTAL: 4 SUCCESS
20 11 2018 20:08:02.848:INFO [Chrome 70.0.3538 (Windows 10 0.0.0)]: Connected on
 socket hLeUgWEYjMs-sZQXAAAB with id manual-4511
20 11 2018 20:08:03.240:WARN [Chrome 70.0.3538 (Windows 10 0.0.0)]: Disconnected
```

Figure 6.9: Unit test running on CLI

Karma displays the unit test result in the browser as shown in the following figure:

Figure 6.10: Karma displaying the unit test results in the browser

Unit Testing a Service

Services are very easy to unit test. To test a service, you set the providers metadata property with an array of the services that you'll test or mock, using **TestBed**.

Let's see a typical generated service test spec file:

```
import { TestBed } from '@angular/core/testing';
import { TestService } from './test.service';


describe('TestService', () => {
  beforeEach(() => TestBed.configureTestingModule({}));


  it('should be created', () => {
    const service: TestService = TestBed.get(TestService);
    expect(service).toBeTruthy();
  });
});
```

From the preceding snippet, it can be observed that **TestBed** loads the corresponding dependencies so that they are available during the tests. Then, the suits function (**describe()**) takes in **TestService** as parameter so that all specs that are related to the service can be grouped. The spec function accepts a title, which is **'should be created'**, and a function containing one expectation, **expect(service).toBeTruthy().**

Testing a Service Class

Now, let's proceed to creating a service function in the service used (**TestService**) in the preceding snippet, and then write a unit test for the function as shown in the following snippet:

```
// service functions returns 2
getTwo(){
return 2
}
```

```
// unit test for the function
  it('return 2', () => {
    const service: TestService = TestBed.get(TestService);
    expect(service.getTwo()).toEqual(2);
  });
```

Testing HTTP Services

Angular provides **HttpClientTestingModule**, which is a testing module that permits mocking HTTP requests by providing you with the **HttpTestingController** service. We shall see how to use **HttpTestingController** to create a test for a HTTP request service if given a service file:

```
import { Injectable } from '@angular/core';
import { HttpClient } from '@angular/common/http';
import { Observable } from 'rxjs';

export interface Data {
  userId: number;
  id: number;
  title: string;
  completed: boolean;
}

@Injectable({
  providedIn: 'root'
})
export class TestService {
  mockData = 'https://jsonplaceholder.typicode.com/todos'

  constructor(private http: HttpClient) { }
```

```
    getPost(id): Observable<Data> {
      return this.http.get<Data>(this.mockData+'/'+id);
    }
}
```

From the preceding snippet, we can see a **getPost** function using an HTTP **get** request; our purpose is to write a unit test for the function. Therefore, to create a test for the HTTP request, we need to open the **spec.ts** file and perform the following steps:

1. Add **HttpClientTestingModule** and its **HttpTestingController** to the import section:

    ```
    import { HttpClientTestingModule, HttpTestingController } from '@angular/
    common/http/testing';
    ```

2. Add **HttpClientTestingModule** to the import the property of the **TestBed**
    configuration object:

    ```
    describe('TestService', () => {
      beforeEach(() => TestBed.configureTestingModule({
        providers: [TestService],
        imports: [
          HttpClientTestingModule ],
      }));
    ```

3. Write a spec function for the HTTP service function:

    ```
    it('expects service to fetch data based on post id',
    inject([HttpTestingController, TestService],
      (httpMock: HttpTestingController, service: TestService) => {
        // create fake data
        const fakeData = {
          "userId": 1,
          "id": 1,
          "title": "delectus aut autem",
          "completed": false
        }
        // We call the service
        service.getPost(1).subscribe(data => {
          expect(data.id).toBe(1);
          expect(data.title).toBe('delectus aut autem');
          expect(data.userId).toBe(1);
          expect(data.completed).toBe(false);
        });
        // We set the expectations for the HttpClient mock
    ```

```
        const req = httpMock.expectOne('https://jsonplaceholder.typicode.
    com/todos/1');
        expect(req.request.method).toEqual('GET');
        // Then we set the fake data to be returned by the mock
        req.flush(fakeData);
      })
  );
  // run every test and make sure expectations are met
  afterEach(inject([HttpTestingController], (httpMock:
  HttpTestingController) => {
    httpMock.verify();
  }));
```

Getting Started with E2E Testing with Protractor

The e2e testing of an application involves testing the functionality of an application by simulating the behavior of an end user. For example, an e2e test can be written to check whether the expected string is returned after the click of a button, or if a certain element is rendered as expected. The major concern with e2e tests is they can run slowly, thereby leading to a source of false positives that fail tests because of timeout issues. Protractor is the framework developed by the Angular team to implement e2e testing. It runs tests in a real browser against your running application, interacting with the application as a user would.

The following example implements e2e testing on the title of an Angular app using protractor:

```
import { browser } from 'protractor';
describe (' App title test', () => {    it('Title should be correct', () =>
{
const appUrl = 'https://localhost:4200;
const expectedTitle = 'App Starter';
browser.get(appUrl);
browser.getTitle().then((actualTitle) => {       expect(actualTitle).
toEqual(expectedTitle);
  });
    });
  });
```

Before we move on to the next section, we will briefly compare unit and e2e tests on the basis of the following parameters:

- **Speed**: Unit tests run quickly because they basically operate on small chunks of code and thus they run faster compared to e2e tests, which run in a browser.

- **Reliability**: The major concern with e2e test is that they run slowly, thereby leading to source of false positives that fail tests because of timeout issues. Time out issues can result from using more dependencies and complex interactions. However, even if a well-written unit test fails, you can trust that there's a problem with the code.

- **Code quality**: An e2e test happens via the browser and it does not directly interact with the code. However, a unit test does so, therefore it helps to ensure that a code is well written and easy to test. Writing unit tests can help identify needlessly complex code that may be difficult to test. As a general rule, if you're finding it hard to write unit tests, your code may be too complex and may need to be refactored. However, writing e2e tests won't help you write better-quality code per se.

Cost-effectiveness: Because e2e tests take longer to run and can fail at random, a cost is associated with that time. It also can take longer to write such tests, because they may build upon other complex interactions that can fail; therefore, development costs can be higher when it comes to writing e2e tests.

Mimicking user interactions: Mimicking user interactions with the user interface is where e2e tests shine. Using Angular protractor, you can write and run tests as if a real user were interacting with the user interface. You can simulate user interactions using unit tests, but it'll likely be easier to write e2e tests for that purpose because that's what they're made for.

Interacting with Elements

In the last section, we saw the bare minimum files needed to write our first protractor test. In this section, we'll introduce two new protractor APIs: `element` and `by`. These APIs help you interact with the template content of the web application. By the end of this section, we'll have created some test scenarios around creating a new contact.

Using the "by" API to locate web elements

Let's assume we have the HTML of our pages as shown in the following:

```
<input class="contact-email" id="email" type="email">
```

We want to find a web element using **by.css**, so the protractor will be as follows:

```
let e1 = element(by.css('.contact-email')); let e2 = element(by.
css('#contact-email')); let e3 = element(by.css('input[type="email"]'));

by.id
```

If we need to find a web element by ID and have the following HTML:

```
<input class="contact-email" id="contact-email" type="email">
```

Then, for the preceding snippet, the protractor will be as follows:

```
let email = element(by.id('contact-email'));

by.buttonText by.partialButtonText
```

Let's observe another example. Say we were to find a button with matching text for the following HTML:

```
<button>Submit Contact</button>
```

Then, for the preceding snippet, the protractor would be as follows:

```
let fullMatch = element(by.buttonText('Submit Contact')); let partialMatch =
element(by.partialButtonText('Submit'));

by.linkText by.partialLinkText
```

Other e2e examples involve finding a link by matching text, finding a web element by **xpath**, which is a locator strategy, and finding a web element using **by.binding()** in Angular.

Exercise 27: Performing an E2E Test for a Default Angular CLI Application to Find an Element Using By.CSS

In this exercise, we will be writing an e2e test for a default Angular application by finding an element using **by.css()**. You must have completed the exercises in the previous chapters. To get started, create an application with the name **e2etestapp**, and perform the following steps:

> **Note**
>
> The code files for this exercise can be found here: http://bit.ly/2WrTowJ.

1. Open the **app.components.html** file to decide the element to be tested using the following code:

```
<!--The content below is only a placeholder and can be replaced.-->
<div style="text-align:center">
```

```html
    <h1>
      Welcome to {{ title }}!
    </h1>
    <img width="300" alt="Angular Logo" src="data:image/svg+xml; ">
  </div>
  <h2>Here are some links to help you start: </h2>
  <ul>
    <li>
      <h2><a target="_blank" rel="noopener" href="https://angular.io/
tutorial">Tour of Heroes</a></h2>
    </li>
    <li>
      <h2><a target="_blank" rel="noopener" href="https://github.com/
angular/angular-cli/wiki">CLI Documentation</a></h2>
    </li>
    <li>
      <h2><a target="_blank" rel="noopener" href="https://blog.angular.
io/">Angular blog</a></h2>
    </li>
  </ul>
```

2. Open the **app.po.ts** protractor file, and write the following function:

```typescript
import { browser, by, element } from 'protractor';

export class AppComponentPage {
  navigateTo() {
    return browser.get('/');
  }

   getParagText () {
    return element(by.css('app-root h1')).getText();
  }

  getParagText2() {
    return element(by.css('app-root h2')).getText();
  }

  getParagText3 () {
    return element(by.css('app-root li h2 a')).getText();
  }
}
```

3. Open the **e2e** folder to access the test file named **app.e2e.spec.ts** and observe the following code, which has the default e2e code for testing the content in the title:

```
import { AppPage } from './app.po';
describe('workspace-project App', () => {
  let page: AppPage;
  beforeEach(() => {
    page = new AppPage ();
  });
  it('should display welcome message', () => {
    page.navigateTo();
    expect(page.getParagText()).toEqual('Welcome to packtTest!');
  });
```

4. Write the following test to display the content in the **H2** tag:

```
it('should display content in h2', () => {
  page.navigateTo();
  expect(page.getParagText2()).toEqual('Here are some links to help you start:');
  });
```

5. Write the following test to display the content in the **a** tag:

```
it('should display content in a', () => {
  page.navigateTo();
  expect(page.getParagText3()).toEqual('Tour of Heroes');
});
```

6. Go to the terminal and run **ng e2e**. You will obtain the following output:

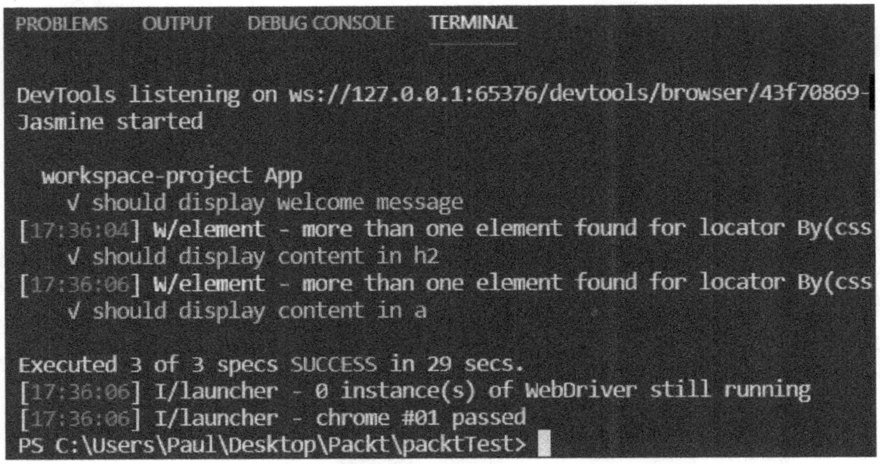

Figure 6.11: Final output of e2e testing

As can be seen in the preceding output, we have successfully completed e2e testing and located web elements using the **by.css()** method.

Activity 17: Performing Unit Tests on the App Root Component and Blog-Post Component

You have been tasked to write a unit test for the app root component and the **blog-home** component in the **Blogging Application** project. Once finished, you should have all service functions and components tested successfully. Before beginning the exercise, ensure that all previous exercises and activities have been completed. You can use any IDE of your choice; open the **Blogging Application** project and perform the following steps:

> **Note**
>
> The code files for this activity can be found here: http://bit.ly/2GVJ9LX.

1. Open root component test file, **app.components.spec.ts**, and import the required modules.

2. Mock the **app-header**, **router-outlet**, and **app-footer** components into the **app.components.spec.ts** file.

3. Write the suits functions for **AppComponent**.

4. Write the assertion and matcher functions to evaluate true and false conditions.

5. Open the **blog-home.component.spec.ts** file (in the **blog-home** folder) and import the modules.

6. Mock the **app-title-header** components in the **blog-home.component.spec.ts** file.

7. Write the suits functions in the **blog-home.component.spec.ts** file.

8. Write the assertion and matcher functions to evaluate true and false conditions.

9. Run **ng test** in the command line.

> **Note**
>
> The solution for this activity can be found on page 335.

Summary

The book began by describing the **MongoDB**, **Express**, **Angular**, and **Node** (**MEAN**) architecture. The MEAN technology components were described in terms of their features/advantages, limitations, and scenarios in which they are best used. We ran the Node server and implemented various Node features such as **callbacks**, **event loops**, **event emitters**, **streams**, **buffers**, and the **filesystem** in the first chapter.

In the second chapter, we introduced RESTful APIs and their designs concepts, performed operations on MongoDB Atlas, and implemented some features of the Express framework on Node applications. The chapter activities aimed at implementing Node, MongoDB Atlas, and Express together to develop a **RESTful API** that performed **CRUD** operations.

The third chapter introduced us to frontend development using the Angular **CLI**. We implemented various features such as directives, components, modules such as templates and reactive forms, and routers. The fourth chapter introduced us to Node application security practices and to the different forms of authentication/authorization strategies for Node applications. We learned how to grant user access to the RESTful API and perform user authentication on a Node application. This was done by implementing token-based authentication using **JWT** and **Passport** middleware in addition to applying local and social application strategies.

The fifth chapter taught us Angular **declarable** (**pipes** and **custom directives**), in addition to observables and reactive extension. The chapter wrapped up with Angular application bootstrapping and modularity, where we implemented modules, such as feature modules and lazy loading modules, in various exercises and activities.

In this chapter, we first described Angular animations by understanding some animation functions provided by the Angular animation modules. The animation functions were used to implement animation on elements and route transitions. In the latter part of the chapter, we briefly learned about some newly added features, such as CLI imports, Angular budget, virtual scroll, drag and drop, and Angular elements.

After this, we looked at optimizing Angular applications. In this section, we learned why performance optimization is important and briefly about described some tools used for checking and analyzing the performance of web applications. We later looked at how load time and runtime performance can be optimized.

The final section took us through testing Angular applications. We looked at how the two main types of tests, unit and e2e testing, are implemented using the provided modules, tools, and frameworks. Thus, this book has provided you with the basic elements of the MEAN stack for building robust web applications.

Appendix

About

This section is included to assist the students in performing the activities in the book.
It includes detailed steps that are to be performed by the students to achieve the objectives of the activities.

Chapter 1: Introduction to the MEAN Stack

Activity 1: Creating an HTTP Server for a Blogging Application

1. Create a new folder at an appropriate location in your system and rename it **Blogging Application**.

   Open the newly created **Blogging Application** folder from your code editor (Visual Studio) and create a **server.js** file, as shown in the following screenshot:

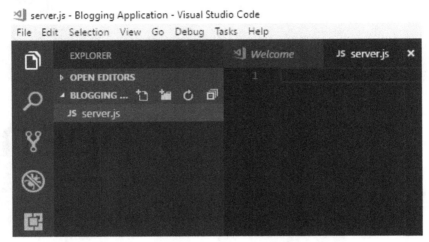

Figure 1.19: Creating the server.js file

2. Declare and assign HTTP using the following command:

```
var http = require ('http');
```

3. Declare and assign the hostname and port number:

```
const hostname = '127.0.0.1';
const port = 8000;
```

4. Create the HTTP server:

```
const server = http.createServer((req, res) => {
res.statusCode = 200;
res.setHeader('Content-Type', 'text/plain');
res.end('Blogging Application\n');});
```

5. Call the server to listen to localhost on the specified port:

```
server.listen(port, hostname, () => {
console.log ('Server running at
http://${hostname}:${port}/');});
```

6. Run the server by first pressing *Ctrl* + to open the integrated command-line terminal in Visual Studio and then type the following:

    ```
    >node server.js
    ```

    You will obtain the following output:

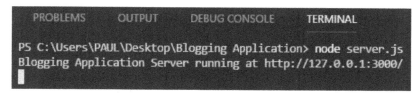

Figure 1.20: Running the server on the command-line interface

7. Go to your browser and type **http://localhost:3000** in the URL address bar. You should obtain the following output:

Figure 1.21: Final output of the activity

Activity 2: Streaming Data to a File

1. Go to your Desktop and create a new folder and rename it **StreamingProgram**.

2. Open the newly created **StreamingPrgram** folder from your code editor (Visual Studio) and create **stream.js**, **readTextFile.txt**, and **writeTextFile.txt,** as shown here:

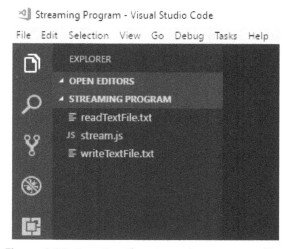

Figure 1.22: Creating the streaming program files

3. Load and import the filesystem module into the stream.js file using the following code:

```
var fs = require('fs');
```

4. Create a readable stream by calling the **createReadStream()** function on the **readTextFile.txt file** using the following code:

```
Const readableStream = fs.createReadStream('readTextFile.txt');
```

5. Create a writable stream by calling the **createWriteStream()** function on the **writeTextFile.txt** file using the following code:

```
Const writableStream = fs.createWriteStream('writeTextFile.txt');
```

6. Call the **on()** function on the **readableStream()** method. Then, pass data as the first argument and then attach a callback, as shown in the following code:

```
readableStream.on('data', function (data) {
console.log('Hey!, I am about to write what has been read from this file
readTextFile.txt');
});
```

7. Call the **write()** method on the **writeableStream()** method to write data inside the **readableStream()** callback using the following code:

```
readableStream.on('data', function (data) {
console.log('Hey!, am about to write what has been read from this file
readTextFile.txt');
var txt = ' Written!'
    var newdata = data + txt; //Append text string to the read data
    if (writableStream.write(newdata) === true) {
    console.log('Hey!, am done writing, Open the file writeTextFile.txt to
see what has been written');
        }
    else
    console.log('Writing is not successful');
});
```

8.   Press *Ctrl+* to open the integrated command-line terminal in Visual Studio and run the program by typing in the following code:

```
node stream.js
```

You will obtain the following output:

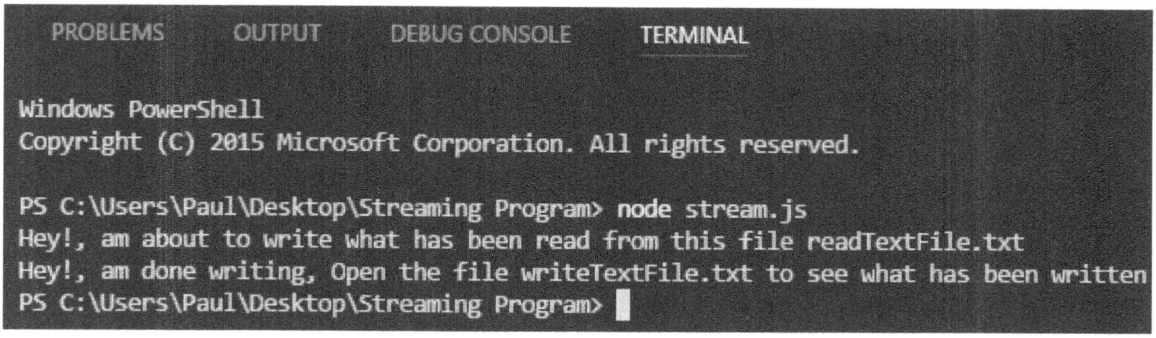

Figure 1.23: Running the streaming program

Then, open the **writeTextFile.txt** file to confirm the text that was read and written into it.

Chapter 2: Developing RESTful APIs to Perform CRUD Operations

Activity 3: Connecting the Node application with MongoDB Atlas

1. Create a subfolder named config and create a `db.js` file inside config folder.

   First, open server folder in the Blogging Application folder by using the keyboard combination Ctrl + O or Ctrl + k from Visual Studio Code and enable the integrated terminal with Ctrl + '. To accept default npm commands, create a `package.json` file using the following code:

   ```
   npm init
   ```

2. Install mongoose and import Mongoose.

   To install and import Mongoose, first open the `db.js` and type the following:

   ```
   npm install mongoose -- save
   ```

   To import Mongoose, type the following code:

   ```
   const mongoose = require("mongoose");
   ```

3. Assign a MongoDB connection string to `uri` and declare the options settings using the following code:

   ```
   var uri = "mongodb+srv://username:password@cluster0-0wi3e.mongodb.net/
   test?retryWrites=true";


   const options = {
       reconnectTries: Number.MAX_VALUE,
       poolSize: 10,
       useNewUrlParser:true
     };)
   ```

4. Connect the application to MongoDB Atlas using the following code:

   ```
   mongoose.connect(uri, options).then(
     () => {
       console.log("Database connection established!");
     },
     err => {
       console.log("Error connecting Database instance due to: ", err);
     }
   );
   ```

5. Create a folder named api (inside config), a subfolder models (inside api) inside it, and then create an `Article.js`.

   Code for creating the api folder:

   ```
   mkdir api
   ```

   Code for creating the models folder:

   ```
   mkdir models
   ```

   Code for creating the `Article.js` file:

   ```
   touch Article.js
   ```

6. Declare the schema and assign a schema class in the `Article.js` file. First we import Mongoose using the following code:

   ```
   const mongoose = require("mongoose");
   ```

   To declare and assign schema, we use the following code:

   ```
   const Schema = mongoose.Schema;
   ```

   To create the schema instance and add schema properties, use the following code:

   ```
   const BlogSchema = new Schema({
     title: {
       type: String,
       required: true
     },
     body: String,
     tag: {
       type: String,
       enum: ['POLITICS', 'ECONOMY', 'EDUCATION']
     },
     createdOn: {
       type: Date,
       default: Date.now
     }
   });
   ```

7. Create the default Mongoose model.

    To create the model, we first call mongoose on `model()` function to use the default mongoose connection using the following code:

    ```
    mongoose.model();
    ```

    Then, pass the model name as the first argument:

    ```
    mongoose.model("ArticleModel");
    ```

    Pass the schema name(BlogSchema) as the second argument:

    ```
    mongoose.model("ArticleModel", BlogSchema);
    ```

    Make model exportable using the following code:

    ```
    module.exports = mongoose.model("ArticleModel", BlogSchema);
    ```

8. Create an `output.js` file and import model using the following code:

    ```
    const Article = require("../models/Article");

    if(Article){
        console.log('Model Succesfully Imported');
    }
    ```

9. Run the `output.js` file to confirm whether the model has been imported using the following code:

    ```
    node output
    ```

    You will obtain the following output:

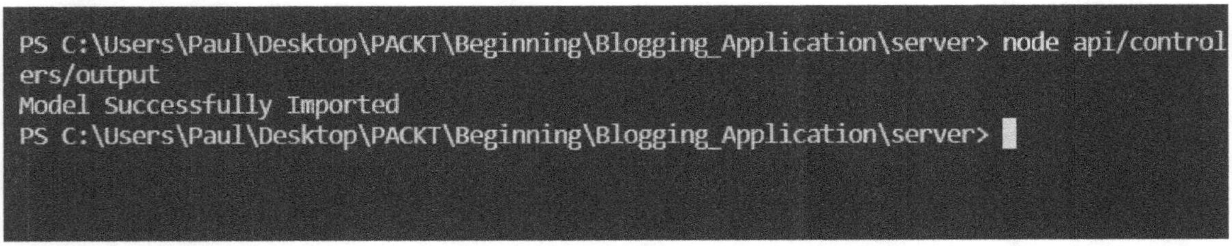

```
PS C:\Users\Paul\Desktop\PACKT\Beginning\Blogging_Application\server> node api/control
ers/output
Model Successfully Imported
PS C:\Users\Paul\Desktop\PACKT\Beginning\Blogging_Application\server>
```

Figure 2.18: Model successfully imported

10. Run node db.js inside the config folder to test the connection using the following code:

```
node db.js
```

You will obtain the following output:

Figure 2.19: Testing the connection

Activity 4: Creating Controllers for API

1. Create a folder named controllers as a subfolder inside api, and then open the controllers folder and create an `articleListController.js` file.

    To create the controllers folder, use the following code:

    ```
    mkdir controllers
    ```

    To create the `articleListController.js`, use the following code:

    ```
    touch articleListController.js
    ```

2. Open the articleListController.js file and import the model using the following code:

    ```
    const Article = require("../models/Article");
    ```

3. Create a controller to list all articles using the following code:

    ```
    exports.listAllArticles = (req, res) => {
      Article.find({}, (err, article) => {
        if (err) {
          res.status(500).send(err);
        }
        res.status(200).json(article);
      });
    };
    ```

4. Create a controller to create new articles using the following code:

```
exports.createNewArticle = (req, res) => {
  let newArticle = new Article(req.body);
  newArticle.save((err, article) => {
    if (err) {
      res.status(500).send(err);
    }
    res.status(201).json(article);
  });
};
```

5. Create a controller to read articles using the following code:

```
exports.readArticle = (req, res) => {
  Article.findById(req.params.articleid, (err, article) => {
    if (err) {
      res.status(500).send(err);
    }
    res.status(200).json(article);
  });
};
```

6. Create a controller to update articles using the following code:

```
exports.updateArticle = (req, res) => {
  Article.findOneAndUpdate(
    { _id: req.params.articleid },
    req.body,
    { new: true },
    (err, article) => {
      if (err) {
        res.status(500).send(err);
      }
      res.status(200).json(article);
    }
  );
};
```

7. Create controller to delete articles using the following code:

```
exports.deleteArticle = (req, res) => {
  Article.remove({ _id: req.params.articleid }, (err, article) => {
    if (err) {
      res.status(404).send(err);
    }
    res.status(200).json({ message: "Article successfully deleted" });
  });
};
```

Activity 5: Creating the API Express Route and Testing a Fully Functional RESTful API

1. Create a routes folder within the api folder and create an `articleListRoutes.js` file using the following code:

```
touch articleListRoutes.js
```

2. Open the `articleListRoutes.js` and create a route function using the following code:

```
module.exports = function(app) { }
```

3. Import controller into route function using the following code:

```
module.exports = function(app) {
var articleList = require('../controllers/articleListController');
}
```

4. Create route for **get** and **post** requests on `/articles` using the following code:

```
module.exports = function(app) {
  var articleList = require('../controllers/articleListController');
app
  .route("/articles")
  .get(articleList.listAllArticles)
  .post(articleList.createNewArticle);
}
```

5. Create route for **get**, **put**, and **delete** requests on `/articles/:articleid` using the following code:

```
module.exports = function(app) {
  conts articleList = require('../controllers/articleListController');
app
  .route("/articles")
```

```
    .get(articleList.listAllArticles)
    .post(articleList.createNewArticle);
  app
    .route("/articles/:articleid")
    .get(articleList.readArticle)
    .put(articleList.updateArticle)
    .delete(articleList.deleteArticle);
  }
```

6. Install Express and the **bodyParser** module using the integrated command line.

   To do this, first open server folder in the Blogging Application folder by using the keyboard combination Ctrl + O or Ctrl + k from VSC and enable the integrated terminal with Ctrl + '. Then, install Express and the bodyparser module using the following code

```
npm install express - save
npm install bodyparser - save
```

7. Create a **server.js** file in the Blogging Application/config folder and then import Express and the **body-parser** module using the following code:

```
const express = require("express");
const bodyParser = require("body-parser");
```

8. Create the Express application using the **express()** function:

```
const app = express();
```

9. Define the connection port

```
const port = process.env.PORT || 3000;
```

10. Call the **bodyParser** middleware on the created Express app using the following code:

```
app.use(bodyParser.urlencoded({ extended: true }));
app.use(bodyParser.json());
```

11. Import the **db** connection:

```
require("./config/db");
```

12. Add CORS (Cross-Origin Resource Sharing) headers to support cross-site HTTP requests

```
app.use(function(req, res, next) {
  res.header('Access-Control-Allow-Origin', '*');
  res.header('Access-Control-Allow-Methods',
'GET,PUT,POST,DELETE,PATCH,OPTIONS');
  res.header('Access-Control-Allow-Headers', 'Content-Type, Authorization,
Content-Length, X-Requested-With');
  // allow preflight
  if (req.method === 'OPTIONS') {
      res.send(200);
  } else {
      next();
  }
});
```

13. Import the route using the following code:

```
conts routes = require('./api/routes/articleListRoutes');
```

14. Call route on the Express application using the following code:

```
routes(app);
```

15. Listen to the Express server

```
app.listen(port, () => {
  console.log('Server running at http://localhost:${port}');
});
```

16. Run **server.js** inside the server folder to test the connection using the following code:

```
node server.js
```

You will obtain the following output:

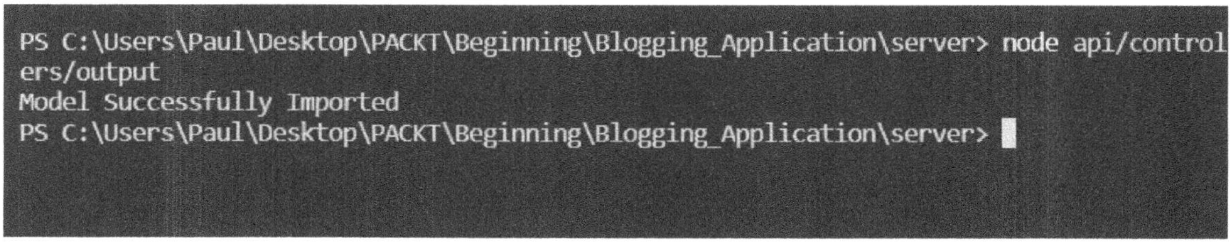

```
PS C:\Users\Paul\Desktop\PACKT\Beginning\Blogging_Application\server> node api/control
ers/output
Model Successfully Imported
PS C:\Users\Paul\Desktop\PACKT\Beginning\Blogging_Application\server>
```

Figure 2.20: Database connection established

17. Open Postman and test the API.

18. Post a new article to `localhost:3000/articles` using the POST request as shown:

Figure 2.21: Implementing the POST request

19. Get the posted articles by id on `localhost:3000/articles/:id` using the GET request as shown:

Figure 2.22: Implementing the GET request by id

20. Get all posted articles by id on `localhost:3000/articles` using GET request as shown:

Figure 2.23: Implementing the GET all posts request

21. Update posted articles by id on `localhost:3000/articles/:id` using the PUT request as shown:

Figure 2.24: Updating using the PUT request by id

22. Delete posted articles by id on `localhost:3000/articles/:id` using DELETE request as shown:

Figure 2.25: Implementing the DELETE request

Chapter 3: Beginning Frontend Development with Angular CLI

Activity 6: Designing the Frontend and Components for the Blogging Application

1. Create a new Angular project named **blog** by pointing your CLI to the **Blogging Application** directory, and create an Angular CLI application with the name blog using the following code:

    ```
    ng new blog
    ```

2. Import the bootstrap theme and its resources from http://bit.ly/2DI7UsR by opening the link, and download the bootstrap theme and resources into the **blog/src/assets** folder.

3. Update **index.html** with the necessary resource links using the following code:

File name: index.html

```
<!doctype html>
<html lang="en">
<head>
  <meta charset="utf-8">
  <title>Blog</title>
  <base href="/">
  <meta name="viewport" content="width=device-width, initial-scale=1">
//[…]
<script type="text/javascript" src="assets/js/main.js"></script>
</body>
</html>
```

Live link: http://bit.ly/2HDFQuT

4. Create the **header** components and update the HTML template with the theme's header using the following code:

File name: header.component.html

```
ng generate component header
<nav class="navbar navbar-expand-lg navbar-dark absolute_header">
  <div class="container">
    <a class="navbar-brand" href="#">
      <img class="etcodes-normal-logo" src="assets/images/logo-light.png"
```

```
width="84" height="22" alt="Logo">
      <img class="etcodes-mobile-logo" src="assets/images/logo.png"
width="84" height="22" alt="Logo">
    </a>
    <button class="navbar-toggler hamburger-menu-btn" type="button"
data-toggle="collapse" data-target="#navbarNavDropdown" aria-
controls="navbarNavDropdown"
//[…]
              </ul>
            </li>
          </ul>
        </li>
      </ul>
    </div>
  </div>
</nav>
```

Live link: http://bit.ly/2Rt5h1Q

5. Create the **title-header** component using the following code:

```
<div class="bg-img-71 py-100px py-md-200px mb-80px">
  <div class="container">
    <div class="row">
      <div class="col-lg-6 offset-lg-3 text-center all-text-content-
white">
        <h1>MEAN Stack Courseware Blog Application Project</h1>
        <p>Aenean lacinia bibendum sed consectetur. Etiam porta sem
malesuada magna mollis euismod. Fusce
              dapibus pertinax vix, varius cursus turpis dign issim id
aliquam habemus tractatos.</p>
      </div>
    </div>
  </div>
</div>
```

6. Create the **blog-home** components and update the HTML template with the theme's content:

File name: **blog-home.component.html**

```
ng generate component blog-home
            <!-- Blogs -->
```

```
<title-header></title-header>
            <div class="container">
                <div class="row">
                    <div class="col-lg-12">
                        <div class="row blog_posts stander_blog">
                            <div class="col-md-6 col-lg-4">
                                <article>
                                    <div class="post_img card-blog-img">
                                        <img src="assets/images/home-27/2.
jpg" alt="Card image cap">
                                        <a href="blog-standard-two-col-
right-sidebar.html">
                                            <span class="card-blog-meta">
//[…]
                                </div>
                            </div>
                        </div>
                    </div>
```

Live link: http://bit.ly/2FXWZh9

7. Create the **footer** components and update the HTML template with the theme's footer:

File name: **footer.component.html**

```
ng generate component footer
<footer class="web-footer footer bg-color-blackflame all-text-content-
white">
    <div class="footer-widgets pt-85px pb-55px">
        <div class="container">
            <div class="row large-gutters">
                <div class="col-lg-5 mb-30px">
                    <div class="footer-widget">
                        <h3>Paulappz</h3>
                        <p class="pt-20px pt-lg-155px">© 2018 Paulappz
Themes</p>
//[…]
                </div>
            </div>
        </div>
    </div>
```

```
        </footer>
```

Live link: http://bit.ly/2UnBZ6s

8. Create the `view-post` components and update the HTML template:

File Name: view-post.component.html

```
ng generate component view-post
  <div class="page-container scene-main scene-main--fade_In">
          <!-- view post -->
          <div class="container">
              <div class="row">
                  <div class="col-md-12">
                      <div class="post_img">
                          <img src="assets/images/b3.jpg" alt="Card
image cap">
//[…]
                      </div>
                  </div>
              </div>
          </div>

          </div>
```

Live link: http://bit.ly/2FWIJoP

9. Update the root component template with the following code:

```
<div id="main-content" class="bg-color-gray">
  <app-header></app-header>
  <div class="page-container scene-main scene-main--fade_In">
    <app-blog-home></app-blog-home>
    <app-footer></app-footer>
  </div>
</div>
```

10. Run **ng serve -o** to start the application. You will obtain the following output in the browser:

Figure 3.16: Blog application theme update

11. Update the root component template with the following code:

```
<div id="main-content" class="bg-color-gray">
  <app-header></app-header>
  <div class="page-container scene-main scene-main--fade_In">
    <view-post></view-post>
    <app-footer></app-footer>
  </div>
</div>
```

You will obtain the following output in the browser:

Figure 3.17: Blog application theme update

Activity 7: Writing Services and Making HTTP Request Calls to an API

1. Create a service file for blog post articles by running the following command:

```
ng generate service service/article
```

2. Update **app.module.ts** file by importing the provider for **ArticleService** using the following code:

```
import { BrowserModule } from '@angular/platform-browser';
import { NgModule } from '@angular/core';
import { AppComponent } from './app.component';
import { BlogHomeComponent } from './blog-home/blog-home.component';
import { HeaderComponent } from './header/header.component';
import { FooterComponent } from './footer/footer.component';
import { ArticleService } from './service/article.service';
import { HttpClientModule } from '@angular/common/http';
import { ViewPostComponent } from './view-post/view-post.component';
import { TitleHeaderComponent } from './title-header/title-header.
component';

@NgModule({
  declarations: [
    AppComponent,
    BlogHomeComponent,
    HeaderComponent,
    FooterComponent,
    ViewPostComponent,
    TitleHeaderComponent
  ],
  imports: [
    BrowserModule,
    HttpClientModule
  ],
  providers: [ArticleService],
  bootstrap: [AppComponent]
})
export class AppModule { }
```

3. Write the interface class in a newly created **posts.ts** file using the following code:

```
export interface Post {
    photo: string;
    title: string;
    body: string;
    tag: string;
}
```

4. Import the **Injectable**, **HttpClient**, **Post**, and **Observable** modules using the following code:

```
import { Injectable } from '@angular/core';
import { HttpClient, HttpHeaders } from '@angular/common/http';
import { Post } from '../posts'
import { Observable } from 'rxjs';
```

5. Declare **Url** variables and assign string values in the **ArticleService** class as shown:

```
articlesUrl = 'http://localhost:3000/articles';
articleUrl = 'http://localhost:3000/article/';
article: any;
httpOptions:any;
```

6. Inject **HttpClient** and set **HttpHeaders** using the following code:

```
constructor(private http: HttpClient) {
    this.httpOptions = new HttpHeaders({
        'Access-Control-Allow-Origin':'*',
        'Access-Control-Allow-Methods':'PUT, POST, GET, DELETE, OPTIONS',
    });
}
```

7. Write the CRUD service functions:

```
getArticles(): Observable<Post> {
    this.article = this.http.get<Post>(this.articlesUrl);
    return this.article;
}
getArticle(id: number) {
    return this.http.get(this.articleUrl + id);
}

/** POST: add a new article to the database */
```

```
PostArticle(article: Post): Observable<Post> {

    return this.http.post<Post>(this.articlesUrl,
      { 'title': article.title, 'body': article.body, 'tag': article.tag,
'photo': article.photo }, {
        headers: this.httpOptions
      })
  }

  deleteArticle(id: number):
    Observable<{}> {
    return this.http.delete(this.articleUrl + id, {
      headers: this.httpOptions
    })
  }

  updateArticle(id: number, article: Post): Observable<Post> {
    return this.http.put<Post>(this.articleUrl + id, { 'title': article.
title, 'body': article.body, 'tag': article.tag, 'photo': article.photo
},{
      headers: this.httpOptions
    })
  }
}
```

8. Update the **blog-home** components class file with the following code:

```
import { Component, OnInit } from '@angular/core';
// Import service
import { ArticleService } from '../service/article.service';
@Component({
  selector: 'app-blog-home',
  templateUrl: './blog-home.component.html',
  styleUrls: ['./blog-home.component.css']
})
export class BlogHomeComponent implements OnInit {
  articles:any=[];
//Inject service
  constructor(private articleService:ArticleService) { }
  ngOnInit() {
 this.articleService.getArticles()
```

```
    .subscribe(
      res => {
        for(let key in res){
          this.articles.push(res[key]);
        }
      },
      err => {
        console.log("Error occured");
      }
    );
    }
    }
```

9. Update the **blog-home** components template file with the following code:

File name: blog-home.component.html

```
<app-title-header></app-title-header>
    <div class="container">
        <div class="row">
            <div class="col-lg-12">
                <div  class="row blog_posts stander_blog">
                    <div class="col-md-6 col-lg-4"    *ngFor="let article
of //[…]


                    </div>
                </div>
            </div>
        </div>
```

Live link: http://bit.ly/2TjT1FQ

10. Update the **root** component template with the following code:

```
<div id="main-content" class="bg-color-gray">
  <app-header></app-header>
  <div class="page-container scene-main scene-main--fade_In">
    <app-blog-home></app-blog-home>
    <app-footer></app-footer>
  </div>
</div>
```

11. Run **ng serve -o** on the command line to view the following output:

Figure 3.18: Blog-home page of the application

12. Update the **view-post** components class file with the following code:

```
import { Component, OnInit } from '@angular/core';
import { ArticleService } from '../service/article.service';
@Component({
  selector: 'view-post',
  templateUrl: './view-post.component.html',
  styleUrls: ['./view-post.component.css']
})
export class ViewPostComponent implements OnInit {
  id: any;
  article: any;
  constructor( private articleService: ArticleService) { }
```

```
ngOnInit() {
    this.id = '5b9426b70e473447f400eeb9' // id of first post from API
    this.articleService.getArticle(this.id)
      .subscribe(
        res => {
          console.log(res)
          this.article = res;
        },
        err => {
          console.log("Error occured");
        }
      );
  }
}
```

13. Update the **view-post** components template file with the following code:

File name: view-post.component.ts

```
<div class="page-container scene-main scene-main--fade_In">
          <!-- Blog post -->
          <div class="container">
              <div class="row">
                  <div class="col-md-12">
                      <div class="post_img">
                          <img src="https://{{article.photo}}" alt="Card
image cap">
//[…]
                      </div>
                  </div>
              </div>
          </div>

          </div>
```

Live link: http://bit.ly/2VqoaoB

14. Update the **root** component template with the following code:

```
<div id="main-content" class="bg-color-gray">
  <app-header></app-header>
  <div class="page-container scene-main scene-main--fade_In">
    <view-post></view-post>
    <app-footer></app-footer>
  </div>
</div>
```

15. Run **ng serve -o** to start the application. You should obtain the following output:

Figure 3.19: View-post page of the application

Activity 8: Creating a Form Application Using the Reactive/Model-Driven Method

1. Create an Angular CLI application named Reactive form:

   ```
   ng new reactive-form
   ```

2. Create a component and name it **PacktStudentReactiveForm**:

   ```
   ng generate component reactive-form/ PacktStudentReactiveForm
   ```

3. Register the reactive forms module in **app.module.ts** and add it to import properties to activate the reactive form using the following code:

   ```
   import { ReactiveFormsModule } from '@angular/forms';
   import { FormsModule } from '@angular/forms';

   imports: [
       BrowserModule,
       FormsModule,
       ReactiveFormsModule
     ],
   ```

4. Import the **FormControl** and **FormGroup** modules into the reactive form component (**packt-student-reactive-form.component.ts**):

   ```
   import { FormGroup, FormControl, Validators, FormBuilder } from '@angular/
   forms';
   import { Component, OnInit } from '@angular/core';
   ```

5. Declare and initialize the array in the reactive components class, as follows:

   ```
   courseTitles = ['MEAN Stack', 'MEVN Stack', 'MERN Stack'];
   ```

6. Create **FormGroup** and **FormControl** variable instances:

   ```
   myform : FormGroup;
   name : FormControl;
   courseTitle : FormControl;
   duration : FormControl;
   constructor() { }
   ```

7. Create functions to initialize and validate using the following code:

   ```
   ngOnInit() {
     this.createFormControls();
     this.createForm();
   }
   ```

```
createFormControls() {
  this.name = new FormControl('Paul Adams', Validators.required),
  this.courseTitle = new FormControl(this.courseTitles[0], Validators.
required),
  this.duration = new FormControl('6 days')
}
createForm() {
  this.myform = new FormGroup({
    name: this.name,
    courseTitle : this.courseTitle,
    duration: this.duration
  });
}

submitted = false;

onSubmit() { this.submitted = true; console.log(this.name) }
newStudent() {
  this.myform.reset();
}
```

8. Register the control and form group in the html form template of the reactive component (**packt-student-reactive-form.component.html**) using the following code:

File name: **packt-student-reactive-form.component.html**

```
<div class="container">
    <div *ngIf="!submitted">
        <h1>Packt Course Form</h1>
//[…]
      </select>
                <div *ngIf="courseTitle.invalid" class="alert alert-
danger">
                    courseTitle is required
                </div>
            </div>
            <div class="form-group">
                <label for="duration">Course Duration</label>
                <input type="text" class="form-control" id="duration"
formControlName="duration">
            </div>
```

```
                <button type="submit" class="btn btn-success"
        [disabled]="">Submit</button>
                <button type="button" class="btn btn-default"
        (click)="newStudent();">New Student</button>
            </form>
        </div>
```

Live link: http://bit.ly/2WutecX

9. Add a **submitted** view to the template:

```
        <div *ngIf="submitted">
            <h2>You submitted the following:</h2>
            <div class="row">
                <div class="col-xs-3">Name</div>
                <div class="col-xs-9  pull-left">{{name.value}}</div>
            </div>
            <div class="row">
                <div class="col-xs-3">Course Duration</div>
                <div class="col-xs-9 pull-left">{{duration.value}}</div>
            </div>
            <div class="row">
                <div class="col-xs-3">Packt Course Title</div>
                <div class="col-xs-9 pull-left">{{courseTitle.value}}</div>
            </div>
            <br>
            <button class="btn btn-primary" (click)="submitted=false">Edit</
        button>
        </div>
    </div>
```

10. Update the components style sheet (**packt-student-reactive-form.component.css**)
    and the main application style sheet (**style.css**) using the following code:

```
// packt-student-reactive-form.component.css
.ng-valid[required],
.ng-valid.required,
.has-success {
    /* border-left: 5px solid #42A948; */
    /* green */
}

.ng-invalid:not(form) {
```

```
    /* border: 1px solid #a94442; */
    /* red */
}

// style.css
/* You can add global styles to this file, and also import other style files
*/
@import url('https://unpkg.com/bootstrap@3.3.7/dist/css/bootstrap.min.
css');
```

11. Update the root template file (**app.componets.html file**) by hosting the form component **src/app/app.component.html** using the following code:

```
src/app/app.component.html
< app-packt-student-reactive-form ></ app-packt-student-reactive-form >
```

12. Launch the application by running the following snippet in the command-line terminal and go to the address **localhost:4200**:

```
ng serve --open
```

You will obtain the following output:

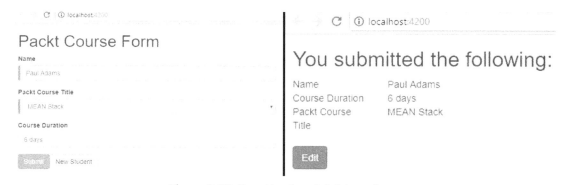

Figure 3.20: Reactive/model-driven form

Activity 9: Creating and Validating Different Forms Using the Template and Reactive-Driven Method

1. Create the **User Login** form component using the following code:

    ```
    ng generate component login
    ```

2. Update the **User Login** form component class and update the HTML template to be reactive/model-driven using the following code:

    ```
    import { Component, OnInit } from '@angular/core';
    import { FormGroup, FormControl, Validators, FormBuilder } from '@angular/
    forms';
    @Component({
      selector: 'login',
      templateUrl: './login.component.html',
      styleUrls: ['./login.component.css']
    })
    export class LoginComponent {
      loginForm: FormGroup;
      displayMessage: string;
      submitted = false;
      constructor(private formBuilder: FormBuilder) {
        /* Declare Reactive Form Group here */
        this.loginForm = this.formBuilder.group({
          email: ['', [
            Validators.required,
            Validators.pattern("[^ @]*@[^ @]*")
          ]],
          password: ['', [
            Validators.minLength(8),
            Validators.required
          ]],
        });

      }

      submitForm() {
        this.submitted = true;
        /* Change the display message on button click / submit form */
        if (this.loginForm.valid) {
          this.loginUser();
        }
    ```

```
    }

    loginUser() {
    console.log('Logged In sucessfully')
    }
  }
```

The template is updated with the following:

File name: login.component.html

```
<title-header></title-header>
<div class="" style="padding-bottom: 3rem!important;">
  <div class="row">
    <div class="col-md-6 mx-auto">
      <!-- form card login -->
      <div class="card rounded-0">
//[…]
      <!-- /form card login -->
    </div>
  </div>
</div>
```

Live link: http://bit.ly/2B8XFfK

Update the **app** component template with the following snippet and run **ng serve** to view the **User Login** form output:

```
<div id="main-content" class="bg-color-gray">
  <app-header></app-header>
  <div class="page-container scene-main scene-main--fade_In">
    <app-login></app-login>
    <app-footer></app-footer>
  </div>
</div>
```

You will obtain the following output once you type `http://localhost:4200/login` in the browser:

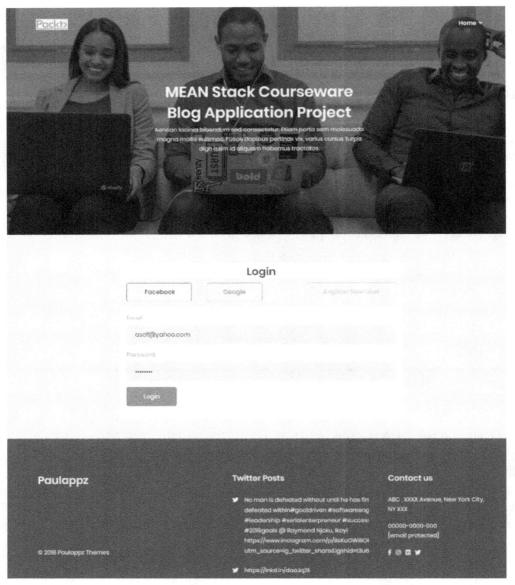

Figure 3.21: Reactive login form

3. Create the **User Registration** form component:

```
ng generate component register
```

4. Create an exportable user class file in the **app** directory using the following code:

```
export class Users {
    constructor(
    public fullName: string,
    public email: string,
    public password: string
) { }
}
```

5. Update the **User Registration** form component class and update the HTML template to be template-driven.

The class is updated as follows:

```
import { Component, OnInit } from '@angular/core';
import { Users } from '../users';

@Component({
  selector: 'app-register',
  templateUrl: './register.component.html',
  styleUrls: ['./register.component.css']
})
export class RegisterComponent implements OnInit {
  model = new Users('', '', '');
  constructor(/*private auth: AuthService,
    private router: Router*/) { }
  ngOnInit() {
  }
  onSubmit() {
      this.registerUser();
  }
  registerUser() {
console.log('Registration Successful')
    }
```

The template is updated as follows:

```
File name: register.component.html
```

```
<title-header></title-header>
```

```
<div>
  <div class="row">
    <div class="col-md-6 mx-auto">
      <!-- form card login -->
      <div class="card rounded-0">
        <h3 class="mb-0" style="text-align:center">Register  Admin
User</h3>
        <div class="card-header">
        </div>
        <div class="card-body">
          <form (ngSubmit)="userForm.form.valid && onSubmit()"
//[…]
      <!-- /form card login -->
      </div>
    </div>
  </div>
</div>
```

Live link: http://bit.ly/2Wul1p2

6. Update the **app** component template with the following snippet and run **ng serve**
to view the **User Registration** form output:

```
<div id="main-content" class="bg-color-gray">
  <app-header></app-header>
  <div class="page-container scene-main scene-main--fade_In">
    <app-register></app-register>
    <app-footer></app-footer>
  </div>
</div>
```

You will obtain the following output once you run **http://localhost:4200/register** in the browser:

Figure 3.22: Template-driven Register form

7. Create the **Post Create/Edit** form component and an exportable **Posts** class:

```
ng generate component create
export class Posts {
    constructor(
    public title: string,
    public body: string,
    public tag: string,
    public photo: string,
    ) { }
}
```

8. Update the **Post Create/Edit** form component class and update the HTML template to be template-driven.

The class is updated as follows:

```
import { Component, OnInit } from '@angular/core';
import { Posts } from '../post';
@Component({
  selector: 'app-create',
  templateUrl: './create.component.html',
  styleUrls: ['./create.component.css']
})
export class CreateComponent implements OnInit {
  tags = ['POLITICS', 'ECONOMY', 'EDUCATION','STORY','TECH'];
  model = new Posts('','','','');
  submitted = false;
  constructor() { }
  onSubmit() {
    this.submitted = true;
  console.log(this.model)
}
  ngOnInit() {
  }
}
```

The template is updated as follows:

File name: create.component.html

```
<title-header></title-header>
<div class="py-5">
  <div class="row">
```

```
        <div class="col-md-6 mx-auto">
          <!-- form card login -->
          <div class="card rounded-0">
              <h3 style="text-align:center" class="mb-0">Create Post</h3>
              <div class="card-header">
                </div>
            <div class="card-body">
              <form (ngSubmit)="postForm.form.valid && onSubmit()"
    //[…]

              <button type="submit" class="btn btn-success">Submit</button>
            </form>
          </div>
          <!--/card-block-->
        </div>
        <!-- /form card login -->
      </div>
    </div>
  </div>
```

Live link: http://bit.ly/2HGg3SD

9. Update the **app** component template with the following snippet and run **ng serve** to view the **Post Create/Edit** form output:

```
<div id="main-content" class="bg-color-gray">
  <app-header></app-header>
  <div class="page-container scene-main scene-main--fade_In">
    <app-create></app-create>
    <app-footer></app-footer>
  </div>
</div>
```

You will obtain the following output once you type `http://localhost:4200/create` in the browser window:

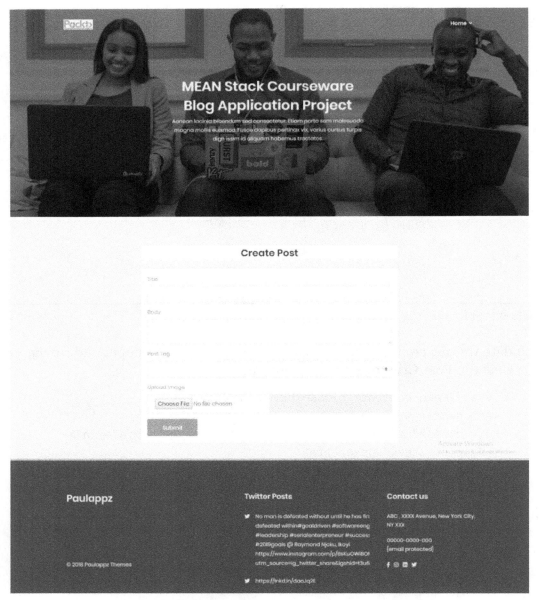

Figure 3.23: Template-driven post create/edit form

Activity 10: Implementing a Router for the Blogging Application

1. Import **RouterModule** into the **app** module file (**app.module.ts**) and update the import property:

```
import { RouterModule, Routes } from '@angular/router';

imports: [
    BrowserModule,
    HttpClientModule,
    RouterModule.forRoot(appRoutes),
    FormsModule,
    ReactiveFormsModule,
    BrowserAnimationsModule
  ],
```

2. Configure the route in **app.module.ts** as follows:

```
const appRoutes: Routes = [
  { path: 'blog', component: BlogHomeComponent,
    data: { title: 'Article List' }},
  { path: 'blog/post/:id',      component: ViewPostComponent },
  { path: 'login', component: LoginComponent},
  { path: 'register', component: RegisterComponent},
  { path: 'create', component: CreateComponent},

  { path: '',
    redirectTo: '/blog',
    pathMatch: 'full'
  },
  // { path: '**', component: PageNotFoundComponent }
];
```

3. Add **router-outlet** to the **app.component.html** file:

```
<div id="main-content" class="bg-color-gray">
  <app-header></app-header>
  <div class="page-container scene-main scene-main--fade_In">

    <router-outlet></router-outlet>

    <app-footer></app-footer>
  </div>
</div>
```

4. Add the router link to the **blog-home** component:

File name: blog-home.component.html

```html
<title-header></title-header>
    <div class="container">
        <div class="row">
            <div class="col-lg-12">
                <div  class="row blog_posts stander_blog">
                    <div class="col-md-6 col-lg-4"    *ngFor="let article
of articles">
                        <article>
                            <a routerLink="post/{{article._id}}">
                            <div class="post_img card-blog-img">
                                <img src="https://{{article.photo}}"
//[…]

                </div>
            </div>
        </div>

    </div>
```

Live link: http://bit.ly/2CSjEaQ

5. Start the server and serve the Angular application using the CLI with the following commands:

```
> node server.js
> ng serve -o
```

6. Open the browser and input `http://localhost:4200/blogin` in the URL address bar to view the router in action.

You will obtain the following output:

Figure 3.24: Blog post route

If you click on one of the posts, it will navigate to the view-post page, as shown:

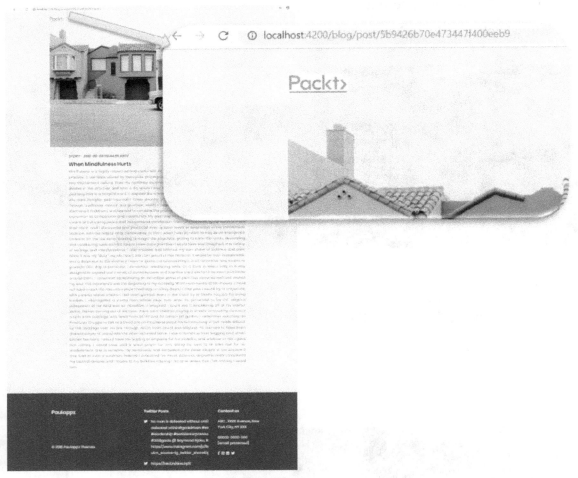

Figure 3.25: Route to view-post page

Chapter 4: The MEAN Stack Security

Activity 11: Securing the RESTful API

1. Create an admin user model by creating a file named **userModel.js** inside the **api** folder and input the following code:

```
const mongoose = require("mongoose"), // loading modules
bcrypt = require('bcryptjs'),
Schema = mongoose.Schema;

const UserSchema = new Schema({ // Schema Instance
  fullName: {
    type: String,
    trim: true,
    required: true
  },
  email: {
    type:String,
    unique:true,
    lovercase:true,
    trim:true,
    required:true
  } ,
  hash_password: {
    type:String,
    required:true
  },
  createdOn: {
    type: Date,
    default: Date.now
  }
});

UserSchema.methods.comparePassword = function(password){  //password
confirmation
  return bcrypt.compareSync(password, this.hash_password);
}
module.exports = mongoose.model("User", UserSchema); //user model
```

2. Create an admin user controller by creating a file called **userController.js** inside the **controllers/api** folder input using the following code:

File name: userController.js

```
const User = require("../models/userModel"); // Import userModel,
    jwt = require('jsonwebtoken'), // load jasonwebtoken module
    bcrypt = require('bcryptjs');  // load bcryptjs module for password
hashing

exports.register = (req, res) => { // exportable function to register new
user
    let newUser = new User(req.body);
    newUser.hash_password = bcrypt.hashSync(req.body.password, 10);
    newUser.save((err, user) => {
        if (err) {
            res.status(500).send({ message: err });
        }
        user.hash_password = undefined;
        res.status(201).json(user);
    });
};

//[…]

exports.loginRequired = (req, res, next) => {
    if (req.user) {
        res.json({ message: 'Authorized User!'});
        next();
      } else {
        res.status(401).json({ message: 'Unauthorized user!' });
      }
};
```

Live link: http://bit.ly/2DJEs5S

3. Update the route file (**articleListRoutes.js**) in the routes directory (**server/api/controllers**) with the following code:

```
'use strict';
module.exports = function(app) {
  var articleList = require('../controllers/articleListController');
  var userHandlers = require('../controllers/userController');

  // articleList Routes
  app
  .route("/articles")
  .get(articleList.listAllArticles)
  .post(userHandlers.loginRequired, articleList.createNewArticle);

  app
  .route("/article/:articleid")
  .get(articleList.readArticle)
  .put(articleList.updateArticle)
  .delete(articleList.deleteArticle);

  app
  .route("/articles/by/:tag")
  .get(articleList.listTagArticles);

  app
  .route("/auth/register")
  .post(userHandlers.register);

  app
  .route("/auth/sign_in")
  .post(userHandlers.signIn);

};
```

4. Update the **server.js** (inside the **server** folder) file with the following code:

```
'use strict'
const express = require("express");
const bodyParser = require("body-parser");

// db instance connection
require("./config/db");
var User = require('./api/models/userModel'),
```

```
        jsonwebtoken = require("jsonwebtoken");

const app = express();

const port = process.env.PORT || 3000;
app.use(bodyParser.urlencoded({ extended: true }));
app.use(bodyParser.json());

//CORS (Cross-Origin Resource Sharing) headers to support Cross-site HTTP
requests
app.use(function(req, res, next) {
    res.header('Access-Control-Allow-Origin', '*');
    res.header('Access-Control-Allow-Methods',
'GET,PUT,POST,DELETE,PATCH,OPTIONS');
    res.header('Access-Control-Allow-Headers', 'Content-Type,
Authorization, Content-Length, X-Requested-With');
    // allow preflight
    if (req.method === 'OPTIONS') {
        res.send(200);
    } else {
        next();
    }
});

app.use((req, res, next) => { // Verify JWT for user authorization
    if (req.headers && req.headers.authorization && req.headers.
authorization.split(' ')[0] === 'JWT') {
        jsonwebtoken.verify(req.headers.authorization.split(' ')[1],
'RESTfulAPIs', (err, decode) => {
                if (err) req.user = undefined;
                req.user = decode;
                next();
            });
    } else {
        req.user = undefined;
        next();
    }
});


// API ENDPOINTS
var routes = require('./api/routes/articleListRoutes'); //importing route
```

```
routes(app);

// LISTENING
app.listen(port, () => {
  console.log('Server running at http://localhost:${port}');
});
```

5. Run the server using **node server** on the CLI and open Postman for testing.

6. Test for registration by typing in **localhost:3000/auth/register** on the address bar. You will obtain the following output:

Figure 4.15: Screenshot for registration

7. Attempt the login required path and post request on **localhost:3000/articles**. You will obtain the following output:

Figure 4.16: Screenshot for posting articles

8. Attempt user login by typing in **localhost:3000/auth/sign_in** on the address bar. You will obtain the following output:

Figure 4.17: Screenshot for sign in

9. Set the authentication key on the header and input the value in JWT token format, as shown here:

Figure 4.18: Screenshot for setting the authentication key

10. Attempt the login required path and post request on `localhost:3000/articles`. You will obtain the following output:

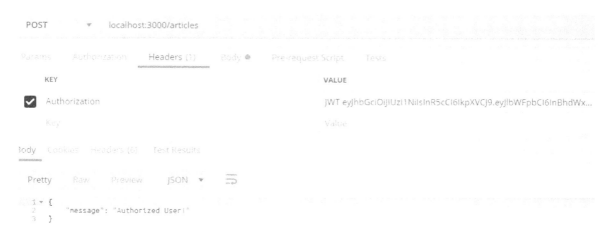

Figure 4.19: Screenshot for articles

Thus, from the preceding outputs, it can be clearly observed that we have successfully secured the RESTful API we developed in the previous exercise. We also managed to provide admin access for creating, updating, and deleting data.

Activity 12: Creating a Login Page to Allow Authentication with Twitter Using Passport Strategies

1. Create a **package.json** file and install **express**, **body-parser**, **mongoose**, **passport-twitter**, and **passport** by running the following code:

    ```
    npm init
    npm install express body-parser mongoose passport-twitter passport
    express-session -save
    ```

2. Create a **server.js** (using **touch server.js** on the CLI) file and import **express** and **body-parser** using the following code:

    ```
    const express = require("express");
    const bodyParser = require("body-parser");
    const session = require('express-session');
    ```

3. Create an Express application, assign a port number, and use the **body-parser** middleware on the Express application using the following code:

    ```
    const app = express();
    const port = process.env.PORT || 4000;
    app.use(bodyParser.urlencoded({ extended: true }));
    app.use(bodyParser.json());
    ```

4. Create a **config** folder using the following code:

    ```
    mkdir config
    ```

5. Create a database by first creating a file named **db.js** (using **touch db.js** on the CLI) in the **config** folder directory and input the following code:

    ```
    const mongoose = require("mongoose");

    var uri = "mongodb+srv://username:passowrd@cluster0-0wi3e.mongodb.net/
    test?retryWrites=true";

      const options = {
        reconnectTries: Number.MAX_VALUE,
        poolSize: 10
      };
    // Connect to the database using the following code
    mongoose.connect(uri, options).then(
        () => {
          console.log("Database connection established!");
        },
    ```

```
    err => {
      console.log("Error connecting Database instance due to: ", err);
    }
  );
```

6. Create an **api** directory and three subfolders named **controllers**, **models**, and **routes** using the following code:

```
mkdir api
mkdir - controllers && mkdir - models && mkdir - routes
```

7. Create a model file inside the **controller** directory (using `touch userModel.js` on the CLI) and then create the schema and model:

```
const mongoose = require("mongoose"),
const Schema = mongoose.Schema;
const UserSchema = new Schema({
twitter       : {
    fullName    : String,
    email       : String,
    createdOn: {
      type: Date,
      default: Date.now
    },
  },
});

//Create a mongoose model from the Schema
mongoose.model("User", UserSchema);
```

8. Create a passport file inside the **config** directory (using `touch passport.js`) and then create a Twitter strategy using the following code:

File name: passport.js

```
const  TwitterStrategy = require("passport-twitter").Strategy;
const mongoose = require('mongoose'),
const User = mongoose.model('User');

// Create an exposed function
module.exports = function (passport) {}
serialize the user for the session
    passport.serializeUser(function (user, done) {
        done(null, user.id);
```

```
        });

    deserialize the user
        passport.deserializeUser(function (id, done) {
            User.findById(id, function (err, user) {
                done(err, user);
            });
        });

//[…]
        } else {
            done(null, user);
        }
      });
    }
  ));
  }
```

Live link: http://bit.ly/2FXYfki

9. Create a route file inside the **routes** directory (using **touch route.js**) and then create an exposed function as an exportable module that takes in **app** and **passport** using the following code:

```
module.exports = function(app,passport)  {
app.get('/auth/twitter',
  passport.authenticate(' twitter ', {scope:"email"}));

app.get('/auth/ twitter /callback',
  passport.authenticate('twitter', { failureRedirect: '/error' }),
  function(req, res) {
    res.redirect('/success');
  });

}
```

10. Update the **server.js** file with the following code:

```
//db instance connection
require("./config/db"); app.get('/success', (req, res) => res.send("You
have successfully logged in"));
app.get('/error', (req, res) => res.send("error logging in"));
```

11. Import and initialize passport using the following code:

```
const passport = require("passport");
// Authentication configuration
app.use(session({
    resave: false,
    saveUninitialized: true,
    secret: 'bla bla bla'
  }))
app.use(passport.initialize());
app.use(passport.session());
```

12. Update the API endpoint using the following code:

```
var routes = require('./api/routes/route'); //importing route
routes(app,passport);
app.listen(port, () => {
    console.log('Server running at http://localhost:${port}');
});
```

13. Run the server (using **node server** on the CLI), open a browser, and test this by typing in **localhost:4000/auth/twitter** on the browser address bar. You will obtain the following output:

Figure 4.20: Successful authentication using Twitter

Chapter 5: Angular Declarables, Bootstrapping, and Modularity

Activity 13: Communicating Between Two Components Using Observable

1. Create the **app-header** component using the CLI, as shown here:

```
ng generate component app-header
```

2. Create the **app-content** component using the following CLI command:

```
ng generate component app-content
```

3. Create the user model and interface in **user.model.ts** using the following command:

```
export interface User {
  firstName: string;
  lastName: string;
}
```

4. Create the user service and update the server:

```
ng generate server user
import { Injectable } from '@angular/core';
import { BehaviorSubject } from 'rxjs';

@Injectable()
export class UserService {
  private user = new BehaviorSubject<boolean>(false); //create user as
behavior
  cast = this.user.asObservable(); //cast user as observable

  constructor() { }

  User(newUser) {
    this.user.next(newUser);
  }
}
```

5. Define the user and inject **service** into the **app-header.component.ts** class using the following code:

```
import { Component, OnInit } from '@angular/core';
import { User } from '../user/user.model';
import { UserService } from '../user.service';

@Component({
```

```
    selector: 'app-header',
    templateUrl: './app-header.component.html',
    styleUrls: ['./app-header.component.scss']
})
export class AppHeaderComponent implements OnInit {
  user: User = {
    firstName: 'Paul',
    lastName: 'Oluyege'
  };
  isLoggedIn: boolean;
  constructor(private usersService:UserService) { }
```

6. Define the user and inject **service** into the **app-content.component.ts** class using the following code:

```
import { Component, OnInit } from '@angular/core';
import { User } from './/../user/user.model';
import { UserService } from '../user.service';

@Component({
  selector: 'app-content',
  templateUrl: './app-content.component.html',
  styleUrls: ['./app-content.component.scss']
})
export class AppContentComponent implements OnInit {
  user: User = {
    firstName: 'Paul',
    lastName: 'Oluyege'
  };
  isLoggedIn: boolean;
  constructor(private usersService: UserService) { }
```

7. Write **ngOnInit()**, **login()**, **signup()**, and **logout()** methods for the **app-header.component.ts** class, as shown here:

```
ngOnInit() {
    this.usersService.cast.subscribe(user=> this.isLoggedIn = user);
  }

  login() {
    this.isLoggedIn = true;
    this.usersService.User(this.isLoggedIn);
  }
```

```
  signup() {
    this.isLoggedIn = true;
    this.usersService.User(this.isLoggedIn);
  }

  logout() {
    this.isLoggedIn = false;
    this.usersService.User(this.isLoggedIn);
  }

}
```

8. Write **ngOnInit()**, **login()**, **signup()**, and **logout()** methods for the **app-content. component.ts** class, as shown here:

```
ngOnInit() {
    this.usersService.cast.subscribe(user => this.isLoggedIn = user);
    this.isLoggedIn = false;
  }

  login() {
    this.isLoggedIn = true;
    this.usersService.User(this.isLoggedIn);
  }

  logout() {
    this.isLoggedIn = false;
    this.usersService.User(this.isLoggedIn);
  }
}
```

9. Update the **app-header.component.html** template using the following code:

```
<div class="app-header">
  <div class="title" routerLink="/">Packt MEANStack Courseware</div>
  <div class="profile-dropdown" *ngIf="isLoggedIn">
    <div class="initials">
      {{user.firstName.charAt(0)}}{{user.lastName.charAt(0)}}
    </div>
  </div>
  <div class="action-btns" *ngIf="!isLoggedIn">
    <button class="app-btn login-btn" (click)="login()">Login</button>
    <button class="app-btn signup-btn" (click)="signup()">Signup</button>
  </div>
```

```html
  <div class="action-btns" *ngIf="isLoggedIn">
    <button class="app-btn logout-btn" (click)="logout()">Logout</button>
  </div>
</div>
```

10. Update the **app-content.component.html** template using the following code:

```html
<div class="app-content">
  <div class="user-profile" *ngIf="isLoggedIn">
    Hi {{user.firstName}} {{user.lastName}}! Welcome to MEANStack class
  </div>
  <div class="action-btn">
    <button class="app-btn" *ngIf="!isLoggedIn" (click)="login()">Login</
button>
    <button class="app-btn" *ngIf="isLoggedIn" (click)="logout()">Logout</
button>
  </div>
</div>
```

11. Update styles for both components (**app-header** and **app-content),** as shown here:

```scss
// app-content-component.scss
.app-content {
    padding: 40px;

    .user-profile {
      margin-bottom: 20px;
    }
  }
// app-header-component.scss
.app-header {
    background: #e94e06;
    height: 44px;
    color: white;
    padding: 6px 10px;
    display: flex;
    flex-direction: row;
    align-items: center;
    box-shadow: 0 3px 5px -1px rgba(0,0,0,.2), 0 6px 10px 0
  rgba(0,0,0,.14), 0 1px 18px 0 rgba(0,0,0,.12);
    .logo {
```

```
//[…]
          }
        }
      }
    }
```

12. Update the **app.component.html** template with the following code:

    ```
    <app-header></app-header>
    <app-content></app-content>
    ```

13. Run **ng serve** on the CLI and open the browser on **localhost:4200** to see the output and test it, as shown in the following screenshot:

Figure 5.10: Synchronization of two components

Activity 14: Creating a Lazy Loaded Application

1. Create an Angular project with the name **users,** as shown here:

   ```
   ng new users --routing
   ```

   Note that the **--routing** flag generates a file called **app-routing.module.ts**, which is one of the files you need for setting up lazy loading for your feature module.

2. Create a **users-list** feature module with routing:

   ```
   ng generate module users-list  --routing
   ```

3. Add a **user-list component** to the feature module using the following code:

   ```
   ng generate component users-list / users-list
   ```

4. Create a **users-details** feature module with routing using the following code:

   ```
   ng generate module users-details  --routing
   ```

5. Add a **user-detail** component to the feature module using the following code:

   ```
   ng generate component users-detail / users-detail
   ```

6. Globally install the **json-server** on your system using **npm** or **yam**:

   ```
   npm install -g json-server
   ```

7. Create a new JSON file named **db.json** and fill it with data from https://api.myjson. com/bins/10v4ns. Then, launch this file on the **json-server** using the following code:

    ```
    json-server --watch db.json
    ```

8. Add a **user-list** service using the following code:

    ```
    ng generate service service/users-list
    ```

9. Update the routes array in **AppRoutingModule** with the following code:

    ```
    import { NgModule } from '@angular/core';
    import { Routes, RouterModule } from '@angular/router';

    const routes: Routes = [
      {
        path: 'userslist',
        loadChildren: './users-list/users-list.module#UsersListModule'
      },
      {
        path: 'userslist/:id',
        loadChildren: './users-detail/users-detail.module#UsersDetailModule'
      },

      {
        path: '',
        redirectTo: '',
        pathMatch: 'full'

      }
    ];

    @NgModule({
      imports: [RouterModule.forRoot(routes)],
      exports: [RouterModule]
    })
    export class AppRoutingModule { }
    ```

10. Configure the feature module's routes in **users-list-routing.module.ts** by first importing the component at the top of the file with the other JavaScript import statements and then add the route to **UserListComponent**:

Here is the code for importing the component:

```
import { NgModule } from '@angular/core';
import { Routes, RouterModule } from '@angular/router';
import {  UsersListComponent} from './users-list.component'

const routes: Routes = [
    { path: "", component: UsersListComponent},
];


@NgModule({
  imports: [RouterModule.forChild(routes)],
  exports: [RouterModule]
})
export class UsersListRoutingModule { }
```

11. Configure the feature modules for **users-detail-routing.module.ts** using the following code:

```
import { NgModule } from '@angular/core';
import { Routes, RouterModule } from '@angular/router';
import {  UsersDetailComponent} from './users-detail.component'

const routes: Routes = [
    { path: "", component: UsersDetailComponent},
];

@NgModule({
  imports: [RouterModule.forChild(routes)],
  exports: [RouterModule]
})
export class UsersDetailRoutingModule { }
```

12. Create the user model and update it with the following code:

```
ng generate cl model/user
export class Users {
  first: string;
  second: string;
  id: number;
```

```
    phone:string;
    picture:string;
    email:string;
  }
```

13. Write the service functions, as shown here:

```
import { Injectable } from '@angular/core';
import { Users } from "../model/users.model";
import {HttpClient} from '@angular/common/http';
import { Observable } from 'rxjs';

@Injectable()
export class UsersListService {
  dataurl = "http://localhost:3000/results";
  constructor(private http: HttpClient) { }


  public getUsers(): Observable<Users[]> {
    return this.http.get<Users[]>(this.dataurl);
  }

  public getUser(id: string): Observable<Users> {
    return this.http.get<Users>('${this.dataurl}?id=${id}');
  }

}
```

14. Update and inject the service into **users-list.component.ts** using the following code:

```
import { Component, OnInit, OnDestroy } from '@angular/core';
import { Router } from '@angular/router';
import { Users } from "../model/users.model";
import { UsersListService } from "../service/users-list.service";
@Component({
  selector: 'app-users-list',
  templateUrl: './users-list.component.html',
  styleUrls: ['./users-list.component.css']
})
export class UsersListComponent implements OnInit {
  userlists: Users[];
  constructor(private router: Router, private usersService:
UsersListService) { }
```

```
    ngOnInit() {
      this.usersService.getUsers().subscribe((user: any) => {
        this.userlists = user;
        console.log(this.userlists);
      });
    }


  }
```

15. Update and inject service into **users-details.component.ts,** as shown here:

```
import { Component, OnInit } from '@angular/core';
import { ActivatedRoute } from "@angular/router";
import { Router } from '@angular/router';
import { Users } from "../model/users.model";
import { UsersListService } from "../service/users-list.service";

@Component({
  selector: 'app-users-detail',
  templateUrl: './users-detail.component.html',
  styleUrls: ['./users-detail.component.css']
})
export class UsersDetailComponent implements OnInit {
  user: Users;
  constructor(private router: Router, private route: ActivatedRoute,
private usersService: UsersListService) { }

  ngOnInit(): void {

    this.usersService.getUser(this.route.snapshot.params["id"]).
subscribe((user: any) => {
      this.user = user;
    });


  }
```

16. Style the **user-list** component using the following code:

```
.selected {
    background-color: #CFD8DC !important;
    color: white;
  }
//[…]
    .list-type1 ol.selected:hover {
      background-color: #BBD8DC !important;
      color: white;
    }
```

17. Style the **users-details** components using the following code:

```
@import url(https://fonts.googleapis.com/
css?family=Raleway|Varela+Round|Coda);
@import url(http://weloveiconfonts.com/api/?family=entypo);

[class*="entypo-"]:before {
  font-family: 'entypo', sans-serif;
}
//[…]
.previous {
    background-color: #f1f1f1;
    color: black;
}
```

18. Update the **app.component.html** template, as shown here:

```
<router-outlet></router-outlet>
```

19. Go to **localhost:4200** and then test for **/userslist** and **/userslist/1**, as follows:

Type **localhost/4200/userslist** on the browser address bar and observe the number of resources requested, as shown here:

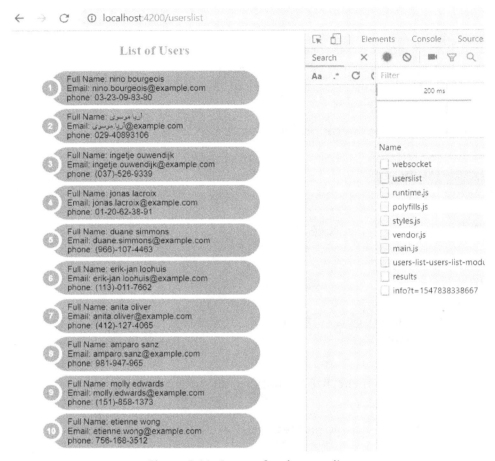

Figure 5.11: Output for the user list

20. Type **localhost/4200/userslist/1** on the browser address bar and observe the number of resources requested, as shown here:

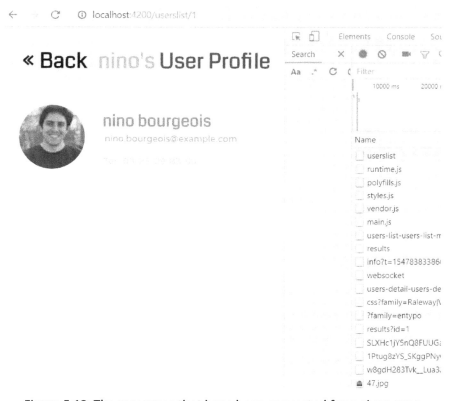

Figure 5.12: The resources that have been requested for a given user

Chapter 6: Testing and Optimizing Angular Applications

Activity 15: Animating the Route Transition Between the Blog Post Page and the View Post Page of the Blogging Application

1. Import the routing module into the **app.routing.module** file using the following code:

```
import { BrowserAnimationsModule } from '@angular/platform-browser/
animations';
import { BrowserModule } from '@angular/platform-browser';
................. . .
imports: [
    BrowserModule,
    BrowserAnimationsModule
  ],
```

2. Create an **animation.ts** file using touch, and then import animation classes and define animation properties:

```
touch animation.ts
```

Here is the code for importing and defining animation classes:

```
import {trigger,state,style,animate,transition,query,animateChild,group}
from '@angular/animations';

export const slideInAnimation =
  trigger('routeAnimations', [
    transition('HomePage <=> PostPage', [
      style({ position: 'relative' }),
      query(':enter, :leave', [
        style({
          position: 'absolute',
          top: 0,
          left: 0,
          width: '100%'
        })
      ]),
//[…]
      query(':enter', animateChild()),
    ])
  ]);
```

3. Update the animated route in the lazy loading **ap.route.module.tsrouting** configuration, as shown in the following code:

```
import { BrowserAnimationsModule } from '@angular/platform-browser/
animations';
const routes: Routes = [
  {
    path: 'blog',
    loadChildren: './blog-home/blog-home.module#BlogHomeModule',
    data: { animation: 'HomePage' }
//[…]

@NgModule({
  imports: [RouterModule.forChild(routes), SharedModule,
BrowserAnimationsModule],
  exports: [RouterModule]
})
export class AppRoutingModule { }
```

4. Import the animation and router outlet of the root components class in the **app.component.ts** file:

```
import { Component } from '@angular/core';
import { RouterOutlet } from '@angular/router'
import { slideInAnimation } from './animation'
//[…]

prepareRoute(outlet: RouterOutlet) {
  return outlet && outlet.activatedRouteData && outlet.
activatedRouteData['animation'];
}}
```

5. Update the root component template file (**app.component.html**) with the following code:

```
<div id="main-content" class="bg-color-gray">
  <app-header></app-header>
  <div [@routeAnimations]="prepareRoute(outlet)" class="page-container
scene-main scene-main--fade_In">
    <router-outlet #outlet="outlet"></router-outlet>
    <app-footer></app-footer>
  </div>
</div>
```

6. Run the application using **ng serve -o** on the CLI, and then test and observe the page transition on the browser by typing in **localhost:4200/blog/post** in the browser. You will obtain the following output:

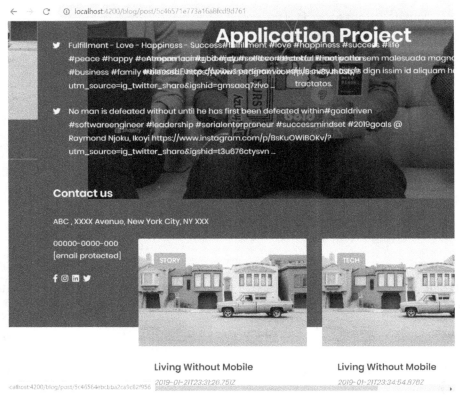

Figure 6.12: Route transition animation between the Blog-Post and View-Post pages

Activity 16: Implementing Router Guard, Constant Storage, and Updating the Application Functions of the Blogging Application

1. **Define a constant for AuthService** and **ArticleService** in the **environment.ts** file with local URL's as shown in the following snippet:

```
export const environment = {
  production: false,
  articlesUrl: 'http://localhost:3000/articles',
  articleUrl: 'http://localhost:3000/article/',
  registerUrl: "http://localhost:3000/auth/register",
  loginUrl: "http://localhost:3000/auth/sign_in"
};
```

2. Import and declare the environment in the **auth.service.ts** file as shown in the following snippet:

```
import { Injectable } from '@angular/core';
import { HttpClient } from '@angular/common/http'
import { Router } from '@angular/router'
import { map } from 'rxjs/operators';
import { environment } from '../../environments/environment'

@Injectable({
  providedIn: 'root'
})
export class AuthService {
  config = environment;
```

3. Import the **BehaviorSubject** class in the **auth.service.ts** file using the following command:

```
import { BehaviorSubject } from 'rxjs';
```

4. Declare **user** as an instance of the **BehaviorSubject** class and then observe using the Angular **asObservable()** method as shown in the following snippet:

```
private user = new BehaviorSubject<boolean>(false);
  cast = this.user.asObservable();
```

5. Write an authentication function in the **auth.service.ts** file to check if any tokens exist as shown in the following snippet:

```
constructor(private http: HttpClient,
  private router: Router) { }

public isAuthenticated(): boolean {
  const token = localStorage.getItem('currentUser');
  if (token) return true
  else return false
}
```

6. Update the **login**, **register**, and **logout** functions with the constant variable and then observe the behavioral variable as shown in the following snippet:

```
registerUser(user) {
  return this.http.post<any>('${this.config.registerUrl}', user)
}

loginUser(user) {
```

```
      return this.http.post<any>('${this.config.loginUrl}', { 'email': user.
email, 'password': user.password })
        .pipe(map(user => {
          // login successful if there's a jwt token in the response
          if (user && user.token) {
            // store user details and jwt token in local storage to keep
user logged in between page refreshes
            localStorage.setItem('currentUser', JSON.stringify('JWT ' +
user.token));
          }
          this.user.next(true);
          return user;
        }));
    }

    logoutUser() {
      // remove user from local storage to log user out
      localStorage.removeItem('currentUser');
      this.user.next(false);
      this.router.navigate(['/blog'])
    }
  }
```

7. Create a new **auth-guard.service.ts** service file to implement the router guard as shown in the following snippet:

```
import { Injectable } from '@angular/core';
import { Router, CanActivate } from '@angular/router';
import { AuthService } from './auth.service';
@Injectable()
export class AuthGuardService implements CanActivate {
  constructor(public auth: AuthService, public router: Router) {}
  canActivate(): boolean {
    if (!this.auth.isAuthenticated()) {
      this.router.navigate(['login']);
      return false;
    }
    return true;
  }
}
```

8. Apply the router guard service to the **app.routing.module.ts** route file as shown in the following snippet:

File name: app.routing.module.ts

```
import { NgModule } from '@angular/core';
import { Routes, RouterModule,CanActivate } from '@angular/router';
import { SharedModule } from './shared/shared/shared.module'
import { BrowserAnimationsModule } from '@angular/platform-browser/
animations';
import { AuthGuardService as AuthGuard } from './service/auth-guard.
service';
  //[…]

  // { path: '**', component: PageNotFoundComponent }
];

@NgModule({
  imports: [RouterModule.forChild(routes), SharedModule,
BrowserAnimationsModule],
  exports: [RouterModule]
})
export class AppRoutingModule { }
```

Live link: http://bit.ly/2XrwQwu

9. Import and declare the environment in the **article.service.ts** file as shown in the following snippet:

```
import { Injectable } from '@angular/core';
import { HttpClient, HttpHeaders } from '@angular/common/http';
import { Post } from '../posts'
import { Observable } from 'rxjs';
import { environment } from '../../environments/environment'

@Injectable()

export class ArticleService {
  config = environment;
```

10. Declare the token and header in the **article.service.ts** file:

```
article: any;
  token = JSON.parse( localStorage.getItem('currentUser') ) ;
  httpOptions:any;

  constructor(private http: HttpClient) {
    this.httpOptions = new HttpHeaders({
      'Authorization': this.token,
      'Access-Control-Allow-Origin':'*',
      'Access-Control-Allow-Methods':'PUT, POST, GET, DELETE, OPTIONS',
    });
  }
```

11. Update the functions in the **article.service.ts** file with constant variables and headers as shown in the following snippet:

File name: **article.service.ts**

```
getArticles(): Observable<Post> {
    this.article = this.http.get<Post>('${this.config.articlesUrl}');
    return this.article;
  }
//[…]

  updateArticle(id: number, article: Post): Observable<Post> {
    console.log(this.token)
    return this.http.put<Post>('${this.config.articleUrl}' + id, { 'title':
article.title, 'body': article.body, 'tag': article.tag, 'photo': article.
photo },{
      headers: this.httpOptions
    })
  }
}
```

Live link: http://bit.ly/2GZehKy

12. Update the **blog-home** component class (**blog-home.component.ts**), template (**blog-home.component.html**), and style (**blog-home.component.css**) using the following code snippets:

The code for updating the **blog-home.component.ts** file is as follows:

File name: blog-home.component.ts

```
//blog-home.component.ts
import { Component, OnInit } from '@angular/core';
import { ArticleService } from '../service/article.service';
import { AuthService } from '../service//auth.service';

@Component({
  selector: 'app-blog-home',
  templateUrl: './blog-home.component.html',
  styleUrls: ['./blog-home.component.css']
})
export class BlogHomeComponent implements OnInit {
//[…]
  }

  logOut() {
    this.authService.logoutUser()
  }

}
```

Live link: http://bit.ly/2tDW3GH

The code for updating the **blog-home.component.html** (template) file is as follows:

File name: blog-home.component.html

```
//blog-home.component.html
<app-title-header></app-title-header>
<div *ngIf='isLoggedIn'>
<a routerLink="/create" style="float: left;margin:-50px 0px 0px
100px;background-color: orangered;color: white" class="button btn">New
Post</a>
<button (click)="logOut()" style="float: right;margin:-50px 100px 0px
0px;background-color: black;color: white" class="button btn">Logout</
button>
</div>

//[…]

              </article>
```

```
                    </div>
                </div>
            </div>
        </div>
    </div>
```

Live link: http://bit.ly/2IAhQsY

The code snippet for the style (**blog-home.component.css**) file is as follows:

```
.button{
border-style: solid;
border-width : 1px 1px 1px 1px;
text-decoration : none;
padding : 8px;
font-size:12px;
margin: 0 auto;
}
```

13. Update the **view-post** component class (**view-post.component.ts**) and the template (**view-post.component.html**) using the following code:

The code for updating the **view-post.component.ts** file is as follows:

File name: **view-post.component.ts**

```
//view-post.component.ts
import { Component, OnInit } from '@angular/core';
import { Router, ActivatedRoute } from '@angular/router';
import { ArticleService } from '../service/article.service';

@Component({
  selector: 'app-view-post',
  templateUrl: './view-post.component.html',
  styleUrls: ['./view-post.component.css']
})
```

```
export class ViewPostComponent implements OnInit {
//[…]
            }
        );
    });
  }
}
```

Live link: http://bit.ly/2ExYdhd

The code for updating the **view-post.component.html** file is as follows:

File name: view-post.component.html

```
<!-- View post -->

<div  class="page-container scene-main scene-main--fade_In">
    <!-- Blog post -->
    <div class="container">
//[…]
                                </p>
                            </div>
                            <div class="separator-line"></div>
                        </article>
                    </div>
                </div>
            </div>
        </div>

    </div>
```

Live link: http://bit.ly/2T3cIT9

14. Update the **login** component class (**login.component.ts**) and the template (**login. component.html**) using the following code:

The code for updating the **login.component.ts** file is as follows:

File name: login.component.ts

```
import { Component, OnInit } from '@angular/core';
import { FormGroup, FormControl, Validators, FormBuilder } from '@angular/
```

```
forms';
import { AuthService } from '../service//auth.service';
import { Router } from '@angular/router'
import { first } from 'rxjs/operators';

//[…]
  }


}
```

Live link: http://bit.ly/2X142WN

The code for updating the `login.component.html` file is as follows:

File name: `login.component.html`

```html
<app-title-header></app-title-header>
<div class="" style="padding-bottom: 3rem!important;">
  <div class="row">
    <div class="col-md-6 mx-auto">
      <!-- form card login -->
      <div class="card rounded-0">
        <h3 class="mb-0" style="text-align:center" class="mb-0">Login</h3>
        <div class="card-header">
          <a href="#" class="btn" style="float:left;margin-
right:10px;color:darkblue;border: 1px solid darkblue">
            <i class="fa fa-facebook-official"></i>
            Facebook
//[…]

          </div>
          <div *ngIf="success" class="alert alert-success">{{success}}</
div>
          <div *ngIf="error" class="alert alert-danger">{{error}}</div>
        </form>
      </div>
      <!--/card-block-->
    </div>
    <!-- /form card login -->

  </div>
```

```
      </div>
    </div>
```

Live link: http://bit.ly/2UaQATe

15. Update the **register** component class (**register.component.ts**) and the template (**register.component.html**) using the following code:

The code for updating the **register.component.ts** is as follows:

File name: **register.component.ts**

```
import { Component, OnInit } from '@angular/core';
import { AuthService } from '../service/auth.service';
import { Router } from '@angular/router'
import { Users } from '../users';
import { first } from 'rxjs/operators';

@Component({
  selector: 'app-register',
  templateUrl: './register.component.html',
  styleUrls: ['./register.component.css']
})
//[...]
  navigateToLogin() {
    this.router.navigate(['/login']);
  }
}
```

Live link: http://bit.ly/2XqhR60

The code for updating the **register.component.html** is as follows:

File name: **register.component.html**

```
<app-title-header></app-title-header>
<div  style="padding-bottom: 3rem!important;">
  <div class="row">
    <div class="col-md-6 mx-auto">
      <!-- form card login -->
      <div class="card rounded-0">
        <h3 class="mb-0" style="text-align:center">Register  Admin
```

```
        User</h3>
        //[…]

            </div>

          </div>
        </div>
```

Live link: http://bit.ly/2IBJoOH

16. Update the **create** component class (**create.component.ts**) and the template (**create.component.html**) using the following code snippets:

    The code for updating the **create.component.ts** file is as follows:

File name: create.component.ts

```
    import { Component, OnInit } from '@angular/core';
    import { Posts } from '../post';
    import { ArticleService } from '../service/article.service';
    import { Router } from '@angular/router'
    import { first } from 'rxjs/operators';

    //[…]
      navigateToBlogHome() {
        this.router.navigate(['/blog']);
      }
    }
```

Live link: http://bit.ly/2GKyDb6

The code for updating the **create.component.html** file is as follows:

File name: create.component.html

```
    <app-title-header></app-title-header>
    <div style="padding-bottom: 3rem!important;">
      <div class="row">
        <div class="col-md-6 mx-auto">
          <!-- form card login -->
          <div class="card rounded-0">
            <h3 style="text-align:center" class="mb-0">Create Post</h3>
```

```
        <div class="card-header">
        </div>
        <div class="card-body">
          <form (ngSubmit)="postForm.form.valid && onSubmit()"
#postForm="ngForm" novalidate>
            <div class="form-group">
              <label for="title">Title</label>
              <input type="text" class="form-control" id="title"
[(ngModel)]="model.title" name="title" #title="ngModel"
                [ngClass]="{ 'is-invalid': postForm.submitted && title.
invalid }" required>
              <div *ngIf="postForm.submitted && title.invalid"
class="alert alert-danger">
                  Title is required
              </div>
            </div>
//[…]
            <div *ngIf="error" class="alert alert-danger">{{error}}</div>
          </form>
        </div>
      </div>

    </div>

  </div>
</div>
```

Live link: http://bit.ly/2XqKKPt

17. Update the **edit** component class (**edit.component.ts**) and the template (**edit. component.html**) using the following code snippets:

The code for updating the **edit.component.ts** file is as follows:

File name: edit.component.ts

```
import { Component, OnInit } from '@angular/core';
import { Router, ActivatedRoute } from '@angular/router';
import { ArticleService } from '../service/article.service';
import { Posts } from '../post';
import { first } from 'rxjs/operators';
```

```
@Component({
  selector: 'app-edit',
  templateUrl: './edit.component.html',
  styleUrls: ['./edit.component.css']
})
//[…]

  navigateToBlogHome() {
    this.router.navigate(['/blog']);
  }
}
```

Live link: http://bit.ly/2Ec53aU

The code for updating the **edit.component.html** file is as follows:

File name: edit.component.html

```html
<app-title-header></app-title-header>
<div style="padding-bottom: 3rem!important;">
  <div class="row">
    <div class="col-md-6 mx-auto">
      <!-- form card login -->
      <div class="card rounded-0">
        <h3 style="text-align:center" class="mb-0">Edit Post</h3>
        <div class="card-header">
        </div>
        <div class="card-body">
          <form (ngSubmit)="postForm.form.valid && onSubmit()"
#postForm="ngForm" novalidate *ngIf="article.length != 0">
            <div class="form-group">
              <label for="title">Title</label>
              <input type="text" class="form-control" id="title"
[(ngModel)]="article.title" name="title" #title="ngModel"
                [ngClass]="{ 'is-invalid': postForm.submitted && title.
invalid }" required>
              <div *ngIf="postForm.submitted && title.invalid"
class="alert alert-danger">
                Title is required
              </div>
            </div>
//[…]
```

```
            </form>
          </div>
        </div>
      </div>
    </div>
  </div>
```

Live link: `http://bit.ly/2BWVjAR`

18. Run **ng serve** to test the **'/blog'** route before and after logging in.

    You will obtain the following output once you test the **'/blog'** route before logging in:

Figure 6.13: The output obtained for the test on the '/blog' route before logging in.

When you test the '/blog' route after logging in, you will obtain the following output:

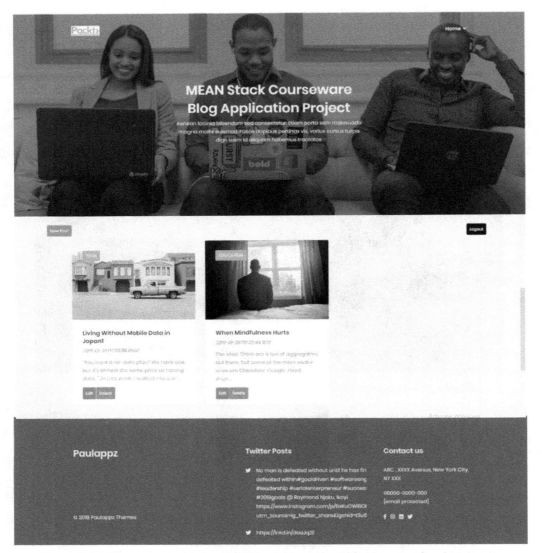

Figure 6.14: The output obtained for the test on the '/blog' route after logging in.

Activity 17: Performing Unit Testing on the App Root Component and Blog-Post Component

1. Open the root component test file, **app.components.spec.ts**, and import the modules, as shown:

```
import { TestBed, async,ComponentFixture } from '@angular/core/testing';
import { AppComponent } from './app.component';
import { Component, OnInit, DebugElement } from '@angular/core';
import { RouterTestingModule } from '@angular/router/testing';
import { RouterLinkWithHref } from '@angular/router';
import { By } from '@angular/platform-browser';
```

2. Mock the **app-header**, **router-outlet**, and **app-footer** components into the **app.components.spec.ts** file the with the following code:

```
@Component({selector: 'app-header', template: ''})
class HeaderStubComponent {}

@Component({selector: 'router-outlet', template: ''})
class RouterOutletStubComponent { }

@Component({selector: 'app-footer', template: ''})
class FooterStubComponent {}
```

3. Write the suits functions for **AppComponent**, as shown in the following code:

```
describe('AppComponent', () => {
  beforeEach(async(() => {
    TestBed.configureTestingModule({
      imports: [ RouterTestingModule.withRoutes([])],
      declarations: [
        AppComponent,
        HeaderStubComponent,
        RouterOutletStubComponent,
        FooterStubComponent
      ]
    }).compileComponents();
  }));
```

4. Write the assertion and matcher functions to evaluate true and false conditions:

```
it('should create the app', async(() => {
    const fixture = TestBed.createComponent(AppComponent);
    const app = fixture.debugElement.componentInstance;
    expect(app).toBeTruthy();
  }));
  it('should have a link to /', () => {
    const fixture = TestBed.createComponent(AppComponent);
    const debugElements = fixture.debugElement.queryAll(By.
directive(RouterLinkWithHref));
    const index = debugElements.findIndex(de => {
      return de.properties['href'] === '/';
    });
    expect(index).toBeGreaterThanOrEqual(-1);
  });
});
```

5. Open the **blog-home.component.spec.ts** file (in the **blog-home** folder) and import the modules:

```
import { async, ComponentFixture, TestBed, inject } from '@angular/core/
testing';
import { HttpClientModule } from '@angular/common/http';
import { Component, OnInit } from '@angular/core';
import { BlogHomeComponent } from './blog-home.component';
import { NO_ERRORS_SCHEMA } from '@angular/core';
import { ArticleService } from '../service/article.service';
```

6. Mock the **app-title-header** components in the **blog-home.component.spec.ts** file, as shown:

```
@Component({ selector: 'app-title-header', template: '' })
class TitleHeaderStubComponent { }
```

7. Write the suits functions in the **blog-home.component.spec.ts** file, as shown:

```
describe('BlogHomeComponent', () => {
  let component: BlogHomeComponent;
  let fixture: ComponentFixture<BlogHomeComponent>;
  let testBedService: ArticleService;

  beforeEach(async(() => {
    // refine the test module by declaring the test component
    TestBed.configureTestingModule({
```

```
        declarations: [BlogHomeComponent, TitleHeaderStubComponent],
        providers: [ArticleService],
        imports: [HttpClientModule],
        schemas: [NO_ERRORS_SCHEMA]
      })
        .compileComponents();
    }));
```

```
beforeEach(() => {
// create component and test fixture

    fixture = TestBed.createComponent(BlogHomeComponent);
    // AuthService provided to the TestBed
    testBedService = TestBed.get(ArticleService);
    // get test component from the fixture

    component = fixture.componentInstance;
    fixture.detectChanges();
```

8. Write the assertion and matcher functions to evaluate true and false, as shown:

```
    it('should create', () => {
      expect(component).toBeTruthy();
    });

    it('Service injected via inject(...) and TestBed.get(...) should be the
    same instance',
        inject([ArticleService], (injectService: ArticleService) => {
          expect(injectService).toBe(testBedService);
        })
      );
    });
    });
```

9. Run **ng test** in the command line. You will obtain an output similar to the following:

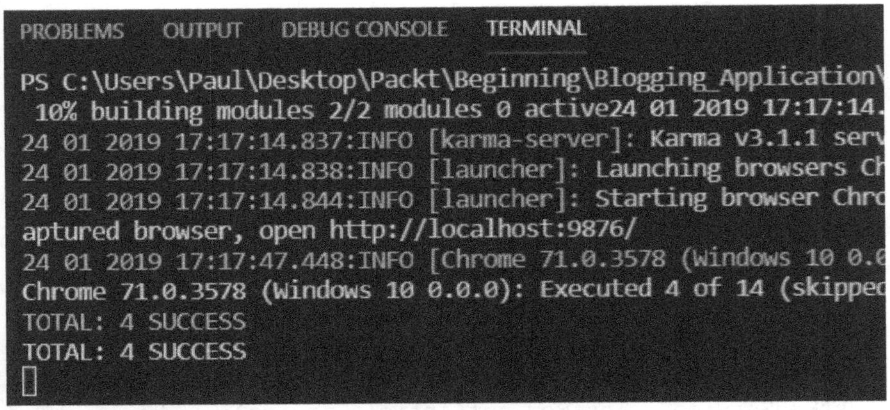

Figure 6.15: Final output on e2e testing on student app

As can be seen in the preceding output, we have successfully performed e2e testing on the **student** app.

Index

About

All major keywords used in this book are captured alphabetically in this section. Each one is accompanied by the page number of where they appear.

www.ingramcontent.com/pod-product-compliance
Lightning Source LLC
Chambersburg PA
CBHW080615060326
40690CB00021B/4708